Affirmed Action

Affirmed Action

*Essays on the Academic
and Social Lives
of White Faculty Members
at Historically Black Colleges
and Universities*

edited by Lenoar Foster, Janet A. Guyden,
& Andrea L. Miller

WITHDRAWN
UTSA Libraries

ROWMAN & LITTLEFIELD PUBLISHERS, INC.
Lanham • Boulder • New York • Oxford

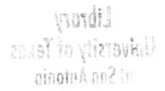

ROWMAN & LITTLEFIELD PUBLISHERS, INC.

Published in the United States of America
by Rowman & Littlefield Publishers, Inc.
4720 Boston Way, Lanham, Maryland 20706
http://www.rowmanlittlefield.com

12 Hid's Copse Road
Cumnor Hill, Oxford OX2 9JJ, England

British Library Cataloguing in Publication Information Available

Library of Congress Cataloging-in-Publication Data

Affitmed action : essays on the academic and social lives of white faculty members at
historically black colleges and universities / edited by Lenoar Foster, Janit A. Guyden &
Andrea L. Miller.
    p. cm.
    Includes bibliographical references and index.
    ISBN 0-8476-9460-7 (cloth : alk. paper) – Isbn 0-8476-9461-5 (pbk. : alk. paper)
    1. Afro-American universities and colleges—Faculty. 2. White college teachers—
United States—Social conditions. I Foster, Lenoar, 1951- II. Guyden, Janet A. 1946-
III. Miller, Andrea L., 1954-

LC2781.5 .A44 1999
378.1'2—dc21

                        99-044767

Printed in the United States of America

Contents

Part 2. Academic Careers at Historically Black Colleges and Universities

Part 3. Transformed and Transforming at Historically Black Colleges and Universities

Appendix

Preface _____

White faculty who teach and administer in historically black colleges and universities in the United States are inescapably drawn into a discussion and appraisal of the state of race relations in the country. The issue of race is a salient feature of the daily life, study, activities, and considerations of faculty and students in these institutions and in the communities in which many historically black institutions are situated. As the diverse other, white faculty and administrators "who have dealt with race at a distance or only on an intellectual level are required to confront the whole issue of race and to explore their own reactions, personal prejudices, and other internal and external barriers to effective interracial relationships" (Smith and Borgstedt, 1985, p.149). White faculty members and administrators cannot successfully practice aversive behaviors that deny their personal values, perceptions, assumptions, and predispositions. For to teach in a historically and predominantly black college or university requires an immersion into the culture that undergirds the very fabric of the lives of students and of the institution.

White faculty who teach and administer in predominantly black higher education institutions confront the reality of diversity that has occupied and challenged academic communities in America for more than three decades. That challenge above all demands that academe "rethink how we educate students and for what means; how we define our scholarship, our discipline, and our departments; and how we organize our education communities, both within our institutions and in relation to the local and larger communities of which we are a part" (Musil, 1996, p.224).

The purpose of this volume is to contribute to the dialogue on faculty diversity in higher education from the perspective of white minority faculty in historically black colleges and universities in the United States. Through these voices, mostly unheard in the national discourse on faculty diversity and rarely documented in the higher education literature on faculty diversity, we hope to illustrate the continuing challenges that diversity poses in higher education institutions and to indicate the benefits that accrue to students and to higher education institutions when committed, dedicated, and ethical efforts are made to create inclusive educational communities. White faculty constitute one-third of the total faculty numbers at historically black colleges and universities (United States Department of Education, 1996). The need to hear these voices is particularly appropriate at this time when issues of faculty, student, and institutional diversity are being challenged and threatened by assaults on affirmative action and other diversity initiatives in higher education institutions throughout the nation.

We believe that historically black colleges and universities are uniquely positioned to offer authoritative models of what diversity, framed and grounded in mutual respect, understanding, collaboration, and appreciation, can mean to the intellectual life of higher education and to the fulfillment of democratic principles. These institutions have historically and successfully educated their students to navigate the wider American society, while imbuing them with a sense of personal pride in their culture and heritage, personal efficacy in their talents and abilities, and personal excellence through educational achievement and community involvement. Importantly, these institutions have prized and valued the importance of mutual interaction with and understanding of different groups, and they have encouraged the involvement and leadership of their students in diverse settings. Central to this educational mission and direction have been the faculty, diverse in its representation and expertise, of historically black institutions.

Overview of the Contents

The introduction provides a broad historical framework for exploring the presence of white faculty in historically black institutions of higher education in the United States. It examines the factors and circumstances that have motivated and sustained that presence and provides a framework for interpreting the contributions of the authors whose work comprise the volume. With the exception of the editors, contributors to this volume are white faculty members and administrators who currently work in historically black colleges and universities (HBCUs), or who formerly held such positions. They represent the experiences of white faculty and administrators in both public and private HBCU institutions.

The volume is organized into three major themes. In part 1, "Teaching and Learning at Historically Black Colleges and Universities," authors explore multifaceted themes that surround the teaching and learning process in HBCU institutions. Specifically, contributors explore the purposes, nature, and consequences of teaching and learning from the institutional perspectives of HBCUs, institutions founded on "principles centered around the belief that Black students must be educated to assume leadership and service roles in the Black community and to succeed in the larger community" (Brazzell, 1996, p.50); that the sense of community empowers, supports, and sustains achievement; and that self-empowerment through an understanding of one's self and pride in one's cultural legacy are powerful prerequisites for success and service.

In chapter 1, Karl Henzy explores the significance of "contact zones" with black students and discusses the consequences of that "contact" from personal and disciplinary perspectives. The consequences of "contact" bear unique learning outcomes for him and for his students. In chapter 2, Matthew Redinger chronicles his personal and disciplinary teaching journey at one private four-year college for African-American women and at one public historically black university. He deconstructs his experiences of disciplinary and personal awareness and growth against backdrops of institutional mandates and student expectations for white faculty teaching at predominantly black institutions, his training as a historian, and glimpses from his earliest years as a child in a culturally homogeneous environment of a western state. Redinger explores the significance of the lessons he learned while teaching at two historically black institutions and the impact those experiences have had on his present position as an assistant professor of history at Montana State University, Billings, and for his interactions with students at his present institution who come from homogeneous living and learning environments. In chapter 3, Fred Bales traverses the terrain of analyzing the communication and actions in our society that supposedly lead to a color-blind society. He admits that the journey is a perilous one, particularly in his field of journalistic communication, which does not enjoy an enviable record of presenting accurate images of people of color nor for recruiting significant numbers of minorities into the field. As a communications professor he explores the responsibility of white journalism/communication professors to equip future black journalists with skills and insights that will make them a force in contemporary communications media. He admits that the task is fraught with misunder-standings and stereotypes that might derail the best efforts. According to Mark Thomson, in chapter 4, retention, achievement, and admissions to some of the nation's most prestigious medical, dental, and graduate schools are educational achievements that routinely occur for African-American students at Xavier University of Louisiana, a historically black and Roman Catholic institution in New Orleans, Louisiana. He discusses the unique and dynamic system of support and mentoring that sustains the achievement and success of students in meeting an institutional mission and expectation of academic achievement and service. In this context, Thomson finds that his own personal cultural insights have been dramatically changed and that this transformation has affected him in ways he could never have previously contemplated. In chapter 5, Amy Sibulkin explores the contextual efficacy of incorporating diverse multicultural issues into teaching and research in psychology at a historically black university. She discusses how teaching at a predominantly black college and university creates an immediacy for considering multicultural and diverse perspectives that may be unlikely to exist at predominantly white higher education institutions. It is both that context and immediacy that HBCU institutions provide that bear both obvious and not so obvious benefits and consequences for teaching and learning by white faculty members in these institutions. In chapter 6, Barbara Jur discusses how she developed a new understanding and appreciation for the "cultural communication power" of mathematics and its consequences for achievement in teaching at a historically black university. She explores how her roles as facilitator and responder in teaching African-American students created a dialogue for understanding and achievement. For Jur and her students mathematics could not be treated as a spectator sport.

In part 2, "Academic Careers at Historically Black Colleges and Universities," authors explore the nature of an academic career at an HBCU institution and the demands, challenges, and opportunities such a career provides for personal and institutional perspectives. They discuss the benefits that have accrued from their affiliation with an HBCU institution and why they continue to live out their academic career in these institutions.

In chapter 7, Barbara Frankle explores the "not always comfortable alliances and alignments" that plunged her into a new vision of education and that have fostered a thirty-year career as a faculty member and administrator at a historically black college. Against a backdrop of youthful naivete and mature involvement, Frankle explores how her association with historically black colleges has transformed her understanding of race and diversity, and how such association over time has aided her in a reformulated idea of what higher education should be doing in the 1990s and in the coming millennium. In chapter 8, against a backdrop of colorful social and political history, Stephen Rozman takes the reader on a twenty-six-year odyssey of personal and professional growth as a faculty member, department chair, and division dean at Tougaloo College in Tougaloo, Mississippi. His story is deeply personal and intimate, and it is tied to both his personal and professional commitment to Tougaloo College and to his life as a resident of the state of Mississippi. Rozman's professional and personal growth and his struggles and accomplishments are framed against his life and activities on the campus of Tougaloo College, renowned for its institutional leadership during the early days of the civil rights movement in Mississippi. In chapter 9, Jesse Silverglate discusses his conscious choice to dedicate his career energies to a life of teaching at a small, religiously affiliated college in Miami, Florida. He explores what this decision has meant for his professional and personal growth as a white faculty member in a predominantly black institution. The outcomes of his decision have included a thirty-year career that has been characterized by unique challenges, enriching personal and professional opportunities, and outstanding accomplishments by his students. In chapter 10, Frederick Frank reflects on the "anger-laser" he has so often encountered as a white professor on a predominantly black university campus. He judges this effect as "a good bit right" from his experiences as a white person in the general society; as a professor who has had significant professional experience on several predominantly white campuses where he has seen up close the negative effects that race can have on the well-being and success of minority students and faculty; and as a white professor on a predominantly black campus where black role models are important to students. Frank explores the complex and not so complex meanings of the "anger-laser" in American society as a whole, in higher education, and in historically black colleges and universities. With candor, some humor, and a bit of historical reference, Roy DeLamotte, in chapter 11, discusses his experiences and emerging insights as a young white United Methodist minister, southern and Mississippian by birth, whose goal was to promote racial equality as a professor at two predominantly black colleges. His discussions of the assumptions, beliefs, and values of black students on the predominantly black campus where he spent the bulk of his academic career, and the assumptions, beliefs, and values of whites and blacks in their interactions with each other in the wider American society are poignant for their truthfulness and for their conclusions.

In part 3, "Transformed and Transforming at Historically Black Colleges and Universities," authors explore the transforming effect of working at an HBCU institution and its consequences for professional and personal growth and development, for teaching and learning, and for the success of students. The authors also propose that higher education, in general, might profit from the behavior of HBCU institutions in their historical legacy of inclusiveness and in their support and nurturing of students on personal and individual levels.

In chapter 12, Toni Anderson and Juliana Lancaster conceptualize "voice" as a complex sense of belonging for minority white faculty in a predominantly black college that includes the opportunity to be heard, respected, understood, and valued in the context of the predominant culture within the institution. They discuss a model of four developmental stages (Silenced, Channeled, Heard, and Transformed) in the evolution of voice that they have experienced as white women minority faculty in a predominantly black college and the reasons for it. Anderson and Lancaster discuss how variables of time, situation, and relationships, not necessarily in any particular order and not a prolonged process, contribute to the minority faculty member's capacity to exercise voice. They explore the cycle, efficacy, and power of their voices in a predominantly black college as minority faculty and discover, unlike the experiences of minority faculty in predominantly white institutions where their voices are generally discounted, that the nurturing and inclusive nature of their institution supported their integration and welcomed their presence and contributions. In chapter 13, Karen Sides-Gonzales explores the theme of "We Are Family" to discuss the spirit of mission, pride, achievement, and success that characterizes the educational experience at St. Philip's College in San Antonio, Texas. Sides-Gonzales contends that the moral spirit and foundation provided by the school's first leader, Miss Artemisia Bowden, daughter of an ex-slave employed by the Episcopal Church to guide the institution, continues to animate the work of the public institution today to educate students inclusively and to educate students successfully for service in the wider community. In chapter 14, Lenoar Foster, Andrea Miller, and Janet Guyden discuss the context, scope, and meaning of faculty diversity in HBCU institutions, and the degree to which such diversity provides institutional viability for the education of students and upholds long-held traditions of educational inclusion by HBCU institutions.

The Audience for This Book

We believe that this volume addresses issues and demands that higher education is being asked to respond to in definitive ways. Among these are the need to: (1) further diversify campuses in order to serve the needs and challenges of an ever increasing diverse population and work force; (2) foster inclusive educational communities where all voices and contributions are heard, valued, supported, and sustained in support of democratic principles; (3) foster the academic achievement and success of students through outcomes-based and experientially-based programs; (4) provide dynamic, meaningful, and support-ive learning environments for student retention and persistence; and (5) ground collegiate education in the needs of community service and outreach at all levels of human interaction (governmental, corporate and non-corporate, local, state, national, and international levels). Higher education administrators and faculty who are charged with responding to the myriad of ethical and value-laden educational decisions that undergird the business of higher education, and to the accountability demands occasioned by the need to respond to these and other issues, will find the environmental and programmatic experiences and projects of historically black colleges and universities to be particularly instructive and worthy of emulation. Higher education scholars and students and educational historians exploring faculty mobility and faculty issues among diverse faculty will find that this volume fills a void in looking at faculty diversity through other "diverse eyes and voices." Scholars studying white identity development will discover personal case studies that point to the need to examine and to eradicate those societal structures that consciously and unconsciously mandate and provide privilege for some but not others in our democratic society. Importantly, administrators, faculty, and students at historically black colleges and universities will readily recognize in the voices contained in this volume how their institutions, working under dire conditions in many instances, have been responsive, productive, and successful in areas of contemporary concern to the higher education enterprise. With this realization HBCU institutions will need to more aggressively assert their expertise and capacities to provide authoritative voices and exemplary models in addressing many of the contemporary issues in higher education relative to faculty and student diversity, support of student retention and persistence, disciplinary and interdisciplinary collaborations for the improvement of teaching and learning, community outreach and service learning, and partnerships that connect postsecondary education to the world of work and professional practice.

References

Brazzel, J.C. (1996). Diversification of postsecondary institutions. In S.R. Komives, D.B. Woodward, Jr., & Associates (Eds.) (1996), *Student services: A handbook for the profession* (pp.43-63). San Francisco: Jossey-Bass Publishers, Inc.

Musil, C.M. (1996). The maturing of diversity initiatives on American campuses: Multiculturalism and diversity in higher education. *American Behavioral Scientist,* 40(2), 222-233.

Smith, S.L., & Borgstedt (1985). Factors influencing the adjustment of white faculty in predominantly black colleges. *Journal of Negro Education,* 54(2), 148-163.

United States Department of Education (1996). *Historically black colleges and universities: 1976-1994* (NCES 96-902, by C.M. Hoffman, T.D. Synder, and B. Sonnenberg). Washington, DC: National Center for Education Statistics.

Acknowledgments _____

We are indebted to Jill Rothenberg, our editor at Rowman & Littlefield Publishers, Inc., for her belief in and support of this project, and for her enthusiastic encouragement during the final stages of the compilation of this volume. We are also indebted to Christine Gatliffe, editorial assistant to Jill Rothenberg at Rowman & Littlefield Publishers, Inc., for her graciousness in responding quickly and efficiently to all of our technical questions during the process of compiling this work. No question was too small or too tedious.

In October 1998, Lenoar Foster and Janet A. Guyden had the privilege of presenting a plenary session to the meeting of the Fifth National HBCU Faculty Development Symposium, the annual meeting of the HBCU Faculty Development Network, in Miami, Florida. Their presentation, "Content Analysis of the Viewpoints of Selected White Faculty Members at HBCUs," and the feedback that was received from it from the diverse group of assembled faculty members from HBCU institutions throughout the country provided important insights and frameworks from which this volume was eventually organized and compiled. They are grateful to all of the faculty members at that conference for their candor, suggestions, and encouragement in this project and for our future research.

We would like to extend our heartfelt thanks and gratitude to the following individuals whose conversations with us and writings to us aided us immensely in the "voicing" process for this work: William Ziegler (Bethune-Cookman College), William Lawless (Paine College), Laura Grady (Paine College), William Castine (Florida A&M University), and Garrett Olmsted (Bluefield State College).

Special thanks are extended to Dr. Deidre D. Labat, vice president for academic affairs at Xavier University of Louisiana, for her enthusiastic support of this project. We are indebted to Dr. Labat for her intellectual realization of the need for such a scholarly contribution as this volume represents and for her work in disseminating our project goals to white faculty at her institution. Too, we are indebted to Lester Sullivan, archivist at Xavier University of Louisiana, for his graciousness and kindness in assisting us with the cover for this volume.

Special thanks are also extended to Karen Gass, administrative assistant in the Office of the Dean, School of Education, at the University of Montana for her generous time, encouragement and patient assistance to the editors in putting together the typed copy for this volume. We were always amazed at Karen's ability to interpret our "hieroglyphic" remarks through the process of putting together the final copy.

Lastly, we are grateful for the encouragement and enthusiasm of our colleagues at each of our home institutions. For it was our belief that they also believed what Garcia (1997) has so astutely stated:

> Our colleges and universities are at the heart of the social conscience of the nation—places where artificial barriers of race, religion, class, sex, sexual orientation, and language can be transcended and where we can inspire and develop leaders who will marshal a just society. Clearly, those involved in higher education must do a better job of educating both the public and policymakers about the importance of an inclusive society, not only for the benefit of people of color, but for us all. (p.3)

References

Garcia, M. (1997). The state of affirmative action at the threshold of a new millennium. In M. Garcia (Ed.) (1997), *Affirmative action's testament of hope: Strategies for a new era in higher education* (pp.1-17). Albany, NY: State University of New York Press.

Introduction

White Faculty at Historically Black Colleges and Universities: A Historical Framework

Janet A. Guyden, Lenoar Foster, & Andrea L. Miller

Historically black colleges have always had a white presence. From the beginning, white participation in black education was the rule rather than the exception as missionary organizations, religious denominations, and individuals took up the mantle of education for slaves and newly enfranchised freedmen. The literature in higher education is replete with research about the experiences of black faculty in majority educational institutions. That literature reports black faculty experiences that include isolation, overt hostility, and relegation to service roles that focus on minority issues. Although white faculty have been a part of the historically black higher education experience from its inception, little has been written about their experiences over time.

In this introductory chapter we provide a historical framework for exploring the presence of white faculty in historically black institutions of higher education in America. The purpose of this exploration will be to examine the factors and circumstances that motivated and sustained that presence and to provide a framework for interpreting the contributions of essayists in this volume.

Underlying Context

The general assumption that surrounds the historical lore of black higher education is monolithic: after the Civil War, schools and colleges were established to provide education for blacks so they would be prepared to find their place in American society. That general assumption disguises the multiple levels of conflict and ambiguity that beset this mammoth undertaking. Despite the existence of slavery as a social institution, a small but growing number of freedmen existed in colonial America. Members of this group actively sought and participated in education. The general attitude regarding the education of slaves was negative, yet slave owners were known to serve their own interests by educating their slaves to work in businesses and skilled crafts. Slaves and freedmen viewed education as the means to enfranchisement and full participation in the American social fabric. They actively sought it independently and through supportive whites. Although liberal whites viewed education for blacks as the means to full, equal participation in American society, other whites viewed the education of blacks as a means of providing an appropriately compliant work force and a resource for the colonization of Africa (Anderson, 1988; Bowles and DeCosta, 1971; Holmes, 1934; Spivey, 1978).

Although Holmes (1934) noted "that at the beginning of the Civil War the Negro, generally considered, began his academic education at zero" (p.8), he also acknowledged that "a considerable number of persons of color received academic instruction in varying degrees" (p.8), from the beginning of slavery in America (1619) to the nineteenth century. Before the Civil War, freedmen, slaves, and sympathetic whites supported efforts to establish educational opportunities for blacks. The formal educational opportunities were limited, but blacks did participate in them and some did earn college degrees. Records also indicate that blacks participated in other educational processes of those earlier times such as apprenticeships, teacher training, enrollment in non-degree courses, study abroad, self education, and education at a limited number of institutions established for blacks (Bowles and DeCosta, 1971).

The earliest higher education institutions established for the education of blacks actually predated 1854, usually identified as the establishment date for Ashmun Institute (Lincoln University) in Pennsylvania. Bowles and DeCosta (1971) identified a series of attempts to establish higher education institutions for blacks by the colonializationists and liberals as early as 1817. The colonializationists made several unsuccessful attempts to establish institutions from 1817 up until the successful establishment of Ashmun Institute in 1854. The liberal factions felt the need to establish colleges to prepare teachers and ministers and began their efforts as early as 1831. By 1839, these efforts resulted in the early beginnings of the Institute of Colored Youth in Philadelphia County (Pennsylvania). The school was incorporated in 1842 and ultimately became Cheney Training School for Teachers (Bowles and DeCosta, 1971). A black principal, Charles Reason, was appointed principal of the Institute for Colored Youth in 1852.

With the onset of the Civil War and the need to provide educational resources for the increasing numbers of blacks seeking refuge in the wake of the Union army, the trickle of educational efforts increased considerably. As Union army generals organized camps to support the needs of freedmen throughout the South, they enlisted the support of northern churches, freedmen's societies, black churches, and free black northern communities. In 1865, Congress created the Bureau of Refugees, Freedmen and Abandoned Lands (the Freedmen's Bureau) and placed it under the leadership of General Oliver O. Howard (Hill, 1984; Holmes, 1934). The bureau worked in coordination with the denominational boards and freedmen's societies to establish and maintain 2,677 schools. Although these schools provided primarily elementary and secondary education, the hope for the future was captured in the use of the words "college" and "university" in many of the names (Anderson, 1988; Bowles and DeCosta, 1971; Holmes, 1934). Some seventy-nine societies were engaged at one time or another in the effort to provide educational aid to the freedmen (Holmes, 1934, p.12).

Developmental Periods of Black Higher Education

Anderson (1988), Bowles and DeCosta (1971), and Holmes (1934) described the historical development of black higher education in phases or periods. These periods, with some modifications, represent a guide to the organization of this historical narrative. Each of these periods encompasses some significant developmental event, or series of events, that mark the evolution of the historically black college.

The first and most active phase ranged from 1865 to the late 1880s, roughly from the close of the Civil War to the end of Reconstruction. By the late 1880s, the progress gained during Reconstruction had begun to stall in the face of a rising Jim Crowism. The second phase spanned the period from the 1890s through approximately 1928. It was marked at the outset by the passage of the Second Morrill Act in 1890 and the *Plessy* v. *Ferguson* ruling that made "separate but equal" the law of the land in 1896. The exhaustive survey of black colleges conducted by the Bureau of Education marked the end of the second phase. The third phase, ranging from the 1930s to 1954, included a period of solidification when the black colleges became established institutions. Black higher education institutions sought and acquired recognition from regional accrediting bodies, and expanded their programs and facilities in response to the influx of students using the GI Bill after World War II. The fourth phase began after *Brown* v. *Board of Education* and continues into the present. The Brown ruling marked the end of separate but equal as the law of the land. It also set the stage for turbulent times for black colleges. With integration looming in the future, many individuals, both black and white, began to question the need for the continuation of black colleges. The presence of white faculty was evident in each of these periods. Their roles varied in each era, and their presence and participation in black higher education was continuous.

The Active Early Period: 1865 to the Late 1880s

During this active first period, the Freedmen's Bureau, the freedmen's societies, northern churches, and the denominational boards of black churches were most active in the establishment of black educational institutions. Anderson (1988) identified a triumvirate of philanthropy that supported black higher education from Reconstruction through the years of the Great Depression and noted the distinct perceptions regarding the relationship of education to the political, economic, and social roles of blacks. *Missionary philanthropy* consisted of "northern white benevolent societies and denominational bodies." *Negro philanthropy* was represented by "black religious organizations." *Industrial philanthropy* was identified as "large corporate philanthropic foundations and wealthy individuals" (p.239).

The dominant northern denominational boards and societies involved in establishing educational institutions during the first phase were the American Missionary Association (AMA), the Freedmen's Aid Society of the Methodist Episcopal Church, the American Baptist Home Mission Society, and the Presbyterian Board of Missions. The black church denominations that were active in establishing institutions in this same time period were the African Methodist Episcopal Church, the African Methodist Episcopal Zion Church, the Colored Methodist Episcopal Church (now the Christian Methodist Episcopal Church), and the black Baptist Church (Anderson, 1988). The industrial philanthropy group consisting of the Peabody Education Fund and the John Slater Fund were active during the early developmental phase, while the General Education Board, the Caroline Phelps-Stokes Fund, and individuals like Anna T. Jeanes and Julius Rosenwald contributed more significantly to the later second phase of black higher education development.

The faculty and administration in schools organized for blacks during the early first phase were made up predominantly of white clergy, missionaries, and teachers trained in the northern tradition. They had begun preparing black teachers to work in the primary and secondary schools with the purpose of lifting up the race. McBride (1977), in his analysis of the changing racial thought at Lincoln University, described the Presbyterian General Assembly's praise for thirty students who had applied to the Committee of Freedmen to work in the South to educate freedmen in 1868. These newly trained black teachers worked in the schools at the primary and secondary levels, but black administrators were rare during this period. Those institutions that were established by the black church denominations were more likely to have black faculty and leadership.

When the Freedmen's Bureau was officially discontinued in 1870, black and white church denominational boards continued the work of establishing and maintaining schools, especially the colleges and universities. Holmes (1934) cited the American Missionary Association's (AMA) policies regarding its role in maintaining a large number of educational institutions. Where its work operating primary and secondary schools duplicated the work of local boards of education, it transferred its work to the local boards. The association sought to advance the effectiveness of its higher education institutions by assisting them to achieve complete independence, or by merging them with other institutions where feasible.

As local boards of education assumed responsibility for primary and secondary education, the early institutions for blacks focused more specifically on college-level work. With the early emphasis on teacher preparation in the secondary-level normal schools, the number of black teachers at the lower levels increased. By the end of Reconstruction in 1870, the number of normal schools and industrial schools had increased and the number of black teachers working at those levels exceeded white teachers for the first time (Holmes, 1934). The missionary fervor that had spurred the initial establishment of the schools for blacks began to wane and financial support became scarce. The white teachers who remained in the black institutions near the end of the first period and through the early second period were deeply committed. As the South reverted to patterns of subjugation, white teachers in black educational institutions were subjected to intimidation and violence. Although their numbers were dwindling, a committed core remained to ensure the beginnings of an established pool of black teachers.

Each of the groups involved in the establishment of higher education for blacks had its own educational philosophy that was predicated upon its perception of the role of blacks in the American society: full participants in the American society or educated workforce participants with limited social roles. The northern missionary and Negro philanthropy groups were focused on liberal education and the development of black leadership to lift the black race. The industrial philanthropy groups were focused on education that would prepare blacks for participation in rebuilding the southern economy and for maintaining their place in a segregated southern society.

Anderson (1988) has deftly explored the subtle differences that existed between the northern missionary and Negro groups. Both groups believed in the power of the classical liberal curriculum to improve the lot of black people and acquiesced in the assumption that deliverance of the race was predicated upon patterning black behavior on the culture and values of white New England. The area over which the two groups disagreed was in the use of black faculty and administrators in the schools. The northern missionary groups exercised a paternalistic control over the educational institutions they established as a function of their Christian duty. As noted earlier, the supply of black teachers at the elementary level began to increase during the latter part of the first educational phase. The colleges and universities that emerged during this first phase were private and largely denominational. The faculties and administrations remained predominantly white. The colleges established by the black denominations were the exception.

The Second Period: 1890 to 1928

The late 1880s were marked by major social and political events of the time. By the late 1880s, Reconstruction had come to an end and local social and political attitudes began to impact education in the South. Hill (1984) noted that progress in public education for blacks stalled after Reconstruction and the United States Supreme Court's 1896 separate but equal decision in *Plessy* v. *Ferguson.* Although black higher education had previously been a private enterprise, the passing of the Second Morrill Act in 1890 set the stage for the development of public black higher education. As separate but equal became the law of the land, southern states passed statutes that forbade the mixing of the races, particularly in the school setting. The availability of black teachers to provide collegiate level education was still problematic. Those few positions were still filled by white faculty in the private black colleges of missionary origins. Bowles and DeCosta (1971) noted that 194 blacks had graduated from northern colleges between 1865 and 1895. That number did not represent the resources necessary to staff the newly emerging, rapidly growing black colleges. Thus, the public and the land-grant black colleges initially provided only secondary, normal, and industrial education.

The combination of the emergence of the public black colleges and the separate but equal doctrine that resulted from *Plessy* v. *Ferguson* led to the development of a closed system of black education that included black higher education. Public elementary and secondary education for blacks had been established during Reconstruction and continued to operate after the resegregation process had emerged. Black teachers replaced white teachers in those schools and the training of black teachers became the primary focus of black colleges. Teachers educated in the black colleges went back into the segregated systems and, in turn, sent even larger numbers to college to be trained as teachers. This cycle led to the expansion of black higher education and an eventual opening for the increased employment of black higher education faculty (Bowles and DeCosta, 1971). By the beginning of the twentieth century, especially in the middle of the second phase, the black education system was fairly isolated from and dependent on the white social, economic, and political structures of the time.

The northern missionary groups were finding it increasingly difficult to support their colleges. As they sought financial support to keep their colleges viable, they approached the industrial philanthropists. This industrial philanthropy group brought two powerful issues to the table. First, its members had significant financial resources, and second, it had a strong orientation to the Hampton/Tuskegee model of industrial education. Private education agencies like the General Education Board, the Carnegie Foundation, and the Rosenwald Fund, key actors in the industrial philanthropy group, became heavily involved in the funding of black higher education as an extension of the work they had begun at the elementary and secondary levels. Initially, the industrial philanthropists saw little utility in providing liberal education for blacks and had no interest in providing help to the missionary groups. Their educational philosophy was predicated upon educating blacks to rebuild the southern economy and for them to exist within the segregated caste system.

The industrial philanthropists were not completely opposed to liberal education. They were interested in retaining a few colleges to prepare black professionals for the closed black society, but they wanted teacher education within the control of the industrial normal schools (Anderson, 1988). Whoever controlled the minds of the teachers potentially controlled the minds of the students who came under their tutelage. By the 1920s, the industrial philanthropists' interest in funding black higher education had increased. The very issue that had initially made them reluctant to support black higher education finally motivated them: teacher education. As state and local authorities raised the standards for teachers, the industrial normal schools were less able to provide teachers who could meet the new standards. In fact, the black higher education institutions were even needed to provide faculty for the industrial and normal schools (Anderson, 1988).

This second period also encompassed an era of black intellectual development. W.E.B. Dubois and Booker T. Washington represented the intellectual touchstones of the two philosophies that vied for control of black higher education. The period provided fertile ground for a vibrant intellectual movement. Individuals like Alexander Crummell and his American Negro Academy, Carter G. Woodson, Paul Laurence Dunbar, Ida Wells Barnett, and Mary Church Terrell were active and productive during this period. Their activities and work set the stage for blacks to control their own intellectual and educational future.

The Third Period: 1929 to 1954

A movement toward autonomy marked the third period in the development of American black higher education. Increasing unrest and protest in the black community after World War I led to an increase in black control of black institutions, including higher education. Klein (1928), in his extensive survey of black colleges, noted the growing tendency to hire black faculty at institutions that previously had a majority of white faculty. He also noted that colleges governed by the black denominations had black faculty from the beginning. Although Klein (1928) did not provide a summary of faculty by race, a review of the first degrees of institutional faculty members provide some indication of the racial makeup of the faculty. For example, of the fourteen faculty members listed for Talladega College (Alabama), five received their baccalaureate degrees from black colleges; six from white colleges; and three had no college listed for the first degree. Given the limit to nonexistent enrollment of blacks in majority institutions at the time, it can be inferred that the six faculty members who received their degrees from white colleges were probably white. In contrast, Miles College in Birmingham, Alabama, governed by the Colored Methodist Episcopal Church, listed seven faculty members; all seven received their baccalaureate degrees from black colleges. It is probably safe to assume that these faculty members were black.

During this third developmental period, black colleges established themselves more firmly as postsecondary institutions. They closed their secondary divisions and acquired recognition from the regional accrediting bodies, albeit through a separate parallel accrediting structure. The land-grant colleges were offering higher education and the state schools established four-year collegiate departments (Hill, 1982). As more of the institutions offered college level work, they recognized the need for accreditation and the need to offer graduate level programs. Both of these tasks required faculty expertise that was not yet available to large numbers of black faculty. Thus, black colleges continued to utilize white faculty, although Klein (1928) noted that their numbers were decreasing.

Enrollment in the black colleges increased during the 1930s as more black students were able to take advantage of increased secondary school opportunities. By the close of World War II, returning black servicemen flooded black college campuses to take advantage of the GI Bill to pursue college degrees. The closed educational cycle that Bowles and DeCosta (1971) have described eventually led to an increased number of black college faculty available to teach in black colleges. The legal separation of the races during this period would have had the impact of excluding white faculty at black public colleges during this same time.

The Fourth Period:
Brown v. *Board of Education* (1954) to the Present

The fourth major period in the development of black higher education began when the Supreme Court of the United States handed down its ruling in *Brown* v. *Board of Education* in 1954. Although the ruling was initially applied to public primary and secondary schools, its application to the broader social context, including higher education, was swift. The civil rights movement pervaded every aspect of American life and integration slowly began to change the contours of the black community. The space age forced the American educational system to reassess its priorities and black colleges, although separated from the dominant system by law and tradition, were no less affected. The war in Southeast Asia split the country as decisively as the Civil War had one hundred years earlier, while the War on Poverty fought within the political and economic confines of America's borders attempted to heal the wounds caused by generations of benign neglect. Through it all, black colleges and their faculties have attempted to adapt to the demands of a changing national context and to meet the expectations of the black community for racial uplift and educational access and excellence.

Black colleges, their faculty, and their students have played varying roles in the social changes of this fourth period. Black colleges were, at any given time, sources of change or reactors to change. As black students' numbers increased on white campuses as a result of desegregation, the students began to push for the inclusion of the black perspective in the curriculum. The resultant rise of the black studies movement on black campuses met with mixed reviews from black social, political, and educational leaders. This ambivalence toward the inclusion and/or expansion of black studies on the black college campuses was a natural outgrowth of these institutions' ambivalence about their roles. For predominantly black colleges that defined their missions, in part, as preparing students to function in the existing environment, black studies programs represented an element of risk. For the colleges that defined their missions as preparing students for liberation and control over their own destinies, black studies programs represented a positive movement toward social agency. In fact, some of the latter group of institutions were already about the education of "race men" and "race women."

In the broader social arena, the black power and the civil rights movements emerged as social-political constructs driven by the energy of college students and faculty. In fact, some white faculty members gravitated toward black colleges and universities because of their interests in the civil rights movement. Although students and faculty were actively involved in the movement, many presidents of the black colleges were less sanguine about their institutions' involvement in a process that could antagonize the existing dominant power structure. It was not unusual for some black colleges to suspend students and dismiss faculty members because of their active participation in civil rights demonstrations, rather than risk the goodwill and resources that flowed from the white-controlled governmental and philanthropic organizations.

White faculty continued to be present in varying numbers on black college campuses throughout the complex social gyrations of this fourth period. Although little research has focused on their numbers or on their roles during this period, evidence indicates that they continued to be an invisible presence. Decker's 1955 study of white teachers at black colleges and other limited studies (Brown and Donovan, 1980; Davis, 1979; Jones, 1973) provide a baseline perspective for examining the presence and contributions of white faculty on black campuses during part of this fourth era.

In his study of fifty-five black colleges in twenty states, Decker (1955) noted that 8 percent of the 3,600 faculty, or 290 faculty, were "non-Negro." Sixty-seven percent of the fifty-five colleges Decker studied reported having interracial faculties, while eighteen of the schools reported no white faculty. He further noted at the time that several black campuses in Mississippi, Alabama, and Georgia indicated that they "were continuing to abide by state laws until the Supreme Court indicated that white students and teachers could be admitted" (p.501). Decker's study also indicated that several schools in his sample had had long historical traditions of having whites serve on their faculties. Chief among these institutions were Howard University in Washington, D.C. that reported during the study that ninety of its 450 faculty were non-Negro; and Fisk University in Nashville, Tennessee, and Lincoln University in Pennsylvania reported "that their faculties of approximately forty members each are about equally divided" (p.501). Of black campuses reporting mixed faculties, Decker (1955) concluded "on the average, 14 percent of the teachers on bi-racial faculties are non-Negro and the median number of white teachers on the bi-racial faculties studied is three" (p.501). Motivations of white faculty for choosing to work on a black campus in Decker's study varied.

> About 40 percent of the teachers had no particular reason for working in a Negro College. As a whole their attitude indicated that "color" as such had no particular meaning to them. Twenty percent were working in Negro colleges because of an interest in race relations, 6 percent had been appointed to their jobs and another 6 percent mentioned missionary type motives. About 8 percent were convinced that exceptional personal and professional opportunities were present and one gentleman wished to prove to himself that "my democratic attitudes are not mere parlor talk." (Decker, 1955, p.502)

Decker (1955) noted that social relationships on black campuses between black and white faculty were a function of personality and interest rather than a function of race. This was evident in the relationships that white faculty enjoyed with their black colleagues and students. He also noted reactions of close family and friends to white faculty working at a black college that ranged from favorable and supportive to negative and apprehensive. Smith and Borgstedt (1985), in their study of factors influencing the adjustment of white faculty in six predominantly black public and private colleges in the South and North, found that negative attitudes and comments from significant others, family members, and friends "attached some stigma to their position" (p.159) in a black college.

Jones (1973) provided an anecdotal case study of the experiences of a white faculty person at a black college in the late 1960s. The combination of Decker's findings and Jones's descriptions illustrate a powerful picture of dichotomies. The white faculty members on Jones's campus had come for different reasons as well. Most remained a year or two and moved on; a few made long-term commitments. Her telling of the ambiguous position of the white faculty member caught between developing trust as a white person in the black community and allaying the suspicions of the white community provided a tension that was palpable.

Davis (1979) and Brown and Donovan (1980) revisited Decker's work and provided additional insights about white faculty on black campuses. Davis's study was conducted at Morehouse College in Atlanta, Georgia. He explored reasons for employment of white faculty at the college, perceptions about the caliber of students, faculty productivity, and plans to remain at the college. Brown and Donovan (1980) conducted their study at Fayetteville State University in Fayetteville, North Carolina, in an attempt to expand the Davis work to a different cultural setting and to determine whether the difference in cultural settings influenced the same variables. The results of both studies were similar and consistent with the outcomes of the Decker study completed in 1955. White faculty members in the Decker study had no particular reason for seeking employment at black colleges or were committed to an interest in race relations. Davis's sample at Morehouse sought positions because of a commitment to the civil rights movement, or because the institution provided positions in a tight job market. All three of the research-based studies indicated that the majority of the white faculty planned to continue in black higher education institutions. Jones (1973) echoed these findings in her anecdotal case study as well.

Increasingly, however, for younger white faculty members seeking first jobs in higher education who come to academe with new understandings of diversity and inclusion, the need to secure a faculty position in a tight higher education market and the availability of faculty positions in predominantly black higher education institutions have come to be cited as chief reasons and motivations for them working in black colleges and universities (Smith and Borgstedt, 1985; Redinger, 1999).

Historically, the black college has been perceived as receptive and hospitable to white faculty. Magner (1993) has noted that black colleges have always prided themselves on being shelters from racial bias, but charges of discrimination and bias against white faculty have increased (p.A20). Court cases have become more common as white faculty attempt to rectify behaviors that they perceive as discriminatory. This raises a significant concern at a time when white faculty make up 27.5 percent of the faculty at four-year historically black colleges and 25.4 percent of the faculty at historically black two-year institutions, a total of 27.4 percent of faculty at all black higher education institutions (Nettles, Perna, and Freeman, 1999). At a time when all of the best talent is needed to develop and deliver the best possible academic programs that black colleges can provide, these colleges stand accused of the same behaviors that the black community has attributed to the dominant white institutions. Will the literature of the future report white faculty experiences that include isolation, overt hostility, and relegation to service roles that focus on minority issues where minority issues are white issues?

Black colleges have progressed through four distinct periods, moving from externally controlled isolation to internally driven control and participation. White faculty have been an integral part of this complex journey. Their roles and motivations have been as varied as the situations along that historic and developmental path. The continuing and ever dynamic missions of predominantly black colleges and universities must include an ongoing appraisal of the roles that can be played by diverse faculty in providing learning environments that will prepare students to meet the challenges, complex and multifaceted, of the future. Diverse faculty, particularly white faculty, and the environments in which they work, function, interact, and contribute to institutional viability and success will provide a measure to black higher education institutions of their ability to promote their long held traditions of inclusion. More importantly, black higher education institutions can serve as models of what true diversity among higher education faculty can mean for the reflection, growth, development, and advancement of individuals as facilitators of truth and learning, and what these perspectives can offer to the students and institutions they serve.

References

Anderson, J.D. (1988). *The education of blacks in the south, 1860-1935*. Chapel Hill, NC: The University of North Carolina Press.

Bowles, F., & F.A. DeCosta (1971). *Between two worlds: A profile of Negro higher education*. New York: McGraw-Hill Book Company.

Brown, C.I., & D.M. Donovan (1980). *White faculty at historically black institutions: A pilot study*. Durham, NC: Institute on Desegregation, North Carolina Central University. (ERIC Document Reproduction Service No. ED 224 368).

Davis, A.L. (1979). White teachers at black colleges: A case study of Morehouse College. *The Western Journal of Black Studies*, 3, 224-227.

Decker, P. (1955). A study of "white" teachers in selected "Negro" colleges. *The Journal of Negro Education*, 24(4), 501-505.

Hill, S.T. (1982). *The traditionally black institutions of higher education, 1860-1982*. Washington, DC: National Center for Educational Statistics.

Holmes, D.O.W. (1970). *The evolution of the Negro college*. New York: AMS Press, Inc. (Reprinted from the 1934 edition).

Jones, A. (1973). *Uncle Tom's campus*. New York: Praeger Publishers.

Klein, A.J. (1929). *Survey of Negro colleges and universities*. Washington, DC: U.S. Department of Interior, Bureau of Education, Bulletin 7, U.S. Government Printing Office.

Magner, D.K. (1993, October 13). Several black colleges accused of racism. *The Chronicle of Higher Education*, p.A20.

McBride, D. (1977). Africa's elevation and changing racial thought at Lincoln University, 1854-1886. *The Journal of Negro History*, 62(4), 363-377.

Nettles, M.T., L.W. Perna, & K.E. Freeman (1999). *Two decades of progress: African Americans moving forward in higher education*. Fairfax, VA: Frederick D. Patterson Research Institute of the United Negro College Fund.

Redinger, M.A. (1999), You just wouldn't understand. In L. Foster, J.A. Guyden, & A.L. Miller, *Affirmed action: Essays on the academic and social lives of white faculty members at historically black colleges and universities* (23-36). Lanham, MD: Rowman & Littlefield Publishers, Inc.

Smith, S.L., & K.W. Borgstedt (1985). Factors influencing adjustment of white faculty in predominantly black colleges. *Journal of Negro Education*, 54(2), 148-163.

Part One _____

*Teaching and Learning at Historically Black
Colleges and Universities*

Chapter 1 _____

Making Connections:
A White Professor at a
Historically Black University

Karl Henzy

What's in a Name?

It was 1993, and I was just starting as an English professor at Morgan State University. I have to admit that I felt nervous, even a little bit more so than is usual for any professor in a new place, because of the racial difference between me and most of my students. Morgan State is a historically black university (HBCU), and I am white. In fact, as I walked into my first classes that September, for the first time in my life I really felt white. I had always thought of myself generically as just a person. Now I was conscious of myself specifically as a white person. (Of course, I was simply experiencing an awareness that many of my students have had to deal with their whole lives, of being in others' eyes specifically persons of a certain race.) At the same time, I felt optimistic about connecting with my students and having a good semester, and certainly the students' faces I observed looked open, willing to give me a chance. The problem started as I began going through the names on the class roll. There were some Kimberleys and some Davids, but there were other names that I had never seen and that I had no idea how to pronounce: Tsanonda, Acem,

Teria, Contrell, Shountee`, Henina, Tavis, Lamorea. As I stumbled through with incorrect pronunciations, one student after another correcting me on their names, I sensed a growing restlessness. And when I still couldn't get their names right the next day and again the next, students began to sound short and clipped as they said their names correctly, their upright postures and tight lips signifying opposition.

And I couldn't blame them. Here I had had visions of wonderful, open discussions of great works of literature by writers both black and white, and I couldn't even get my students' names right. The atmosphere in the class was beginning to seem hopelessly negative, and I was becoming desperate. Frustrated, and with nothing to lose, I finally looked up from the class roll one day at the beginning of class and just said, "Listen everyone, the truth is I grew up in a typical white middle-class suburb, where everyone was named Billy or Betty or Sally or Tommy, so I'm going to have trouble getting your names right for a while, but it doesn't mean I don't like your names. It just means they're new to me, and I apologize for all my mispronunciations, though I can't promise I'm not going to continue misprounouncing for a little while longer."

I half expected my outburst to be the final straw, and could imagine my students drawing up a petition to have me ousted, but the effect was just the opposite. There were chuckles at the note of sarcasm in my voice as I said "Billy or Betty or Sally or Tommy," and I could feel the release from tension spread throughout the room. Because I had been open with them about the limitations of my background, they were willing to give me some slack. The slight change in atmosphere may seem like a small thing, but I feel like it made teaching possible again.

(Interestingly, in later classes when we got to the great epics like *Gilgamesh*, *The Iliad*, and *Son Jara*, in which the hero frequently has a whole collection of names like so many badges earned, we were able to have some good discussions about names and naming—how naming is done differently in different cultures and may take on a variety of meanings.)

Contact Zones

In a paper delivered at the Modern Language Association Literacy Conference in 1990, Mary Louise Pratt develops a theory of what she calls "contact zones," by which she means "social spaces where cultures meet, clash, and grapple with each other" (Batholomae and Petrosky, 1996, p.530). Historically, of course, contact zones have most often occurred "in contexts of highly asymmetrical relations of power." In the university, Pratt says, this has generally meant that whatever cultural differences exist between students, or between students and professors, the classroom "situation is [assumed to be] governed by a single set of rules or norms shared by all participants. . . . whatever students do [or say or think] other than what the teacher specifies is invisible or anomalous"

(Bartholomae and Petrosky, 1996, p.538). In other words, the teacher pretends that differences of background and experience do not exist. It's as if to acknowledge such differences would be to let anarchy into the classroom.

On the contrary, Pratt argues, "contact zones" can become highly productive learning environments when differences are acknowledged because precisely then the students' and professor's understandings of the subject matter can be seen as coming out of specific times and places, and this can lead to greater, not lesser, awareness for both students and professor. It requires participants to develop skills in "communication across lines of difference and hierarchy that go beyond politeness but maintain mutual respect; a systematic approach to the all-important concept of cultural mediation" (Bartholomae and Petrosky, 1996, p.541). I have found, in my experiences teaching literature as a white professor at a historically black university, that in talking about works of literature, discussion of our backgrounds (and there are differences in background between my students, as well as between them and me), and of the assumptions and expectations we have because of these backgrounds, can be essential to making any progress into deeper understandings of the work.

Testing the Teacher

Once we had gotten over the name problem and my students began to trust me enough to want to test me a bit further, they would sometimes ask me confrontational questions. If we were studying, say, Chaucer or Dostoevsky, I might hear, "Why should we have to study these dead white European writers from hundreds of years ago? What can they possibly have to do with us?" (Of course, my African-American colleagues hear this same question.) If the subject, instead, was fiction by Richard Wright or Zora Neale Hurston, the question might be, "What can you, a white man, have to teach us about black literature? What do you know about what it's like to grow up and live as a black person in America?"

I've never considered pulling rank in such cases to be a viable option. If I were simply to declare that such questions are irrelevant, that, for better or worse, I am the teacher and they are the students, I believe that I would lose the entire class. They would study for the tests, certainly, but any possibility for understanding between us would be eliminated, and they'd leave my class, possibly, with resentment not only toward me but also toward literature.

But, in fact, far from wanting to stifle such questions, I consider them to be quite important. Trying to answer them, not immediately with some pat response but patiently exploring them, can create the driving energy for an entire semester. And these explorations have taught me certain things about literature, about myself, and about what it is that I do, that we do, as academics.

When I teach works of literature by African-American authors, I suggest to my students that we can work as collaborators on such texts. Yes, Richard

Wright's *The Man Who Lived Underground*, a required text in our second semester Humanities course, is about the experience of a man who is treated as guilty by the police for a murder he did not commit, only because of his skin color. I do not know what it is like to be the victim of this kind of persecution, while many of my students can tell story after story of being suspected of some crime, or watched closely as a potential thief, on account of their racial difference from the white people who suspected them. On this level, they are the experts on Wright's story, and they can help me to understand the experience Wright depicts.

Wright's story is not raw experience, however. It is an imagined experience that has been shaped and given form as literature. Here I am the expert: I can talk to my students about Dostoevsky's *Underground Man* and about Wright's method of drawing on the work of the Russian writer. I can draw students' attention to the ways Wright breaks up and structures his narrative. I can take students through certain significant passages word by word, helping them to think through precisely what it is that Wright is saying and what he is not saying. I can show them that such passages, from different sections of the narrative, are linked together by parallel phrases and ideas.

My students, then, are able to bring to bear on the text their cultural experience as African Americans, while I bring to bear on the text my expertise, as a literature professor, with the abstractions of pattern, symbol, allusion, and theme, and together we negotiate a loose sense of how Wright brings the two aspects together in his work.

The Culture of Abstraction

These discussions, in turn, have helped me to realize something about myself. My facility with the abstractions, with pattern, is not something in a different category from what I'm saying my students bring to the text: experience. The habit of isolating the pattern, of moving from the particular to the general, is itself a cultural tendency—the culture of academia ultimately, but for me first the culture of my upbringing. I was raised in white middle-class suburbia. My neighborhood consisted of a set of geometrically arranged streets, with green rectangular lawns, and houses in three or four basic patterns, which were simply variations of each other. It was easy for me to see that the house of my friend up the street corresponded to my house, in spite of slight differences. His house faced east, let's say, while ours faced southeast. Where our second bathroom was, they had an extra closet, and so on. Pattern and generality were the context in which we lived.

Not only the architecture of the neighborhood, but the occupations of our parents, the clothes they bought for us from the malls, the food we ate from Betty Crocker recipes, the television shows we watched, all reinforced the idea that variations were slight and insignificant, and that life was dominated by far-reaching patterns of sameness. My safe, comfortable surroundings allowed me the luxury of time to think about these patterns, and the adults in my life valued and encouraged the ability to impose order and recognize archetypes. This is my cultural background: not the German or English cultural traits of my ancestors, but the abstract homogeneity of middle-class suburbia.

It is a cultural background that is much in harmony with the culture of academia as it currently exists. Those well-known SAT relationship questions (purple is to the color spectrum as the musical note F is to what?) are probably culturally biased because they favor abstract ways of knowing. And we academics, not just in English but in all fields, have this kind of thinking reinforced by our training, during the years of graduate school, to find the patterns, to formulate the general statement, and generally to be happy with that. So when I teach my students at Morgan State University about the patterns in Wright's narrative, its similarities with and differences from other narratives, and the generalizations that can be drawn from it, I'm doing something that my cultural background has prepared me for.

Connections

In some ways it's actually more problematic teaching works of literature by European authors, for I've found that its here that my students have pushed me to expand my sense of the relevance of works long familiar to me. Just as I have applied my cultural experience to African-American literature in generalizing about it, I find that my students keep teaching me about the relevance of their cultural experiences for understanding European literature.

One student, for instance, taught me about rap music themes in the context of a discussion of Homer's *Iliad*. In the Greek warriors' intensity about their reputations as fighters, he sensed something he was already familiar with, and he wanted me not just to tell him about Homer, but to listen and learn from him about Public Enemy and KRS-One. Another student, during a discussion of the *Canterbury Tales*, told me about Spike Lee's film, *On the Bus*. Just as Chaucer has many types of characters on the pilgrimage, each with different motivations (some not so spiritual), each telling his or her story, so Lee has many types of men on that bus to the Million Man March, again with different reasons for being there (some not so idealistic), and with different stories to tell. Still another student kept bringing our discussions of Dostoevsky's *The Brothers Karamazov* to his work as a minister of a black church in Baltimore. In the Russian priest Father Zosima's counseling session with the bereaved women he saw himself, and he wanted me to see this too.

As these and other students spoke during class about their experiences, part of me felt like I needed to cut them short, that they were getting too far away from the texts we were supposed to be studying, using up too much class time to talk about themselves. But another part of me sensed that what they were doing was legitimate and worthwhile, that this is what these texts are for. They made possible a two-way exchange of ideas between different cultural experiences, different ways of knowing, mine and my students. They created what Mary Louise Pratt calls a "contact zone" in its most positive sense. And my students helped me to work with them beyond the standard ways of conducting a class that academia had prepared me for.

Teaching at the other institution where I have worked, a state university that attracts primarily middle-class, white students, has been markedly different. Most students there have been interested neither in discussing abstractions (it's too difficult) nor in relating what we are reading to their own lives. What they want to know is: What's going to be on the test? *The Bell Curve* made so much of the fact that the average SAT scores of African Americans are lower than the scores of students of European descent, but what is it that the SATs measure? For it was here in these discussions that I found the most of what I count as intelligence: intellectual curiosity, a passionate engagement with ideas, a readiness to question. And I am grateful to these students for the ways they have pushed me. I will never think again of the *Iliad*, the *Canterbury Tales*, or *The Brothers Karamazov* without thinking of what my students had to tell me about their experiences in relation to these texts. My sense of them has been enriched, and for that I am grateful.

Notes

This essay previously appeared, in a slightly more abbreviated form, in the *Chronicle of Higher Education* on October 10, 1997. The author would especially like to thank *Chronicle* editor Jennifer Ruark, who greatly assisted him in thinking through this essay.

References

Bartholomae, D., & A. Petrosky (Eds.). (1996). *Ways of reading* (4th ed.). Boston: St. Martin's Press.

Chapter 2 _____

You Just Wouldn't Understand

Matthew A. Redinger

"It's different. You just wouldn't understand. After all, you're white." She was right. I did not understand. In many ways, I am just now processing the events of that day in 1994, and beginning to "understand." The dynamic at work in that small, private college for African-American women provided a context of challenge and response, demanding of those participating in the process a constant effort to reexamine the realities—or personal perspectives on those realities—of race, class, and gender. The challenge the institution presented to us was to broaden our mutual perspectives, and our response to that challenge involved a validation of both our superficial differences and, what is more important, our deeper similarities.

My sojourn into the terra incognita of teaching at two historically black institutions began as I neared graduation from the University of Washington in the spring of 1993. I was one of a class of thirteen freshly minted history Ph.D.s and embraced the same improbable dream as the rest of my class: a tenure track job right out of the chute. We all knew that the odds were long—few of the previous year's graduates had landed positions. I began filling the market with applications in the fall of 1992, and following a few interviews at history conferences and a campus visit, graduation and impending unemployment were roaring my way.

In the last week of May 1993, as I performed my weekly scan of the *Chronicle of Higher Education*, I read a job announcement from Bennett College in the North Carolina Piedmont region, advertising for a World Civilization, United States, Asian, and Latin American history instructor. The ad made no mention of tenure, but in my increasingly dire straits, it made little difference. The announcement did, however, mention that the school was "a small residential liberal arts college [that] focuses on producing scholars," and that the school sought applicants "who understand the nature and purpose of a liberal arts college committed to the education of women." The announcement seemed to fit me well.

In the course of my job search, I was careful to research all of the positions for which I applied, but when I went to seek out Bennett College, I could find little information. With anticipation of the opportunity to face the particular challenges and potential insights I could gain from teaching at a women's college, I applied for the job.

In the days after mailing my application and placement file, Bennett remained a mystery. In fact, it was not until the telephone interview three weeks later that I actually discovered that Bennett was a historically black college. I learned this particularly important piece of information when the academic dean asked me how Bennett's mission of educating African-American women would affect the way I did my job. After this question sunk in for a few seconds, I replied that I would, of course, need to adjust the traditional "Great White Man" way of teaching history to make the course meaningful for the women of Bennett College. The phone interview went well, and the day after the interview, the academic dean invited me to come to the campus for a face-to-face interview in late July.

Now that I was actually going to the school for a campus visit, I had to do some hasty consideration of where my life was taking me. I had not completely come to grips with the very real possibility that I would get a job at a black women's college. I was not sure what it would be like to teach at a school that reflected a reality so radically different from the one I lived in the Pacific Northwest. To aid me in this process of discernment, I depended upon the advice of my mentor, who had so frequently in the past employed his insights, logic, and experience to help me cut through the fog of uncertainty. His response to my concerns was "at the most basic of perspectives, it couldn't hurt your curriculum vitae to demonstrate facility in teaching such a specialized student body. Pulling it off would position you well to apply to an institution in which you would like to settle down." With no viable employment alternatives, I prepared for my trip South.

The campus visit was a cordial affair—the people with whom I would eventually work expressed great interest in me and in my perspectives on restructuring a world civilizations course to emphasize Afrocentric themes. I made it clear at the interview that this would be a position into which I would need to grow, since my whole experience in education centered on western civilizations. At the end of the two-day interview, I noticed that none of the members of the search committee had addressed the issue, which at the time seemed most obvious, of my race. During my last scheduled meeting with the dean, I finally broached the subject. I noted that, frankly, I was curious why a college for black women wanted to hire me, "a white kid from Seattle." The dean replied by noting the perceived need of the institution to broaden the perspectives of its students to prepare them for the world. It was with this that I began a long, and frequently painful, yet deeply enlightening, process of re-education and adjustment of my perspectives on race and gender.

Origins of Civilization

From my first day at Bennett, it was clear that I would have to reexamine the "truths" taught me from my first years in college. I spent my college career in white majority schools, studying under a white majority faculty, who largely embraced a white majority perspective. In history classes, this translated into emphasis on the development of western civilization from its Greco-Roman roots. Since Bennett College hired me to teach the world civilizations survey, my previous education required drastic augmentation and analysis. I knew this would be the case from my interview. The chair of the Department of Social and Behavioral Sciences was in the process of beginning an initiative to change the title, and therefore, the fundamental understanding of the study of world civilizations. Under his leadership, the course title changed from "The History of World Civilizations" to "Origins of Civilization." The emphasis was more than semantic. Not only would the course begin with an extensive examination of the rise of humanity from central Africa, but an Afrocentric theme would predominate.

In making the necessary adjustments to my curriculum by which I would guide my class, my narrowed western perspective came into increasingly sharper focus. I had to do more than merely balance my coverage of Mesopotamia, Egypt, Greece, and Rome with examinations of African, Indian, Chinese, and Latin American civilizations. That would simply have resulted in a dilution of that older traditional perspective. What the course required of me, and what I required of myself to insure academic honesty and integrity, was a complete overhaul of my education. This manifested itself in a deeper examination of the underlying realities of world development in ancient times. I read extensively, and sought hidden themes, for I knew that nothing was as simple as it previously seemed. For example, in my college history and philosophy classes, I learned that Socrates, Plato, and Aristotle were founders of the tradition of philosophical development in western society. While I embraced this as a "truth" throughout my academic career, it later became clear that it was not that simple. I discovered, in the midst of this process of reeducation and "un-learning," what I had previously learned that much of the philosophical thought for which we traditionally credit Socrates, Plato, and Aristotle actually had roots in the much older tradition of the Egyptian "Mysteries" (Bernal, 1987; Diop, 1955; Obenga, 1989; Schure, 1973).

This Afrocentric initiative went far beyond the departmental level. It was part of an institutional movement to "Afrocentrize the curriculum." As part of a year long initiative, the college administration invited one of the foremost Afrocentrist authors in the country, Dr. Asa G. Hilliard III, of Georgia State University, to chair a university-wide workshop. The goal of the workshop was to Afrocentrize more than just the institutional curriculum. The administration intended the workshop to reaffirm the institution as a whole—administration, faculty, staff, and students—as dedicated to the proposition that "African people worldwide must not only survive, must not only adapt, but must also sit once more in the seat of creative leadership on a scale that is worthy of [their] immense potential" (Hilliard, 1991, p.1).

My personal responsibility for this effort was to work to incorporate the ideas of such books as Martin Bernal's *Black Athena* into the history curriculum. This task seemed relatively easy compared to those of my colleagues, who had to trace the African roots of disciplines such as psychology, political science, mathematics, accounting, and biology. As easy as my work may have seemed in comparison, it nonetheless involved a strenuous effort to maintain a balance hinging upon such issues as student self-image and the potential difficulties of students' acceptance of these messages coming from a white professor.

In the process of developing the syllabus and lectures for my Origins of Civilization course, I recognized that I could not force upon the students any particular perspective—Afrocentric, Eurocentric, or otherwise. Doing so would have violated the basic ideal of the intellectual freedom of the student. I realized that presenting new material to the students for consideration of alternative perspectives would encourage them to develop perspectives more real and more meaningful for them as individuals. I was surprised to learn that this material was, indeed, new to most of the students in my classes. They, too, had been the products of an educational system that presented Africans as victims in history. Many of my students approached me to express their appreciation for my exposing them to more empowering alternatives. Having a white professor espousing these new perspectives was clearly a consciousness-raising experience for many of my students.

United States History

My other responsibilities at Bennett included primary responsibility for teaching the United States history survey courses. Since I was in the midst of the process of reeducating myself in world history, it was logical that this effort would spill over into my preparation for U.S. classes as well. I found it difficult, however, to discuss Africans in very early U.S. history as other than an oppressed group.

Beyond the fact that the first Africans were brought to what would later become the United States as indentured servants in 1619, I made it clear to my students that the history of African peoples in the Americas was far more complex than any of us learned to believe. After establishing the well-worn context of the oppression of Africans brought to the English colonies, I compared that to slave experiences in other parts of the Americas, particularly those of slaves in Brazil and the sugar plantations of the Caribbean. This helped students develop a context within which they could begin discerning for themselves the nature of slavery in the United States. To emphasize further the complexity of the history of African Americans, we examined the lives and times of Olaudah Equiano and Anthony Johnson.

Olaudah Equiano was an Ibo boy captured in present-day Benin in 1756 and taken to the coast for purchase by white slavers (Edwards, 1988). He survived the Middle Passage and transport to the Bahamas and Virginia before being purchased in England by a British naval officer. As the officer's servant, he traveled widely, from the Arctic to the tropics. Eventually, he bought his own freedom, married an English woman, and lived out his life as a trader and abolitionist leader of the British black community. Equiano is important in my new analysis of early United States history, in part, because his autobiography, first published in 1789, provides one of the most valuable accounts of the horrors of slavery. Equiano is more valuable in that his life is an amazingly comprehensive mini-history of black-white relations in the British Empire. My students at Bennett seemed to find strength in his strength. Such was not the case in our examination of Anthony Johnson.

Johnson was part of the first wave of African indentured servants brought to the English colonies in North America in 1621. Johnson beat the odds—during a time when most people succumbed to disease, poor diet, or Native American hostility, Johnson lived to a ripe old age. During a time when the male-to-female ratio made it highly unlikely that any man in early Virginia would find a wife and keep her, Johnson again defied convention. He married a woman who had been serving on a nearby plantation, and the two celebrated more than forty years of marriage. In time, Johnson bought his own freedom and that of his wife and young family. Up to this point, my students seemed to revel in the exploits of a remarkable black man. When I noted, however, that upon buying his freedom, Johnson moved his family to Virginia's eastern shore, acquired a plantation, and subsequently worked that land in part with purchased African slaves, some of my students appeared betrayed. Somehow, they believed that Johnson, a black man, would be different, but he was not. He clearly represented the attitudes of the land-owning gentry of his time, regardless of wealth or race. In the process of reeducation of my own historical awareness, I reveled in being able to shake up my students' assumptions about race and class.

My own reexamination of both United States history and the origins of civilization went beyond new understandings of the position of race in society. I also experienced a renewed awareness of women's position in history. My students at Bennett College clearly appreciated my efforts to emphasize women's contributions to the fabric of history. From examinations of Sally Hemmings, Sojourner Truth, Ida Tarbell, and Eleanor Roosevelt and many others in United States history, to digging for deeper understandings of women such as the priestesses of Neolithic Earth goddess worship, Cleopatra, Aspasia, Trieu Au, Khadija, and La Malinche in world civilization studies, women assumed a much more egalitarian role in our struggle to grasp the nature of historical knowledge. It is important to note that we were able to project women into a more egalitarian position than before, and not an unqualified status of equality. This is because, in spite of all the reeducation and awareness building we may go through, the unreconstructed nature of the documentary evidence available to scholars of history hampers our full understanding of the influence of women on history. We have much to undo.

The process of reanalysis of what I had once known continued beyond my years at Bennett College. After I left Bennett in 1995, I assumed an adjunct position at a nearby state university (North Carolina A&T University) noted for its engineering programs, which also happened to be a historically black institution. The work I had done to adjust my historical field of vision continued at this much larger publicly funded institution.

I found that the awareness, which arose out of my experiences at Bennett, served me well at my new institution. At Bennett I was stumbling along, trying to understand and embrace my students' experiences as young African Americans as much as I was challenging my students to embrace broader perspectives themselves. By the time I had arrived at my new position, I had two years of experience in this process. As I began teaching the history of world civilizations, I was much more confident that I would have much to offer my students, many of whom had grown up on the same sort of older assumptions about history, fostered by their high school teachers, as I had been spending time undoing in myself. Clearly, the classroom dynamic was different from what it had been at Bennett. At the smaller school, students were, on the whole, extraordinarily passive "recipients" of knowledge. But at the university students were more aggressive in their pursuit of ideas. They challenged me more. As I was drawing them into deeper understandings of the relationships between African and Asian civilizations, they were demanding more of me. They wanted me to spend more time on the details, instead of playing the historical dilettante—a position into which the realities of semester scheduling had forced me. We simply could not do all that we wanted. This process did, however, convince me of the utility of curtailing my discussions of Roman government and medieval Europe in favor of spending more time in Mongol China, Songhay and Swahili Africa, and the Mayan Empire of Central America.

During my time at North Carolina A&T University, I faced a unique opportunity when I got to teach a western civilizations course at another university, a predominantly white branch of the University of North Carolina system. This was a wonderful opportunity for me to see how many of these themes would fly when presented to an audience that much more recognizably resembled the institutions that I had attended as a student, i.e., the institutions at which I learned a more Eurocentric view of history. Unfortunately, the experience did not turn out to be as full a comparison as I had hoped. The curriculum of western civilization history left less room for consideration of other civilization centers such as Africa, India, Asia, and pre-Columbian Latin America. I was able, however, to transfer many of the newer understandings of the position of women and minority groups in western society. This effort reflected favorably in my students' reactions to the course, which many considered to be the first "real history" course they had taken.

Taken altogether, my experiences at historically black colleges and universities proved remarkably fertile intellectually. When presented with a perspective radically different from the one that had been presented to me as the truth, I came to understand that it was not the truth as much as it was a truth. Increasingly, that older truth was less and less valid, particularly as I faced teaching African-American women about the history of world civilizations and the United States. The result of my older, long-held assumptions clashing with newer, more global, and more equitable perspectives was a reaction wholly atomic in nature. Just as energy is produced when an electron smashes into an atomic nucleus, so was a great deal of heat and light created when a broader awareness impacted with my older, more parochial views. The heat of intellectual ferment and the light of pedagogical insight were also self-sustaining. Just as atomic fission creates a chain reaction when placed in an appropriate environment, so did this conflict of perspectives result in a cascading of awarenesses concerning the place of race, gender, and class in global society. The results of that fission of my older education have fertilized the way I pursue my craft several years later, as I try to "rock" the world of my predominantly white, predominantly middle-class students in Montana.

Before I address ways in which my experiences in North Carolina have permanently altered my pursuit of academic excellence, I would like to identify other new awarenesses I gained while at Bennett. The issues are racism and prejudice.

Racism in the Perspective of Time

When I was growing up in small-town Montana, I knew only one African American. I do not even remember his name. I recall that we were friends—as only six- or seven-year-olds can be friends. We played and wrestled, and explored the backyards, creeks, and fields not far from our homes. Then one day, I heard an older boy, a teenager, call him a "nigger." I saw how it affected my friend. The epithet devastated him. Within weeks, he and his family moved out of our neighborhood, and I never saw him again.

In my young mind, a causal relationship existed between the offhanded crudity expressed by that adolescent and my friend's moving away. My friend moved because that kid called him a name. I recall that I was amazed about a number of things. First, I could not understand what could have motivated that teenager to be so cruel to my friend. On another level, I was unclear about how that remark affected my friend. After all, as kids we learned that "sticks and stones" were all that could hurt us. In the perspective available only with maturity and hindsight, I came to know that, of course, my friend did not move as a result of the name-calling. However, another more mature insight is that I have begun to understand how a word can so dramatically affect a person. I know that words have power, and certain words have incredible power behind them. I now am aware of the injustices manifest in systems that perpetuate the exercise of power used to control and to define the "other." These insights emerged in stunning brilliance when I first encountered controlling power after I moved my family to North Carolina and joined the faculty of Bennett College.

Individual Perspectives

My life has changed dramatically. For the first thirty-one years of my life, I thrived in blissful ignorance of some of the most important issues facing a majority of the people on Earth. Life seemed simple, relatively stable, ultimately just and fair. My conception of that simplicity, stability, justice, and fairness faced serious challenges while I was at Bennett. For the first time, I experienced what it was like to be the "other."

At first, it was mildly awkward being one of the few white faces on campus. I had simply never been in the minority. This minority status was merely temporary, however, since I had the opportunity to "escape." The end of the day found me back in a comfortable, familiar world of suburban life. On campus I was clearly among the "few." In the classroom, there was more stability, because that was an environment over which I had a certain amount of control. Although I was a minority of one in the class, I was still the professor.

Most of my students seemed to take my presence on campus in stride. As I learned in informal conversations with some of my students, they were simply "used" to white teachers. Many of them had white teachers from their earliest grades. This seemed unsurprising to me at the time. But I did not expect the comments of an astonishing number of my students who informed me that I was the only white person they saw on a day-to-day basis. Actually, I was the only white person with whom they had any daily contact. They told me that they went to the "black" malls, the "black" grocery stores, and the "black" dance clubs, and they watched the "black" channel on television. I was astonished to hear that they appreciated having me at their school because I proved to them that they could actually relate to a white person one-to-one. The level of segregation in Greensboro, North Carolina, be it informal or institutionalized, voluntary or imposed, took me by surprise. But my surprise did not stop there. I quickly learned that those students who accepted or even appreciated my teaching at Bennett were not necessarily the only students in the college.

I was aware that there must have been a certain level of discomfort or even resentment among the student body that they had to take this required course from a white professor. But I was certainly unprepared for the ways in which some students expressed that resentment.

During my second semester at Bennett, one of the classes I taught was the second half of the United States history survey. Near the end of a lecture on Reconstruction, one student erupted into a loud series of accusations that I was lying to the class. When I confronted her, she claimed that I was clearly "an agent of the Ku Klux Klan assigned to get a job at Bennett so [I] could misinform young African-American princesses about their own history." It simply stupefied me to face such blatant accusations that I embraced a racist agenda. When I asked her about the specific things about which I had lied, she came up with no specific instances. Facts did not matter at that point. When I further pressed her to explain how I was lying, she got to the root of her concerns. She was outraged that she had to pay money to go to a private college for African-American women only to have to take a course from a man—a white man. I sensed that we had arrived at a teachable moment. I turned the issue around to help her see the situation from a new perspective. I asked her what she would say if she was a professor at a predominantly white school, and I complained that I had to pay to take a class from a black woman. Would that not be a racist comment? She agreed that, of course, it would. So then I asked her how the present situation was different. That was when she came back with the comments with which I began this essay: "It's different. You just wouldn't understand. After all, you're white."

When it was clear that I was getting nowhere, I invited her to address her concerns to the chair of my department. She did, and when she did not get the satisfaction she sought, she approached the president of the college with her concerns. I never heard from her again—she dropped out of my course. After this incident, I approached a number of my students whom I trusted and asked them if I had a reputation in the dorms as a racist. They assured me that most students had no problems with my race—although they did note a clear perception that I was a hard professor. I can take being called "hard." It is another issue for students to label me a racist. I think one of the reasons that students' comments struck me so was because of my efforts to embrace a more comprehensive, more inclusive perspective of world and United States history.

This experience of racism on an individual level came as quite a shock to me. My only previous experience of racism was of a very offhanded sort. Except for the above noted experience of racial prejudice directed at my childhood friend, I had had little direct contact with prejudice, and had never before faced prejudice on such a personal level. But this individual brand of racism paled next to a more insidious, more damaging form of institutional racism manifested by the administration of the school.

Since Bennett was my first full-time teaching experience, I somehow naively expected my colleagues and the administration would see me as simply that—a professional colleague. It quickly became clear, however, that the administration saw things differently. From the first regular faculty meeting in the autumn semester of 1993 the stability and safety of collegiality evaporated.

Institutional Perspectives

The first faculty meeting appeared relatively uneventful and routine. Discussions of attendance policies, student services, student retention, and semester schedules dominated the agenda. When the president of the college took the floor, however, the nature of the meeting changed. After an obligatory round of introductions, greetings, and well-wishing, the president turned her attention to her expectations of the faculty. In the course of her comments, she singled-out—pointed to—the white faculty in the audience and said, "You owe us. You owe us for the generational advantages which you have enjoyed and of which we have been deprived." It was quite clear from her remarks that it was not to the administration, nor to the school that we owed a higher level of service, but to African Americans as a whole. She claimed that our ancestors had established conditions that kept her ancestors suppressed. For hours after the meeting, her words rang in my ears. After the meeting, I visited with another white faculty member, and we discussed those "generational advantages" to which we had been blind and to which the president, as representative of all African Americans, demanded that we remedy. As we looked back on our personal histories, we saw stories of farmers breaking the land, of businessmen scrimping and saving to feed their families, of struggles to survive in the Great Depression. Those "generational advantages" were not very evident to our eyes.

With the passage of time, I have come to rationalize the words the president spoke that day. Clearly, she was speaking of opportunities that my ancestors, my family, and I have enjoyed in our own struggles for survival. These opportunities included access to the land those early Redinger farmers broke and access to business opportunities that allowed my grandfather to open an insurance office in Spokane, Washington, in the 1940s. While these opportunities seemed disguised behind generations of hard work, I can view them now as opportunities unavailable to most African Americans in United States history.

This awareness did not mask the shock and disillusionment I felt after hearing the president enunciate the higher expectations she held for her white faculty members. In spite of the fact that I am now aware of the sorts of things to which she was referring, that does not obscure the fact that this was a bald-faced expression of institutional racism. When members of one race face special treatment, be it higher expectations, lower pay, or different opportunities, for reasons of their skin tone—not for reasons of abilities, competencies, or the lack thereof—that is racism. A particularly objectionable element of her racism was that she characterized us, the faculty members of European descent, as being one with those whose families actually owned slaves in the nineteenth century. Stereotyping is only the most superficial form of racial prejudice.

In my second year at Bennett, I had the opportunity to do battle against the inherent injustice and ignorance behind the act of stereotyping the "other." I organized a panel discussion of an issue that struck at the heart of the lives of my students at Bennett: the meaning and mean-spiritedness of the publication of Richard Herrnstein's and Charles Murray's *The Bell Curve: Intelligence and Class Structure in American Life* (1994). In organizing the panel discussion, I invited colleagues—black and white, female and male—from the departments of economics, psychology, biology, and sociology to join me in examining the argument put forth in this controversial book. This panel discussion was very productive and evocative of an ongoing dialogue at the college for several days following the event. The diversity of the panel was an important element of the success of the program. By demonstrating to Bennett's students that we, as professional academics, stood steadfastly in opposition to the message of the book as it impacted the African-American community, I believe we went far to undo the atmosphere of tension and divisiveness fostered by attitudes such as those expressed by the college's president in that early autumn 1993 faculty meeting.

Taken as a whole, my experiences at Bennett College were at once both very painful and incredibly enlightening. The enlightenment and growth with which I came out of the Bennett experience were very much a result of the pain. The most uncomfortable element of my time at the school was my immediate experience of racial prejudice. By feeling, first hand, what it is like to experience prejudice resulting from being in the minority in a given population, I gained a renewed sensitivity of many of the issues with which African Americans deal on a daily basis in American society. That sensitivity had developed within me the understanding that while my experience as a "minority" was remarkably similar to those of many African Americans today, it was also fundamentally different. The clearest difference was that, on a daily basis, I could "escape" that experience and reenter a familiar world.

I also viewed my time in North Carolina as an opportunity for mutual education. In accepting the position at Bennett, I assumed the responsibility of undertaking a complex process of reeducation, and the result of this process is a richer examination of history in the courses I teach. At the same time, I attempted to engender in my students a broader perspective that includes them and their families and communities in the scope of United States and world history as integral ingredients. On a more fundamental level, I attempted to break down barriers of race and gender by proving to my students that young black women and older white men could engage in respectful, thoughtful, fruitful discourse on issues that affected us all.

Beyond Bennett

When I had the chance to return to the state of my birth to teach at a college in Montana, I jumped at the opportunity. But in packing up my offices in North Carolina, I boxed up more than simply books, pens, and class notes. It was clear to me that I was also packing up a whole gamut of new experiences and perspectives. As I said before, I was a different person than I had been three years before. It was not yet clear to me how these new insights and awarenesses would translate to what was essentially my old world. It was clear, however, that they would change forever the ways I pursued my career.

In terms of the curriculum into which I moved, I had little choice but to jettison much of the course material I had accumulated in North Carolina. Instead of world civilizations (or origins of civilizations), my primary responsibilities are to teach the undergraduate series on western civilization. The limited time I have to explore western civilization and the steadily increasing class sizes and grading responsibilities have both left precious little room for deep and detailed exploration of African, Asian, or Latin American civilizations. Nonetheless, I rarely miss an opportunity to link western civilization with developments in other parts of the globe. Moreover, race was only the most immediate element of my own reeducation. I also call on my students to engage in deeper analysis of the positions of women in society. From the earliest accounts of the first farmers and priestesses in Catal Hüyük and Egypt to Madam Jiang and "Rosie the Riveter" in World War II, women have emerged in a much more real way as playing pivotal roles in the development of western civilization. In much the same way, my current western civilization classes provide students with a more personal understanding of the lives of people of color. For instance, we examine, in a much more profound and inclusive way than before, the lives of Africans in the Middle Passage and the struggles of Aztec, Filipino, and Vietnamese peasants as they suffered under Spanish,

American, and French imperialists. This is not the history I studied in my undergraduate days in Montana colleges and universities!

In much the same way, my approaches to United States history have changed. I found it much easier to translate the awarenesses and sensitivities I had gained in North Carolina to U.S. history classes in Montana than it was for the western civilization courses. My students and I are keenly aware that women and minorities play much more important roles in my history classes than I had learned as an undergraduate.

I recognized my need to challenge many older beliefs planted in the minds of Montana youth from the earliest years, and nurtured in the largely homogeneous society in which most of my students were born and raised. I was not prepared for the reactions of some of my students as we explored this intellectual frontier. One of my current responsibilities is to teach a three-course series of upper division modern United States history courses. In the fall of 1996, I had the chance to teach the Birth of Modern America, 1877-1914. In keeping with the newer perspectives I had gained in North Carolina, we spent a great deal of time examining the histories of African-American sharecroppers and tenant farmers in the post-Reconstruction period and the rise of the Black Farmers' Alliance in the 1890s. We also examined the conditions that made the establishment of the National Association for the Advancement of Colored People necessary in 1909 and the role played by African Americans in World War I. After several such lectures, one of my students spoke up and said, "What is this? A black history class?"

It was then that I realized the insular and parochial nature of the lives of many Montana students. Indeed, I realized that before I went to North Carolina, I myself embraced such a narrow view of United States history. After this comment, we explored the diverse nature of American society. While I was initially shocked by the blatant Eurocentricity of the remark, we were able to turn it into a jumping-off point for discussion of what, after all, is American society. What I was trying to emphasize was that, in the words of a former colleague at Bennett College, "THEY'RE US." "Our" (European-American) history and "their" (African-American) history are one and the same. We cannot possibly understand how or why we have developed as we have as a nation without examining the lives of the people who make up this nation. I had clearly changed what I believed about history.

Such insights into the agency of women and African Americans in history are the most important elements of change that I brought to Montana from North Carolina. This is particularly true for my United States history classes. In a more general vein, however, my North Carolina experience has changed my societal assumptions. Because of the enlightenment I gained in the South, I enjoy a heightened sensitivity to people, regardless of their race, class or gender, and the integral part they play in society today.

My time teaching in HBCUs made me a better professor, and a better man. I enjoy perspectives, awarenesses, and sensitivities that have enriched and leavened both my work as a professor and my life as a citizen of this country. The depth of these awarenesses and perspectives would not have been, I believe, entirely attainable had I not had the opportunity to immerse myself in the African-American community. Having gone through the experience, I know that I could not have reached my present level of understanding without ripping myself out of my old world and entering into a new one. But on a more profound level, I am also convinced that besides being unattainable, these perspectives were, in the context of my own early college education, unknowable. Without benefiting from perspectives more broad than those that I embraced as a student, I would have remained ignorant of the incredible complexity and interwovenness of the lives of Americans black, white, Asian, or Hispanic. The history I learned in college in Montana was fundamentally flat and colorless (except, of course, for the red that came from accounts of blood shed in wars led by "Great White Men"). Because of my own experiences, I have the chance to help my own students discover for themselves how "colorful" their own histories are. Maybe that angry young woman at Bennett in the spring of 1994 was right. Maybe I just "didn't understand." But I think I am beginning to learn.

References

Bernal, M. (1987). *Black Athena: The Afroasiatic roots of classical civilization, Vol. 1: The fabrication of ancient Greece, 1795-1985.* New Brunswick, NJ: Rutgers University Press.

Diop, C.A. (1955). *The African origin of civilization: Myth or reality.* New York: Lawrence Hill and Company.

Edwards, P. (Ed.).(1988). *The life of Olaudah Eequiano, or Gustavus Vassa the African.* White Plains, NY: Longman Publishing Company.

Herrnstein, R. and C. Murray (1994). *The bell curve: Intelligence and class structure in American life.* New York: The Free Press.

Hilliard, A.G. (1991) *Free your mind: Return to the source African origins—A selected bibliography and outline on African-American history from ancient times to the present.* Unpublished manuscript.

Obenga, T. (1989). African philosophy of the Pharaonic period. In I. Van Sertima (Ed.), *Egypt revisited* (pp.286-290). New Brunswick, NJ: Transaction.

Schure, E. (1973). *The mysteries of ancient Egypt: Hermes/Moses.* Blauvelt, NY: Multimedia Publishing Corporation.

Chapter 3 _____

Communicating and Learning the Right Message

Fred Bales

All teachers play roles. In varying degrees they are mentors, role models, drill sergeants and counselors, besides being the conveyors of knowledge. As much as we would wish otherwise, these roles are complicated by race. Thus, the following essay attempts to describe scenes from the life of a recently arrived white faculty member at a historically black institution of higher education.

Scene I: She came to my office after the last class of the semester. She had been absent for more than two weeks and was behind in three or four writing assignments. She was there to explain. An older sibling had run into trouble with the law in another state and she was the only family member who could take her mother there to help out. She knew she was in academic trouble, and she promised to turn in some assignments. She was in a hurry because she had to explain all this to another faculty member. She was trying to focus on school work but broke down, just slightly, as she said that she had to put the family problem behind her so that she could pass her classes.

Had I encountered similar student dilemmas during my tenure at a state university with a majority white student population? Yes, but such cases seem especially poignant at a black university. Why? In my case, one explanation recalls my experience with another minority group: Native Americans. At my previous university, I learned that family and tribal obligations came first with

Native Americans, even if the time away meant academic failure. There is no question about these obligations or any hesitation in meeting them, and, indeed, I usually felt that I was on the defensive in pointing out to Native American students the reasons for their Ds and Fs because of excessive absences and the failure to complete course requirements. My talk of their having committed "academic suicide" no doubt seemed odd to them. Their answers to questions about their recent whereabouts appeared casual to a white teacher, hearing them refer to a family illness or a tribal event. In fact, the answers were so matter-of-fact that it seemed they thought it strange that anyone would object to their long absences.

Now, in a different setting, I ask myself: Is this a general pattern with minority groups, or am I straining to see a pattern in a few cases involving those perceived as different? There is no answer to that question, at least not for me at this juncture. But the point is not so much about reaching a definitive conclusion as in recognizing the fact that the question arises at all, indicating that I am perceiving others as different and therefore seeing myself as different.

General Relationships with Students

Scene II: It was my first week of teaching at Xavier University of Louisiana in New Orleans, Louisiana, and I was in the stairwell walking to the second floor to teach a class. There was the expected noise and hubbub as students around me verily shouted and laughed, but I sensed something unusual from other times in the midst of other students outside classrooms. Yes, mine was the only white face in sight. I was immersed for a brief moment in a scene where I was the different one. Shortly thereafter, I read something about black people often facing an all-white world and that more whites should experience the reverse phenomenon of existing in an all-black world. Although brief, my visit to that world placed me in an atmosphere where many African Americans live out every day of their lives.

So, in my second year at a historically black institution of higher education—a term I had barely known until I was interviewed for a job at one— I cannot answer my own questions about differences between students here and those I knew before. But I sense a difference. And one possible generalization is that the problems of all people, regardless of skin color, tend to be alike, except that members of minority groups may be visited with more problems demanding immediate action.

Scene III: A good student was living off campus and having problems with break-ins, more than one. She wanted to live near school but the neighborhood near school has a high crime rate. Is it any accident that my new school is located in a less desirable neighborhood, at least when desirability is related to criminal activity? Probably not. And some general observations indicate that historically black colleges and universities (HBCUs) around the country were consigned to building their campuses in neighborhoods avoided by white majorities. The student mentioned above eventually missed about two weeks of class time to straighten out her living arrangements. Could she have accomplished that in less time? Probably. But how could I be sure? Questions, questions. Regardless, the student was forced to resolve a basic element of everyday life—housing—that members of the majority group are not as likely to encounter because of different physical environments.

One traditional image of white faculty at black schools, especially southern black schools, portrays teachers on a mission, as in missionaries (Brubacher, 1997). This image presupposes that the missionary is from somewhere else (the North, as I am originally) and that the aim is to help people who are different into some condition that the missionary views as "advanced." Although an educational mission invites less criticism of paternalism under these circumstances than a religious mission, for example, the question cannot be avoided.

Why am I at an HBCU? I certainly don't think of myself as a missionary. Do others think of me that way? I explain that I came here because of sundry pushes and pulls that accompany many career moves. I could take early retirement at my previous school. I felt myself growing stale in my job. I wanted to move from a flagship state university to a small liberal arts school, which was my undergraduate experience. I wanted to move closer to family east of the Mississippi River. I wanted to trade the vagaries of a public school, especially its dependence on funds from a state legislature, for the vagaries of a private school and its greater dependence on tuition money. I wanted to stay somewhere in the southern half of the country. I liked the people in the department when I interviewed and liked the job description presented. I liked the big city and its special culture. No other opportunity seemed to match what I wanted, regardless of racial composition. Still, was there no sense of doing something out of the ordinary by coming to an HBCU? Ultimately, I think I feel a sense of fulfillment in working at a place that some of my old academic friends would not consider desirable because of its racial history and its racial present. I know that, but I don't talk about it with these colleagues.

Juxtaposed against the missionary model are those relationships anchored upon humaneness, involving human interactions where true partnerships are established. In short, in the scholastic setting mutual learning through mutual respect should be the model, so that students are not only learners but also teachers to those who seek to teach them. That ideal has been ably stated by the renowned entertainer Josephine Baker: "Surely the day will come when color means nothing more than skin tone, when religion is seen uniquely as a way to speak one's soul; when birthplaces have the weight of a throw of the dice and all men are born free, when understanding breeds love and brotherhood." Those words appeared on a desk calendar—one of those offering a saying of the day—and that particular date was ripped out and placed on my office door, much to the approval of one of my neighbors, a black colleague in my department.

At the moment, we fall short of Josephine Baker's ideal. Whatever progress has been measured off in moving toward a color-blind society, gaps remain even on progressive college campuses. What disturbs me about analyzing this condition is the peril of stereotyping and basing generalizations upon limited experience. Yet it is important that people like me contribute to the dialogue that needs nurturing if the ideal is to be approached. Cognizant of those risks, I offer some provisional observations.

The Question of Definitions

Much ado has surrounded the term African American, including whether to hyphenate the two words. As a teacher, my philosophy has been to let people name themselves, remembering all the fuss over Irish Americans and Italian Americans and the like. But Africa is special. It is a continent, not a country, and many of my students cannot trace their roots as I can, or even as Alex Haley could. The identity is with a major continent and what that means about the nature of their ancestors' arrival to this country. The depth of that meaning was enhanced by the film *Amistad*.

Scene IV: An African-American colleague gave me two tickets for the opening of the film in New Orleans, the city of its second premiere, and as she discussed the upcoming event she expressed anxiety over the well-publicized shipboard horrors depicted in the "middle passage" scene. Anguished, she shook her head. I never have had—nor ever will have—that degree of emotional identification with an event from my family's past or my race's past. There is no parity, even with indentured servants. And although I would have seen *Amistad* wherever I might have been teaching, the film would not have conveyed its special meaning to me had I not been at a black university and experienced the personal contact with an African-American colleague. In the broader sense, this incident and others again demand that I examine my mission at this university: What can I bring to my teaching at this place? Why am I here? Such questions could be addressed anywhere, but they carry a special intensity at a black institution.

What Is the Right Language?

Scene V: I am walking to my car in the parking lot and in front of me are two students I know. They are laughing and talking. I am reasonably sure they are speaking English, but just what they are saying might as well be Greek to my ears. Their spoken language at this moment is not what I know as "standard English." And I understand that this must influence their writing of "standard English."

Because I teach writing classes in a journalism program, I have an opinion about the formal English language capabilities of young African-American men and women. Too many are deficient by the measure of formal English. Many exceptions exist to remind us that students regardless of race have the capability to write when given adequate grounding. In fact, the whole range of communication skills needs to be fostered among African-American students, not only because some are in deficit and not only because all college students should attain these skills, but because of the emphasis upon African-American students of ability to serve as future leaders of their communities. Although I understand the points of those who talk about Black English, my role is to insist on standard English in my classes. At a minimum, the rules of the language must be known before they can be broken. This is especially true if the rules are broken and the resulting "language" has only a vocabulary but not a grammar.

Despite feeling "right" about my insistence on standard English, I wonder whether my students translate my approach as "White English" taught by a white teacher. Transferring the possible resentment to other academic settings offers some insights. There is talk, for example, about only women being qualified to teach women's studies or African Americans having the sensitivity to teach African American studies. But would anyone seriously argue that only white people can teach standard English? Also, the idea that African Americans teaching standard English to African Americans may avoid credibility problems does not appeal to me as credible. Maybe it should. Thankfully, my African-American colleagues support the teaching of standard English to our students and often join me in bemoaning the lack of general competence in standard English. That reaffirmation of my role has proved helpful to me in this question of which language to teach and to defend. In this setting, colleges are colleges, teachers are teachers, and students are students, regardless of race.

Scene VI: He limped into my classroom the first day, dragging his left leg, braced at the knee. I sought him out after class and he told me that he had been the victim of an accidental shooting. I did not press for details. His agony continued as he missed classes and a few assignments, and once I asked him about how he managed getting to class. He lived with relatives far away from campus and had to walk, he said. As we concluded the semester, I asked him about his progress with the knee. Things were not much better, he said, noting that he had to have his brace fitted at a charity hospital where he was depressed by all the patients who, in his view, were not being well cared for. He felt that he, too, was not getting the best equipment for his condition. I could detect no self-pity in his words, but rather a realistic evaluation about the place where he had to receive medical treatment.

Because of income differentials and single-parent situations, many African-American students come from economically impoverished backgrounds. At Xavier University of Louisiana, a private, historically black and Roman Catholic institution, tuition is a big hurdle, although it is less than the tuition at many other private schools. And even when students receive financial aid, as a majority do, this may mean that more than other students they have to hold outside jobs to meet the costs that multiply during four—or more—years of college. At some point, students who come from low-income families may feel alienated in the sense that they lose faith in their capabilities to control their own lives. If the world is seen as a chaotic place where events occur randomly and if that world is perceived as white controlled, then the potential tensions between African-American students and white faculty become evident.

I would reiterate that the circumstances outlined above are not unique to African-American students at historically black institutions; no, these forces play out with some students of all races and ethnic backgrounds in almost all academic settings. The contemporary reality, however, seems to be that these claims on students appear with more regularity for African-American students and to a greater degree for African-American students. This impression is gained from the "case load" brought to me by students caught up in non-academic problems affecting their academic lives. My unofficial counter tells me that the incidence of such dilemmas is proportionately higher in my present position than in my previous one where the majority of students were white.

Against the above background, faculty at historically black institutions have to weigh a student's promise for post-college achievement against current performance. What does one do with the student who demonstrates a gift for performing academically and who shows leadership potential but who misses an inordinate number of classes and even a few assignments? If a student has outside problems but does good work—when work gets done—how does a faculty member reward that effort while maintaining standards and ensuring fairness to others who fully meet course requirements? My tentative position on that is to encourage potential leaders but to mark them down significantly on my final grade report. I have no precise answer, though, for dealing with the ultimate dilemma of the student who straddles the line between passing or failing a course. At some point, responsibility has to be taught along with subject matter, and some students, regardless of ability or promise, need to learn the lesson of failure. When asked about this, I remind such students that their problem is of their own making and that they have committed, in the words mentioned above, "academic suicide."

The decision-making process in grading becomes more acute with another type of student: the one who is bright but who never faced academic challenges in high school. This type, again not unknown anywhere, seems to perceive homework as a threat to their very honor. Anything that is due can be dashed off in class while the lecture-discussion occurs. This places them at some disadvantage as they miss crucial points relevant to the next exercise and so on, and so on. The problem in my experience is exacerbated with some African-American students because of academic experiences at the public school level. It may be harder than ever for bright African-American students to adjust to a learning environment where they cannot excel, or even pass the course, by employing their wits alone. In such cases, resentment toward the teacher may arise, and if that teacher is white an extra dose of alienation may surface. I never have encountered that resentment directly, but I wonder about its presence and grant the possibility of it arising sometime. When and if this occurs, I have to trust in my African-American colleagues in the belief that they, too, have shared my perspective on the student's performance and that this would be reflected in current grades or an overall grade point average.

Discipline Specific Considerations

Besides the general circumstance of being a white faculty member at a historically black university, I teach in a field renowned for its own short-comings in attracting minorities in the workplace and with a historical failure to represent minorities to the general population in media content.

Ties to a specific vocation overlay the teaching of journalism anywhere but have special consequences for teachers of African-American students. The mainstream news media for years have professed a desire to promote diversity within their newsrooms. One organization, the American Society of Newspaper Editors, in 1978 set a goal of having newsrooms reflect the general national population by race, ethnicity, and gender by the year 2000 (Shipler, 1998). Besides being the right thing to do, this goal may well represent good business practice as almost 26 percent of the country is African American, Hispanic, Asian American or Native American—and growing—and the overall spending power of minorities has been predicted to reach $650 billion by the turn of the century (Williams, 1992). As early as nine years after the newspaper editors' goal was announced, growing concern was expressed that the likelihood of reaching this goal was receding, especially in regard to African-American journalists (Rosenfeld, 1987). Now, the goal for 2000 has been forsaken and the talk focuses on achieving 20 percent by 2010. "While the complexion of major newsrooms has shifted from the virtually all-white hue of thirty years ago, the rate of change has not slowed; the representation of African Americans on news staffs has stagnated at a low plateau of under 6 percent," reports the American Society of Newspaper Editors. And African Americans moving into managerial ranks remain too scarce to be counted as a reform completed" (Shipler, 1998, p.26).

This dilemma is hardly new and various professional organizations have made attempts with uneven degrees of success to attract minorities. A special report from the Dow-Jones Newspaper Fund (1982) set forth the dilemma that still haunts the profession: "The minorities newspapers want to reach are visible. The newspapers that are interested in minorities are visible. But something is keeping them apart. Is it talent? Is it commitment? Is it personality? Is it culture?

Is it the image of newspapers as a promising career field? It could be all of the above. But the fact is, individuals and groups have spent a lot of money and time over the past 15 years to turn a tide of minority writers and editors toward newspaper work as a career. No one has been truly successful" (p.1). This circumstance cannot be attributed entirely to the intransigence of white journalists. In a 1996 survey, 77 percent of editors surveyed said that "a news staff should reflect society in terms of racial-ethnic makeup," and another 86 percent thought that a diverse newsroom staff strengthens news coverage and credibility (Shipler, 1998).

With the relative dearth of African-American journalists in print and broadcast newsrooms, what special obligations are conferred on journalism faculties? The comment above about language deficiencies among large numbers of African-American students is a starting point. If African-American students are to succeed in media and media-related occupations, they cannot do so without above-average language skills. This means that journalism faculty are obligated to engage in remedial English teaching in some cases. These lessons can be learned through grinding and repetitious exercises, exaggerated in some cases by the complexities of Black English and the spoken equivalent that—whatever its merits—is not standard and tends to present special teaching problems in written communication.

Even when students reach adequate levels of preprofessional skills, a white faculty member may be hesitant to advise students to enter a field that traditionally has been low paying and unreceptive to the broader concerns of African Americans. During my college days, I worked one summer on a small city daily where the main news about black people was church events, crimes, or obituaries. Brought home to me that summer was the familiar lament: "The only way for a black person to get into the news is to commit a crime or die."

And that state of affairs has not exactly changed. Talking about the demise of a prominent African-American newspaper, the *Richmond Afro-American*, journalist Hollie West (1996) wrote in the Freedom Forum Report that the black press still is needed as an advocate for black people. Why? "Mainstream dailies show too much of a concern with mainly black pathology, not the hopes and dreams of African Americans. It's up to black Americans to see that their full story is told" (p.4). Further, the history of the black press demonstrates a mission to explain the black community to itself and to involve blacks in control of their own communities. In that respect, the black press was a precursor of the popular current movement of "community journalism." Although this role for journalism has engendered much debate among members of the majority community, it is an old story in the black press where the cult of objectivity often was set aside in favor of communicating in a nonobjective way the goals and aspirations of the audience. That history is a noble one and one that should be continued and recognized by those so keen nowadays for the mainstream press to engage its community more directly.

On the other side, who will tell that story in the mainstream media? One criticism of those publications and broadcast outlets incorporating blacks into their operations is that black staff members are used as sounding boards to ensure race sensitive stories. There is nothing wrong with this, per se, and even a lot right with this concern for avoiding stereotypes and other insensitive nuances. But to the special burdens of African-American journalists it adds the burden of education. As one editor said of this attitude among his peers: "That notion bothers me a lot. We're going to keep a few blacks around so they can save us from embarrassing ourselves. You should be hip enough and clued in enough to see this yourself" (Shipler, 1998, p.32).

These observations place a white faculty member of African-American journalism students squarely in the proverbial middle. This is a location not unknown no doubt to African-American faculty at white-dominated schools, and one well chronicled by Richards (1998). It would be facile to urge black students to work for black-oriented media so that a more complete story of black society can be chronicled daily or weekly. That is a special kind of calling; it may provide a more comfortable work environment and it should not be denied those who would opt for that outlet. Nevertheless, black needs are not the only needs. White people have as much need to hear black voices as black people need the opportunity to speak their voices. Thus, when possible, a white faculty member often thinks in terms of placing young black journalists into predominantly white newsrooms, knowing that these young blacks will be pioneers, or the generation after the pioneers, in a field where racism abides and where these young men and women will undergo conditions never known by that same white faculty member. It's asking a lot.

On the content side of the media, black sources still are too much ignored in news stories. And here lies opportunity. If more young black journalists and other media workers can enter the field, then it should follow that more black people will be chosen as sources for newscasts as well as for newspaper and news magazine stories. The dearth of black spokespeople as experts on television network news continues. The 10th annual Women, Men, and Media Study (1998) found that 92 percent of the experts called on to analyze, interpret or spin the news in a sample of network TV programs were white. "Individuals of either sex, any age and all races can be heard from on the network news, as long as they are not wielding power or offering expertise. The networks' 'golden rolodexes' of expert consultants are badly in need of updating" (p.1).

Another media failing, historically, is the nature of minority group portrayals. One simple pattern of the evolution of minority representation has featured this sequence: initially, no presence or little presence at all; later, some small presence but one that reinforces stereotypes of the minority group; finally, a rounded view of the minority group that continually reinforces its humane concerns and aspirations. Despite some progress, reaching that last stage presents a constant struggle cutting across all forms of mass media. For example, a content analysis of advertisements and editorial photographs in black and mainstream magazines has shown that blacks in advertisements had lighter complexions and more Caucasian features than those in editorial photographs. And compared with their male counterparts, black females in advertisements were lighter in skin color (Keenan, 1996).

Even in local television news where advances are evident, Campbell (1995) showed that "enlightened forms of racism" characterized newscasts by perpetuating racial myths leading to a distorted picture of life for Americans of color. "Though news organizations have made efforts—some sincere, some not—to change that picture, those efforts have not been entirely fruitful. America's racial myths endure despite the best intentions of the news media. It may well be that the very nature of those media—and of the society in which they exist—may not allow them to function in a manner that will contribute to the more accurate portrayals of life outside of the mainstream" (Campbell, 1995, pp.135-136).

Layered over all of this concern about my profession is the old philosophical dispute in black education enunciated by W.E.B. DuBois and Booker T. Washington, pitting advocates for vocational education against those favoring liberal arts education. That can be reconciled, I believe, by arguing for both—at least in the setting of a small liberal arts college with a journalism program. For that reason, it is important to teach professional or pre-professional subjects at a liberal arts institution.

Final Thoughts

Sweeping conclusions are hazardous with any academic exercise. They may even turn out to be disastrous when a faculty member is newly immersed in another culture in another academic setting. What follows represents provisional conclusions, implying my right to change and to be changed by further experience in a place that provides new insights almost daily.

When a white person comes into a black related setting, he or she is forced to think about race. The reality we all live with is that race continues to matter in the United States, on both sides. At Xavier University of Louisiana, demographics published by the administration present several breakdowns, and race is among them. For instance, from official university annual reports I am told that 36 percent of the faculty here are black and 90 percent of the students are black. I also know that 35 percent of the faculty are women, along with about 75 percent of the students. Further, the student-faculty ratio is 14 to 1. Perhaps some day only the latter fact will need to be published. For the foreseeable future, however, we keep score on race and gender so that progress can be measured.

One insight into racial composition came last year when I headed a search committee for two positions in our department. I can vouch that no one placed any pressure on me to seek out strong black candidates or to hire particular black applicants. But I can also allow that I did consciously work to attract a pool of black candidates. Self-pressure was there as it was when I tried to discern who of the forty or so job candidates were black. Finally, I acknowledge some degree of pride in the outcome because we were able to hire two black females for our openings. Incidentally, another black female turned us down for a better paying position.

This episode placed me in the odd position of overseeing a search in which I would not have been selected as a finalist had I been an applicant. The institution's need to hire more black faculty was much on my mind when I applied to teach at the university, and I was told that in my case recent hires of black faculty had brought the department into some semblance of balance and that I would have a chance at the job. The balance of black and non-black faculty is a delicate issue, I would argue, because of the illogical possible extremes: either an all-white faculty or an all-black faculty. But between these unrealistic extremes, what is the "ideal" ratio? Half and half, remembering that the non-black category comprises faculty with roots in Asia and the Indian subcontinent and elsewhere? And how is a goal of faculty mix to be quantified?

Whether black or non-black, faculty at predominantly black institutions usually are duty bound not only to educate black students but also to prepare them for careers and leadership after graduation. My university's mission statement is clear on this: Xavier University of Louisiana is Catholic and historically black. The ultimate purpose of the university is the promotion of a more just and humane society. To this end, Xavier prepares its student to assume roles of leadership and service in society. This preparation takes place in a pluralistic teaching and learning environment that incorporates all relevant educational means, including research and community service. In their roles as advisors, white faculty need to urge black students to aspire to management positions in any field. Change will come best when the change makers change. So, the entry-level job has to be promoted as a foot in the door to something higher up the ladder, and black students need to be prepared for the glass ceiling and to be supplied with the means to smash through it. The lesson should be taught that true empowerment means attaining positions at decision-making levels.

On the practical side of my field, both white and black journalism faculty need to extend a hand into the public schools and identify future leaders. That is particularly incumbent upon faculty in urban areas. One successful method of accomplishing that has been urban journalism workshops for high school students. More than 10 percent of workshop participants who have graduated from college are working for newspapers and another 20 percent in media fields (Newspaper Fund Special Report, 1982). Those figures represent far more success in terms of media employment than the average numbers of black-educated students taking jobs after college.

The field of communication in its broadest sense of information will be one of the key arenas for leadership in the foreseeable future. This belief defines information as work that involves gathering, processing, and disseminating information as one's main job activity, plus the activities of those who design and produce the communication technologies used by other information workers. When communication is linked to information in that fashion, information workers may be or may become the dominant pool in America's work force. Those in the communication disciplines can no doubt do more to emphasize to black students that information is the primary resource in modern society, and that positions of influence in mass communication professions are an important part of the Information Revolution. Because a society's story-tellers exercise great control over the direction of that society, blacks and other minorities need to be among those telling the stories of America to America.

The goal of going beyond education to skills required for leadership and service is not an empty one. Bowen and Bok (1998) found black graduates from U.S. colleges and universities defined as "elite" were significantly more likely than their white peers to be involved in civic activities. In the case of black men that was true especially in the community, social service, youth, and school arenas, and for black women in community, social service, alumni or alumnae, religious and professional groups. Such a broader mission for any teacher at a black school puts an extra weight on the shoulders of the white faculty member, aspiring not just to be the best white person I can be, but the best person I can be, period. That is because we need to reach common ground as human beings, identifying many of the same goals while agreeing on the imperative of using proper means to reach those goals.

In summary, people in college are challenged in ways they haven't been challenged before, and by people they haven't met before. Important in that experience is the contact with people of all types, including minority faculty if you are a white student and white faculty if you are a minority student. Graduates will set sail into an increasingly diverse world where people of different races will be mixed together in the workplace. If students are not exposed to diversity in college, they likely will not be able to work as successfully with people of different races when they join the larger society after graduation. As Bowen and Bok (1998) note,

> As the United States grows steadily more diverse, we believe that Nicholas Katzenbach and Burke Marshall are surely right in insisting that the country must continue to make determined efforts to "include African Americans in the institutional framework that constitutes America's economic, political, educational and social life." This goal of greater inclusiveness is important for reasons, both moral and practical, that offer all Americans the prospect of living in a society marked by more equality and racial harmony than one might otherwise anticipate. (p.285)

Thirty years ago the Kerner Commission in its oft-quoted report talked about America as comprising two societies, "one black and one white." No sane person would suggest that these words were trumpeted as a desirable goal that had been achieved, or as some self-congratulatory paean to America's two nations. The words, of course, were uttered in the context of harsh censure on a society that had failed to reconcile all of its disparate elements, racial and otherwise. And one way to accelerate the contributions of black citizens into a truly multilayered mainstream is to retain a mix of faculty by race, gender, and ethnicity for all students everywhere. That condition, by the way, not only exists for the benefit of the students, but also for the faculty, who likewise need to learn and to grow by encountering those of another race.

Scene VII: I am teaching in a classroom where I cannot identify the race of my own students or my own race. The students exist without race consciousness, thinking of race only in some historical context. In that time and place, race doesn't matter.

The above is only a dream, an ideal. It hasn't happened anywhere I know about in the American experience, but it is a dream worth dreaming.

References

Bowen, W.G. & D. Bok (1998). *The shape of the river: Long term consequences of considering race in college and university admissions.* Princeton, NJ: Princeton University Press.

Brubacher, J.S., & W. Rudy (1997). *Higher education in transition: A history of American colleges and universities* (4th edition). New Brunswick, NJ: Transaction Publishers.

Campbell, C.P. (1995). *Race, myth and the news.* Thousand Oaks, CA: Sage Publishers.

Dow-Jones Newspaper Fund (1982). *A special report on newspaper fund programs for minorities.* Princeton, NJ: The Fund.

Keenan, K.L. (1996). Skin tones and physical features of blacks in magazine advertisements. *Journalism & Mass Communication Quarterly,* 73(4), 905-912.

Rathbun, E.A. (August, 1998). Woman's work still excludes top jobs. *Broadcasting & Cable,* 22-27.

Richards, P.M. (Autumn, 1998). A stranger in the village: A black professor at a white college. *Journal of Blacks in Higher Education,* 21, 88-93.

Rosenfeld, A. (May/June, 1987). Frustration: 'Preaching to the choir' won't convert our profession into a true reflection of society. *ASNE Bulletin,* 16-17.

Shipler, D.K. (May/June, 1998). Blacks in the newsroom: Progress? yes, but . . . *Columbia Journalism Review,* 26-32.

West, Hollie (March, 1996) A "wake-up call" for black newspapers. *Freedom Forum News,* 4.

West, C. (1994). *Race matters.* New York: Vintage Press.

Williams, B.A. (1992). Sins of omission. *Media Studies Journal,* 6(4), 49-56.

Women, Men, and Media (1988*). Who speaks for America? Sex, age and race on the network news* (ADT Research, Andrew Tyndall, Director). Silver Spring, MD.

Chapter 4 _____

The 'Science' and 'Art' of Teaching and Learning at Xavier University of Louisiana

Mark A. Thomson

Xavier University of Louisiana offers a very unique perspective among the many institutions of higher education that cover the landscape of our nation. There are 222 institutions that incorporate a strong Catholic character into their respective curricula. There are also 103 institutions that, in the policy of "separate but equal" that was propelled by *Plessy* v. *Ferguson* over 100 years ago, have grown out of a desire or need to serve the specific needs of the African-American population of our country. Xavier University of Louisiana is the only institution of higher education to incorporate both facets into its mission. The original mission of Blessed Katharine Drexel and the Sisters of the Blessed Sacrament was to establish a higher education setting where the minority communities of both African American and Native American peoples could be provided with teachers and important role models.

An often overlooked aspect that also makes Xavier University unique is the composition of the faculty. While white faculty make up only about one-third of the total faculty members at historically black colleges and universities (HBCUs), they make up the majority of the faculty at Xavier University (U.S. Department of Education, 1996). On a subtle and subconscious level, I am sure that this demographic factor has had an impact both on my own perspective and experiences at Xavier University, as well as having an impact on the experiences of everyone else here. With no other experience at any other Catholic or black higher educational institutions, I cannot truly separate and distinguish which of my views and experiences have grown out of which aspects of the "Xavier experience."

For a new faculty member at the inception of his or her career, there are many factors that compete for attention and inclusion in the pedagogical "bag of tools" that they will use and develop. The tools enter the bag from many sources, including the many past classroom experiences with both excellent and mediocre instructors. Other tool sources might include theory and method lectures and textbooks, experiences as a teaching assistant in graduate school, panels attended at professional meetings, and other discussions with mentors and colleagues. My experiences at Xavier University for nearly four years have persuaded me to throw away almost all of my old tools and to replace them with new ones.

The methods, or pedagogical tools, employed at Xavier University, especially in the sciences, are explained in some detail below. I am not truly equipped to judge if these techniques are unique to Xavier University, if they are unique to historically black colleges and universities, or if they are prevalent among colleges across the nation. I can simply observe that they are new to me and quite different from my own experiences as a student. The methods I have observed to be particularly effective include a firm attention to course standardization in multisection courses, an active but realistic belief in student abilities, an aggressive approach toward remediation of basic skills that are deficient, and an effort to help students identify those concepts that are most important.

Xavier University's Mission and Purpose

As indicated in the Xavier University Mission Statement, the university strives for "the promotion of a more just and humane society. To this end, Xavier prepares its students to assume roles of leadership and service in society" (Xavier Catalog, p.6). This emphasis on both leadership and service is evident throughout campus life. Student organizations are very strong at Xavier, allowing many opportunities for the acquisition of leadership skills. As is the case at other institutions, many of these organizations are social in nature and include several fraternities and sororities, but I find that a large number of students at Xavier are much more interested in academic organizations such as literary public speaking clubs and student affiliate chapters of professional organizations. Each organization, whether social or academic, is required to plan and participate in several service projects. The high level of activity in serving the community has become clear to me as I review student resumes while writing letters of recommendation. Discussions with other faculty indicate that my observations are not unique.

To coordinate the institutional emphasis on service, a Volunteer Services office was created on campus. Through a student organization, Mobilization at Xavier (MAX), the office helps new students find opportunities in the community and serves as an ongoing resource center for students, student organizations, and people in need in the community. Exposure to the needs of others helps students to realize and appreciate what they already have, while at the same time preparing them for leadership by showing them what they can offer to others.

Because Xavier students are expected to assume roles of leadership, there is a strong commitment on campus to help them magnify what they have to offer by obtaining an advanced degree. Suggestions to students regarding professional schools in medicine or law, as well as other graduate programs at both the master's and doctorate levels, are accompanied by specific and concrete plans to improve the likelihood of admission and success in these programs. Efforts of the individual faculty are coordinated through several specialized student support offices, including the GradStar Office and the Pre-Medical Advisor's Office.

The GradStar office is specifically engineered to assist students wishing to gain admittance into graduate school, either in a master's or a doctorate program in their chosen field. To achieve this goal, the office provides orientation regarding admissions requirements, examinations, letters of support, and expectations. For interested students, several trips are planned each year to visit prospective graduate programs in the region. Efforts of the office are coordinated with a faculty liaison in each department. The liaison collects information on programs in their particular discipline and helps to answer questions of a more specialized nature. The GradStar office also helps to sponsor a campus-wide GAPS day. This is an open house where Graduate and Professional School (GAPS) programs are invited to attend and make presentations to prospective students. The popularity of this program has increased to the point that it now fills an entire day, involving students of every level and discipline on campus. To further aid in preparing for application to graduate programs, the office also sponsors a Graduate Record Exam (GRE) review program that is open to all interested students. While most of the services and activities sponsored by the GradStar office seem directed toward upperclassmen, these resources are also emphasized with the freshman and sophomore students so that preparation and focus can begin as early as possible.

The Pre-Medical Office also provides a strong network of resource materials and assistance for those students interested in pursuing studies in health-related fields such as osteopathic or allopathic medicine, dentistry, public health, physical therapy, or veterinary medicine. Through the efforts of two dedicated advisors, Dr. J.W. Carmichael, Jr., from the chemistry department and Dr.

Jacqueline Hunter from the biology department, and financial support from the Howard Hughes Medical Foundation, students in chemistry, biology, and psychology begin preparing for application to medical school virtually at the inception of their studies at Xavier. While participating in the Biomedical Honor Corps, students in their first semester begin to learn about essentials such as medical school admission requirements, what to provide persons writing letters of recommendation, when to prepare and take the MCAT exam, and how to apply for special summer programs that will improve their preparation for medical school. To further focus the attention of the students, the Pre-Medical office maintains an "open-door" policy for representatives from medical schools across the country. Between forty and sixty health-related programs take advantage of this opportunity to meet and recruit Xavier University students each year. This opportunity also allows the students to learn more about the schools and their specific admission policies so that they can make an informed decision when they apply to schools. As with the GradStar office, the services and opportunities offered by the Pre-Medical office are offered to all interested students.

The Nature of the Educational Experience

With different offices trying to help students focus on different goals for themselves, many might easily become lost without the important guidance of advisors. This is where one of the most important aspects of an educational experience at Xavier University rises to the surface: the development of a personal relationship between advisor and student. During the freshman year, students in chemistry and biology are required to maintain an advisor's card. The student must record his or her grades in each class and discuss them on a weekly basis with the academic advisor. In this way, a close relationship is established from the beginning of the student's studies and built over subsequent years. This relationship acts as a guide for the student because the advisor, in full knowledge of the student's abilities and weaknesses, can immediately begin to discuss plans for graduate or professional school and plans for participation in the summer programs discussed above. The advisor also acts as a liaison to the Pre-Medical and GradStar offices, providing important information in both directions. Because the advisor and the student know each other well, they can work together to tailor the curriculum to meet the post-graduation plans, and they can tailor the post-graduation plans to meet the student's abilities. The advisor is also a full-time faculty member and can help the student understand and take full advantage of the special features incorporated into each course.

While the discipline-based content in the undergraduate curriculum at Xavier University differs only slightly from other programs I have experienced, the pedagogical methods are quite different. These differences include a broader exposure to other disciplines, an emphasis on interdisciplinary approaches, and a gradual change in the level of support provided and the level of achievement expected. There is also an emphasis on course standardization and group work. This academic structure is an interwoven thread throughout the curriculum that allows students to form study groups. They can help each other and gain from the experience, even though they may not be registered for the same section of the class.

While completing a degree at Xavier, students must fulfill two important requirements that help to broaden their education and better prepare themselves for roles of leadership and service. These complements to the discipline-based studies are a required minor field of study (18-21 semester hours) and a broad, extensive core curriculum (66 semester hours) in keeping with Xavier's role as a liberal arts university. For many programs, the required minor is integrated into the course of study as is the case in chemistry where the minor field is either biology or mathematics, depending on the post-graduate plans of the student. The core curriculum builds a strong foundation for the major and minor fields of study while preparing for future extracurricular interests in philosophy, natural and social sciences, history, theology, and foreign languages.

There are several efforts to integrate the core curriculum into the major fields of study. Key among these is the Across the Curriculum Thinking (ACT) Program. This is a program in which eight professors in different disciplines bring their classes together several times each semester to discuss a topic. This allows students to view the topic from the perspective of the other disciplines that include biology, chemistry, communications, English, history, philosophy, sociology, and theology. ACT meetings or "brown bag seminars" often include invited guest speakers and always provide time for student discussion and participation on broad topics such as environmental sustainability, commodification, and generations and traditions. Classroom discussions follow up on the points brought up at the seminars so that the students can develop a greater understanding of the topic throughout the year.

The nature and level of expectation in courses at Xavier University follow a gradient similar to what I have experienced elsewhere with the difference that it covers what I perceive as wider spectrum, often allowing students to distinguish themselves early in their studies. The teaching philosophy at Xavier, especially in the sciences, is to provide extra assistance during the initial years of study while maintaining a high standard of expectation. This extra assistance is gradually removed so that as the student rises to the junior or senior level, much more independence is expected and the students are better prepared to pursue graduate studies. The methods and reasons for this have been well documented and described as the "Triple S"—Standards with Sympathy in the Sciences Program that has been in operation at Xavier for quite some time (Carmichael et al, 1988). Some highlights of this program include the use of faculty prepared handbooks and manuals that emphasize important concepts, weekly quizzes to ensure that students do not procrastinate in their studies, and an overlap with

Xavier's Summer Science Academies. The Summer Science Academies are a set of four programs for high school students to help them prepare for and succeed in their math and science classes. This enables the students to arrive at the university better prepared and more likely to succeed in their studies, either here at Xavier or wherever else they may choose to attend.

Freshman students in the sciences are also provided with an externally funded "Peer Counseling Center." Funding for this center is provided by the Howard Hughes Medical Institute and it allows for the employment of fifteen to twenty exceptional sophomore and junior level students as peer counselors and tutors. Because each of these counselors has excelled in chemistry and biology here at Xavier, they are well equipped to help those freshman students who are having difficulty in the general chemistry and general biology classes. Other outstanding sophomores are also employed as part-time instructors to conduct weekly quiz or drill sections. Either as a tutor or as an instructor, this experience reinforces and refreshes the understanding of the fundamentals for the student, strengthening their overall educational experience.

As the students complete the general courses in biology and chemistry and increase their familiarity with the fundamentals, they can begin to solidify their plans for graduate studies. The expectation, from self, faculty, and parents, is usually that students will not stop with a degree from Xavier University, but that they will go on to pursue and complete an advanced degree in either medicine or science or both. To improve opportunities for successful matriculation into advanced medical and scientific degree programs, Xavier science students are strongly encouraged to take advantage of special programs nationwide and here at Xavier that go beyond the normal classroom and laboratory experiences.

For students interested in health-related fields there exist a large number of summer programs nationwide, especially for minority students. These programs vary greatly and can include a combination of special course work, an intensive MCAT review course, experiences in research labs, or observations and assistance in hospitals and operating rooms. For those students who are more interested in basic scientific research in the fields of chemistry, physics, or biology, several programs have been established at Xavier that provide for close faculty-student interaction on a research project during the academic year. With financial support from the National Science Foundation and the National Institutes of Health, these programs provide stipends and supplies for both the students and the faculty members involved. The students present their findings to their peers and the faculty mentors in a seminar at the end of the semester and follow up the project with full-time research during the summer, either at Xavier or at another research facility elsewhere. Coordination between the research mentor and the academic advisor helps to ensure that participation in the program complements the student's course of study and does not interfere with it. One of the most significant benefits of participation in these programs following the freshman, sophomore, or junior year is that the students can choose, before completely committing themselves, if they are truly interested in a career in medicine or in scientific research.

Results and Consequences of the Methods Used

Assessment is currently a very important topic on most university and college campuses. Together with a mission and a method to accomplish that mission comes a set of desired student outcomes that must be achieved. As stated previously, Xavier University's mission is to promote a more just and humane society by preparing students to assume roles of leadership and service in the community. In the natural sciences, this is not accomplished solely by the completion of a baccalaureate degree, but it also requires moving on to complete a graduate or professional degree. This is currently being accomplished at Xavier with a greater number of students gaining admission into advanced programs and completing those programs every year.

Several strong indicators exist which point to the quality of education and level of preparedness that are being accomplished at Xavier University. According to internal studies done by the Pre-Medical office, students entering Xavier who elect a pre-medicine course of study are more than twice as likely to be admitted into medical or dental school when compared to the national average for students with similar ACT/SAT scores and high school grades. Additionally, more than 90 percent of those who gain admission into medical, dental, or graduate programs finish those programs successfully. This is roughly equivalent to the national average.

Because of the quality and success of previous graduates, students at Xavier are becoming increasingly popular among recruiters. Over thirty medical, dental, and veterinary school recruiters visit the university every year. Most of these recruiters return on an annual basis because they are familiar with standards that we expect of our graduating seniors. Most of these graduating seniors receive multiple offers, allowing them to choose the program that best fits their specific needs and interests rather than being forced to accept something less than what they had hoped for. A further example of this high level of expectation is the early admission agreement that has developed between Xavier University and the Tulane University Medical School. Each year, interested sophomore students apply to a faculty committee that selects five candidates for early admission to the Tulane University Medical School. On the basis of the recommendation of the committee, these students are admitted conditionally on their successful completion of courses at Xavier. This allows the students to concentrate on their classes without spending extra time on MCAT preparation and medical school applications and interviews. To my knowledge, all the students who have been admitted through this program have successfully completed the program at Tulane, or are currently on track to do so.

Learning from Xavier University: A Whole New World

Xavier University has given me a whole new view to a very different culture. Many of the students here are very knowledgeable and culturally confident. They express themselves, verbally and nonverbally, in a loud voice to everyone who will listen. Many times I find myself engrossed in conversations with advisees and students where the topic is far removed from chemistry and I become the student. These conversations have not centered on typical generational differences, but have involved a free exchange of ideas and perspectives. One such example comes to mind involving a graduating senior biology student. Knowing that I am beginning to study jazz, this student brought in some recordings from John Coltrane. This led to a discussion, both with him and with other students, about the role of Coltrane and other jazz artists in helping to develop part of the identity of the Afro-American culture. An ongoing discussion still follows ranging from the music of Sarah Vaughn and Billie Holiday to the west coast and east coast differences of Tupac Shakur and A Tribe Called Quest. The key to interaction with students is one of mutual respect. As a white faculty member, I cannot assume to be a positive part of their cultural history. Therefore, I cannot fill a position as a role model without earning their respect. The first step in earning respect is to give it. The most important part of this is to have a genuine interest in those subjects that interest the students. They see and understand this interest and reciprocate. The result is an ambiance that facilitates learning and even demands it. A thirst for knowledge is passed on because the students have learned how important these other subjects are to me.

The students at Xavier have also fostered in me a greater thirst for knowledge in chemistry. Our students are very demanding of themselves and of the faculty members who teach them. Even at the introductory level, I find students that far surpass my expectations. For these students, anything less than perfection is not satisfactory. They push to achieve all that they can and are quick to object to instructors who do not satisfy that quest for excellence. I rarely pass a week without at least one question that requires me to rethink the presentation of the material. Not every instructor is able to rise to this challenge and the results appear in discussions with advisors. "Vote with your feet" is a phrase often used to describe an intolerance for substandard performance and I have seen it several times in class as well. The students at Xavier are discriminating, demanding, and demonstrative, much more so than any other group of students I have ever worked with. My students have routinely suggested that they would rather change their entire work schedule and academic schedule, including the possibility of summer classes, in order to take certain classes from specific faculty members. They will then work day and night to meet the demands placed on them by that "preferred instructor."

My experiences at Xavier have also moved me in directions of greater social consciousness. Through Xavier, I have participated in enlightening conferences on "Racial Relations in New Orleans" and "Remembering *Plessy* v. *Ferguson*." I have stepped from a world of complete misunderstanding regarding the policies of affirmative action and into a world of recognition that we are not a color-blind society and perhaps never will be. As long as racism exists, segregation will exist, sometimes involuntarily, sometimes voluntarily. In the same fashion, as long as segregation exists, racism will continue to exist because two separate and distinct cultures are rarely willing to accept that which they consider to be inferior. Many people mistakenly believe that different and inferior are the same, and are therefore unwilling to try to obtain something they see no value in. The maintenance of these views is demonstrated by the racial composition of some faculty at some historically black colleges and universities. The error of these views can be easily presented and argued by those fortunate few white faculty members who are able to teach at these historically black colleges and universities. The following poem is one I wrote during my second year of teaching at Xavier and is reflective of much of what I have learned here.

Difference and Diversity

Who are you
what could you possibly offer me
you come from such a different place
different ideas, different customs,
different everything
and it is all wrong
I don't even know
why we are talking

Except that
I have so much to offer you
let me teach you what is right
change your wrong ideas
change your wrong customs
change everything about you
then you can be like me
both the same
both right, neither wrong

Conclusions

My experiences at Xavier University have combined instruction with education to significantly change me forever, to the extent that I refer to my previous experiences as a whole other life. I have developed a sensitivity to issues of minority participation and inclusion that will continue to grow and spill over into other aspects of my professional and personal life. As a local leader in the American Chemical Society, I am starting to participate in minority recruitment and mentoring programs. I have become interested in the history, development, and solution to interracial conflicts. With the greater understanding of the issues of racism and prejudice that I am learning from my students, I am now advocating programs that I never felt were necessary. These programs include affirmative action, cultural sensitivity training, and grants to increase minority participation.

The future at Xavier will increase this social development for me. As I strive to meet the demands of my students, I will follow in the tradition of developing new pedagogical techniques and tools. I will continue to learn from my students about their changing world perspectives. While we may not be able to change the entire world together, we will continue to change our part of it.

References

Carmichael, J.W., J.T. Hunter, D.D. Labat, J.P. Sevenair, & J. Bauer (1988). An educational pathway into biology and chemistry-based careers for black Americans. *Journal of College Science Teaching*, 17 (2), 370-377.

United States Department of Education (1996). *Historically Black Colleges and Universities, 1976-1994* (NCES 96-902, by C.H. Hoffman, T.D. Snyder, and B. Sonnenberg). Washington, DC: United States Department of Education, National Center for Educational Statistics.

Xavier University of Louisiana (1998). *Xavier University of Louisiana Catalog, 1998-2000*. New Orleans, LA: The University.

Chapter 5 _____

HBCUs as a Context for Instruction and Research with A Multicultural Perspective

Amy E. Sibulkin

After obtaining undergraduate and graduate degrees from private, selective, and predominantly white universities, I began a research career at two additional universities of the same type. My first teaching experience began in 1995 in the Department of Psychology at Tennessee State University (TSU), as an assistant professor, teaching both undergraduate and graduate courses. TSU's undergraduate full-time equivalent enrollment is about 84 percent African American at the undergraduate level and about 47 percent African American at the graduate level. Eighty-nine percent of undergraduate psychology majors are African American. In each of my undergraduate psychology classes of approximately forty-five students (most of whom are non-majors), about four students are white. After noting the resources that have informed my thinking about multicultural issues, I will describe how a historically black institution provides a powerful context and stimulus for learning about multicultural issues and for incorporating diversity into teaching and research in psychology.

Multicultural Perspectives: Definition and Resources

I am using the term "multicultural perspective" to mean a sense of inclusiveness. Not everyone is a white Christian heterosexual man, and one can remind students and faculty of this by using inclusive language, such as referring to houses of worship as "churches, synagogues, or mosques" rather than as "churches." Also, one can illustrate how research questions or results may reflect implicit assumptions that should be made explicit. For example, studies that describe gender differences often assume that men's behavior is the norm and women's behavior is the deviation to be explained; studies that find a difference between women and men on the type of explanations they give for success on a task are likely to ask why women give fewer self-serving explanations for their success than men, rather than asking why men give more than women (Tavris, 1992). Further, topics can be introduced in the curriculum that are of interest to non-dominant groups (e.g., effectiveness of different methods of bilingual education), and standard topics can be reassessed for generalizability to other groups. At the same time, there is a tension between contrasting dominant groups with non-dominant groups, on one hand, and recognizing the diversity within groups on the other. Historically black colleges and universities (HBCUs) are a particularly good context for learning about diverse views among African Americans.

In the fifteen years between completing my formal education and beginning my teaching career, textbooks have changed to reflect gender inclusive language. Also, pictures of non-white Americans are conspicuous, and explicit discussion of issues relevant to non-white groups is included. Hence, the start of my teaching career was propitious in terms of the availability of multicultural resources. Further, I was fortunate to begin teaching at a time when organized activities were available to learn how to incorporate multicultural perspectives into liberal arts curricula.

Soon after beginning teaching, I attended two workshops on this topic sponsored by the Ford Foundation. One was held at Spelman College, a historically black college for women in Atlanta, Georgia, and the other was the fifth annual Ford Diversity Conference, hosted by the American Association of Colleges and Universities (AAC&U). Interestingly, the workshop at Spelman was for instructors at HBCUs. It was recognized that most HBCUs were misguided to think that because they were predominantly black that they were sensitive to issues of diversity. Some workshop organizers at Spelman were concerned with students' intolerance. The college chaplain related an incident of students protesting the placing of the Koran in the chapel's prayer room, and concern was expressed for harassment of students who were thought to be lesbian.

The same need to educate students, faculty, and administrators at HBCUs about the advantages of including multicultural perspectives exists as at predominantly white institutions. The Ford Diversity Conference had a stronger emphasis on strategies for institutional change that would support a multicultural curriculum and campus climate. The value of working to enhance multicultural perspectives was recognized by TSU in funding some of the travel expenses to attend these conferences. In my own discipline of psychology, the annual conference of the Association for Women in Psychology (AWP) is very informative about current multicultural issues that are applicable to teaching and research. The membership attending these conferences is diverse with respect to ethnicity and sexual orientation, and the issues discussed help in developing an informed multicultural sensitivity.

Multicultural Perspective in Teaching Psychology

Teaching at an HBCU creates an immediacy for considering multicultural perspectives that is unlikely to exist at a predominantly white institution. The presence of large numbers of African-American students, faculty, and staff continuously focuses attention on issues of diversity, both between groups and within a group. I will give examples from my teaching of general, social, and developmental psychology courses to illustrate issues that take on particular significance in terms of presenting them with sensitivity towards inclusiveness and with an awareness of diversity of views among African-American students.

The topics of prejudice and discrimination are standard in social psychology. Prejudice is defined as the affective component of an attitude, i.e., a positive or negative evaluation of an individual based on group membership. Discrimination is defined as the behavioral component of an attitude; in other words, taking action for or against a person, due to the individual's group membership. I am not as comfortable presenting these issues at an HBCU as I assume I would be at a predominantly white institution. Lacking a sense of what the African-American students expect me to know about their experience, I fear appearing uninformed or insensitive. My goal is to present the academic basis and empirical support for these concepts to students who can use empirical results to inform their own experience. I emphasize the cognitive basis of prejudiced attitudes in terms of the mechanisms of social cognition that maintain stereotypes. Following are some examples of social cognition concepts that inform the study of prejudice.

Social psychology courses provide an ideal context for addressing modern racism. One definition of modern racism is the subtle ways individuals from non-dominant groups are made to feel excluded (Aronson, Wilson, & Akert, 1999). In order to illustrate modern racism, I ask my students to write anonymously an example of an experience of feeling excluded, or of being discriminated against due to membership in some group. (I learned this technique at a discussion group at another university.) I explain that for many students this experience would have been due to skin color. However, for others it may be due to some other group membership, such as gender, religion, or sexual orientation. The purpose is to collect and present examples of modern racism to educate myself and the non-black students in my classes about subtle ways in which African Americans are excluded in American society. Further, the intent is to generate an identification with many African-American students' experiences by having non-black students focus on their own experiences of exclusion. I doubt I would do this exercise at a predominantly white institution, because it would not be possible for the few African-American students in the class to maintain anonymity. Also, white students are likely to think of the African-American students' experiences as exceptions or as oversensitive interpretations of others' behavior as discriminatory (Tatum, 1997).

I recently introduced "stereotype vulnerability," another topic in the social psychology of prejudice. Steele (1997) describes stereotype vulnerability as a fear of behaving in a way that could support a stereotype about a group to which one belongs, even if one does not believe the stereotype. African Americans are vulnerable to the stereotype of intellectual inferiority, and Steele presents experimental results supporting the hypothesis that stereotype vulnerability accounts for lower standardized test scores between African-American and white students, based on studies at a selective university. Although I have not taught at a predominantly white university, I expect that this topic would remain an academic abstraction there, because most of the students have had little personal experience with being assumed intellectually inferior based on group membership, except for women in traditionally male dominated fields. At an HBCU, African-American students relate the concept to their own experiences, and white students in the same class become more knowledgeable about this experience from their fellow African-American students.

"Outgroup homogeneity" refers to seeing members of the group to which one does not belong as more similar to each other than one sees members of one's own group. This concept underlies the belief that "They're all alike." Teaching and learning at an HBCU mitigates outgroup homogeneity by exposing instructors and students to diverse views among African Americans. For example, I was surprised when I introduced the topic of Black English. Textbooks emphasize the view that Black English is a dialect with internally consistent rules of grammar and that it should be considered as different from standard English, rather than as a deficit. However, students disagree among themselves as to what, if any, characteristics should be classified as Black English as opposed to slang. Further, students who classify patterns of speech as slang indicate that this does not deserve the status of a dialect. Although technical classifications regarding forms of speech are best left to informed linguists, the views of students lead both instructors and students to ask more sophisticated questions about definitions of and the social uses of language, such as what is a dialect and what are appropriate contexts for slang (e.g., classroom, meeting, workplace).

Another social psychology concept is heuristics, which are "mental shortcuts," or conclusions drawn from ambiguous social information according to predictable rules. Heuristics are useful as time savers, but often lead to inaccurate conclusions. For example, the "availability heuristic" is the shortcut that says, "If I can easily think of examples of a phenomenon, then that phenomenon is actually more common than one for which I can not easily think of examples." A well-known example is to ask whether there are more words that begin with the letter "k" or more words with "k" as the third letter (Tversky & Kahneman, 1974). Most of us assume more words begin with "k," because we can more easily think of such words, although more actually have "k" as the third letter. Heuristics explain why many white people assume that there are more black than white individuals receiving welfare. When picturing a person on welfare, whites tend to think of a black individual. However, in absolute numbers, there are more whites receiving welfare (which is not surprising given that 83 percent of the U.S. population is white, as compared with 13 percent being black). This example is more complex in that a higher proportion of the black population receives welfare than does the proportion of whites (U.S. Bureau of the Census, 1997). Understanding this social psychology concept of heuristics guards against inaccurate conclusions about social information and also illustrates the critical thinking needed to approach social issues. Although it is not true that "Most welfare recipients are black," it is true that "black individuals are more likely to be on welfare than white individuals." The former shows the dangers of stereotypical thinking; the latter points to the continued legacy of prejudice and discrimination in America. Although I do not know students' responses at a predominantly white university, white students pay more attention to this concept, illustrated in this way, when studying among large numbers of African-American students.

Also intriguing is the diversity of views among African-American students regarding barriers to success in America. Given the larger proportion of ethnic minority group individuals who receive welfare, relative to whites, I was again surprised to discover that many African-American students hold negative attitudes toward welfare recipients, seeing them as lazy and taking advantage of the system. (I assume these remarks were not specific to any particular group receiving welfare.) Students also differ in the extent to which they see racial discrimination as a barrier to success. Using personality and social psychology concepts, one could categorize these views along the dimension of internal and external locus of control, which is the degree to which individuals feel they can control what happens to them ("I can succeed if I try hard"), as opposed to feeling that life events are more influenced by factors outside their control ("No matter how hard you try, discrimination is an obstacle").

Developmental psychology courses provide another challenge for white faculty at HBCUs. A difficult issue to present is the effects of poverty on children's developmental outcomes. On average, children in poverty are at higher risk for a large number of suboptimal outcomes, including low birth weight (Starfield et al., 1991), poorer physical health, lower standardized test scores, fewer years of school completion, and poorer mental health (Huston, 1991; Huston, Garcia, Coll, & McLoyd, 1994; McLoyd, 1998). Developmental psychology instructors stress the deleterious effects of poverty in terms of both the need for national family policies and as part of the explanation for ethnic differences in these developmental outcomes. Since a larger proportion of children from ethnic minority groups are poor, a larger proportion have poorer outcomes. This focus on class differences leads to a consideration of the origins of these class differences and institutionalized inequality. It provides an important alternative to blaming the victim. However, developmental psychology courses provide so many opportunities to show poor outcomes for black children that it is difficult to know how to present this material in a sensitive way.

In addition to topics covered, the mechanics of a course provide opportunities to show sensitivity towards inclusiveness. In test questions that use hypothetical people, I use names that are popular among many African Americans. I also suggest topics for papers and bibliographic retrieval exercises on issues that are likely to be of interest, such as the development of ethnic identity, current research on "doll preference" studies, whether evidence exists for ethnic differences in cognitive styles, and predictors of college graduation rates for African Americans. In illustrating research designs, I use examples of questions about non-dominant groups, in order to normalize less traditional topics and marginal groups. For example, I used the report of a study of sexual orientation of children raised by mothers who identified themselves as lesbians to practice identifying independent and dependent variables. I also used data on the association between the percentage of blacks who were sharecroppers in 1930 (in twelve southern states) and the average number of school days attended by black children to illustrate a negative correlation (Bullock, 1967).

HBCUs as a Context for Research

Opportunities for research at HBCUs must be understood in historical context. Black colleges were designed to teach agricultural and manual arts and to train professionals who would work within the black community as teachers, ministers, doctors, and lawyers (Bullock, 1967; Holmes, 1972). Conducting research was not part of the conceptual or financial picture. Guthrie (1998) gives a brief history of psychology at black colleges. In the 1930s very few black colleges even offered psychology as a major; library and research facilities were minimal or nonexistent, making publications of scholarly work almost impossible. In fact, very few professors held doctoral degrees, given the financial and ethnic barriers to attending predominantly white universities that offered doctoral degrees. The first thirty-two black PhDs in psychology received their degrees over a thirty-year period (1920 to 1950), and all these degrees were granted by northern universities.

Currently, at some HBCUs, such as Tennessee State, faculty are expected to conduct research as part of the university's mission. The American Psychological Association's (APA) 1996 annual convention included a panel on research at HBCUs, which focused on funding opportunities for faculty and resources to enhance undergraduates' research experience. Conducting research at TSU is more difficult than at highly research-oriented universities, given relatively lower levels of research funding, staff support, and high teaching requirements. However, a large benefit of doing research at an HBCU is the easy access to African-American students as research participants. In order to aid faculty and student research, our department has a research participant pool, wherein students and faculty who are conducting research list studies in which students may voluntarily participate. Professional organizations stress the need for research on populations other than white men, and federal Public Health Service funding requires inclusion of individuals from minority groups. However, most white faculty at predominantly white institutions live and work separately from people of color, and this separateness creates a barrier to doing research other than the type to which one was exposed in graduate school. White faculty members at an HBCU are nudged in the direction of doing research that explicitly addresses issues relevant to ethnic minority groups, particularly black individuals, because of the interest generated by being in the presence of a black majority. I think the multicultural climate in liberal arts education and being at an HBCU influenced my current choice of research topic. We are exploring the extent to which the gap in graduation rates between black and white traditional-aged college students is accounted for by different rates of having children and different responses to having a child. We are currently using national archival data. However, the plan is to pursue primary data from African-American students who are attending TSU.

White faculty may receive mixed messages regarding their attempt to be inclusive. On the one hand, the current multicultural climate of inclusiveness, promoted by professional associations and accrediting bodies, encourages research on ethnically diverse issues and the inclusion of research participants who belong to ethnic minority groups. On the other hand, some African-American faculty and students are skeptical of the validity of such research conducted by white faculty and students. Presumably, there is a fear of faulty interpretation of results. At an HBCU, this problem can be ameliorated by having African-American faculty and students with whom to collaborate who are more knowledgeable and sensitive to issues surrounding design, data collection, analysis, and interpretation of studies intended to be inclusive. Qualitative research, which involves extensive interviewing with individuals and groups, often about sensitive issues, would particularly benefit from collaboration between researchers from dominant and non-dominant groups, a context available at HBCUs.

Less than five percent of doctoral degrees in the social sciences are awarded to African Americans (National Science Board, 1996), the result of a history of unequally funded and segregated educational opportunities. The American Psychological Association's Office of Ethnic Minority Affairs seeks to increase the proportion of terminally prepared graduates through association programming. Colleges and universities work to recruit and maintain faculty and graduate students from ethnic minority groups. An HBCU is an ideal place for black and white faculty to contribute to the increase in the number of black psychologists through mentoring black undergraduate psychology majors. As HBCUs move toward more emphasis on faculty research, undergraduates have more opportunities to serve as research assistants, thereby gaining valuable experience in terms of increasing admission to doctoral programs. For example, the TSU administration provides a small amount of funds for projects each year, for which faculty can compete. I used these funds to hire an undergraduate psychology major as a research assistant for the aforementioned study on graduation rates. TSU has been a site for the federally funded Minority Access to Research Careers (MARC) program since 1980. MARC provides undergraduates in the biological and behavioral sciences with research experience (both through courses and individual research with a faculty mentor) in order to enhance their chances of admission to graduate and professional schools. Both black and white faculty serve as mentors. Further, the College of Education at TSU (which includes the Department of Psychology) has received federal funds through Title III for a project to increase applications and acceptances into graduate and professional programs in psychology, education, and related fields. One strategy for accomplishing this goal is to enhance undergraduate research experience. Based on programs such as MARC, we have designed a summer research experience in which undergraduates are paid as research assistants to faculty members. This programmatic experience will commence in the summer of 1999.

Summary

My experience at an HBCU provides a context for teaching and research wherein the motivation to continue the conscious process of educating oneself about diversity is maintained. A number of concepts from my discipline of psychology relate to important multicultural issues, such as stereotypes, prejudice, and the effects of poverty on child outcomes. Although these topics would be covered at a predominantly white institution, the HBCU environment provides the opportunity for instructors and students to move beyond simple illustrations to more complex ones. Had I begun teaching at a predominantly white university, my attention to a multicultural perspective would likely have been limited to textbook examples, which are necessarily brief and simplified. The diversity of students and instructors at TSU provides an unusual data base of experiences for applying academic concepts as well as for challenging them.

The author wishes to acknowledge Dorothy Granberry, professor of psychology, Tennessee State University, for helpful comments while revising this manuscript.

References

Aronson, E., T. Wilson, & R.M. Akert (1999). *Social psychology* (3rd ed.) New York: Longman Publishers.

Bullock, H.A. (1967). *A history of Negro education in the south: From 1619 to the present.* Cambridge, MA: Harvard University Press.

Guthrie, R.V. (1998). *Even the rat was white: A historical view of psychology.* New York: Harper & Row.

Holmes, D.O.W. (1972). *The evolution of the Negro college.* New York: AMS Press, Columbia University Contributions to Education, Teachers College Series No. 609.

Huston, A.C. (Ed.). (1991). *Children in poverty: Child development and public policy.* New York: Cambridge University Press.

Huston, A.C., C.T. Garcia-Coll, & V.C. McLoyd (Eds.). (1994). Children and poverty. *Child Development,* 65(2). (Special issue).

McLoyd, V.C. (1998). Socioeconomic disadvantage and child development. *American Psychologist,* 53(2), 185-204.

National Science Board (1996). *Science & engineering indicators- 1996.* (NSB 96-21). Washington, DC: U.S. Government Printing Office.

Starfield, B., S. Shapiro, J. Weiss, K. Liang, K. Ra, D. Paige, & X. Wang (1991). Race, family income, and low birth weight. *American Journal of Epidemiology,* 134(10), 1167-1174.

Steele, C.M. (1997). A threat in the air: How stereotypes shape intellectual identity and performance. *American Psychologist,* 52(6), 613-629.

Tatum, B.D. (1997). *"Why are all the black kids sitting together in the cafeteria?" and other conversations about race.* New York: BasicBooks.

Tavris, C. (1992). *The mismeasure of woman.* New York: Simon and Schuster.

Tversky, A., & D. Kahneman (1974). Judgment under uncertainty: Heuristics and biases. *Science,* 185, 1124-1131.

U. S. Bureau of the Census (1997). *Statistical abstract of the United States: 1997.* Washington, DC: U.S. Government Printing Office.

Chapter 6 _____

Is Mathematics a Cultural Artifact?

Barbara A. Jur

Is mathematics a cultural artifact? This was not a question I had in mind when I began teaching in the Department of Mathematics at Florida A&M University (FAMU) in 1973. I had accepted mathematics as universal—the one truly catholic discipline that would be understood in approach and symbolism no matter where in the world an instructor taught. As with many unexamined truisms, the universality was wrong—British and American mathematicians cannot even agree where a simple decimal point belongs. But the concepts, if not the approaches, are the substance and the pleasure of mathematics. It is in the approaches, particularly in communication, that I, as a white instructor, learned the deepest lessons about mathematics from my students who were, to a person, African American.

The faculty had only recently become integrated. I had tried to obtain a part-time teaching position in 1971 when I moved to Tallahassee, Florida, with my husband who taught mathematics at Florida State University (FSU). I was not trying to be a "do gooder." I simply wanted to teach college mathematics, holding a newly minted master's degree from Ohio State. FSU required a Ph.D. and there was a question of nepotism. My choices were teaching at FAMU or Tallahassee Community College. I could understand the concern about hiring white faculty at FAMU. The administration did not want to take scarce jobs from black instructors. Need and registration finally worked in my favor.

The FAMU student body was practically 100 percent African American at the time I taught, save one lone white student. I actually met the white student at a meeting later and traded stories. He said he had a great time. Everyone was very friendly and tried to put him at ease. In the Department of Mathematics the faculty was 50 percent African American and 50 percent white. The majority of the faculty held master's degrees. While the faculty ages were evenly distributed, the African-American faculty held higher rank. It was mainly a problem of historical time at the institution since department faculty were not integrated until the 1960s. However, we enjoyed one another's company. We were all committed to teaching our students and were rewarded with positive comments for good teaching.

Tallahassee is home to Florida A&M University (FAMU), Florida State University (FSU), and the state legislature. Traditionally, FAMU was regarded as a teaching institution while FSU was a research institution. Facilities were separate and unequal. FSU was air-conditioned. At FAMU only several of the newer buildings were air-conditioned. Elevator access was a problem. I occupied a fourth floor walk-up office that I shared with an African-American male colleague. Traditions and pride were strong at both universities. There was as much pride in academics and programs as there was in football and marching bands. After I left, the state of Florida mandated integration of the student body for state universities. FAMU had already lost its law school. At the time, discussion centered on moving engineering to FSU and education to FAMU. I suspect there was a great deal of horse trading to achieve integration.

I do not remember my first classes, just vignettes from various classes. I do remember that I consciously decided to address students with the honorific "Mr." or "Miss" and their family name. I wanted to do this to give respect to my students, a respect I wished them to show one another. It seemed to me in the world of the 1970s in the deep South they could benefit from a little respect from a white person. My only class rule was to do nothing that would prevent your fellow students from learning.

My rule was put to the test very early that first term in a fundamental math class. There was a football player, a defensive back, who was acting out, interrupting class, bothering those around him. I told him to leave class if he could not act like a college student.

"Make me!" he challenged.

I looked at all hefty 6 foot 3 inches of him, put my book down and started walking toward him. The silence was deafening. I knew I would take his arm and lead him to the door, but physically I could not move him. He solved my dilemma by picking up his books and leaving. Later, in my office, we talked about his mathematics problems. He had never been successful at math in high school and disliked math because he felt like a failure. I said that it should stop here. I set up a schedule where I tutored him. He went to the math lab and I reviewed his homework with special comments. He worked hard, and we both rejoiced when he passed the class.

I still wonder what was so outrageous about his behavior that I should single him out. My classes were anything but quiet. The uninterrupted lectures of my teaching assistant days were history. Students questioned everything— "How could I do this?" "Why did I do that?" "Where did that come from?" I was first a respondent, and then I learned to ask questions, thanks to a great math text by Harold Jacobs (1970), *Mathematics, A Human Endeavor*. Since I did not like to put individuals on the spot, I took answers from anyone who responded—no hands needed. Sometimes several answered together. Sometimes everyone answered like a Greek chorus. We were in a dialogue. We came to class, we did our work outside of class, we participated.

Did I note any culture based differences between my African-American students and white students I had taught before or since? This is a question that is difficult to answer. First of all, this was their institution. They were the majority. They were comfortable and could be themselves. I was not the only white faculty person, but I was on their ground. I had already taught in a setting where the majority of the students were African American—a maximum security institution for delinquent girls in Ohio. It was my first teaching experience. I enjoyed the students and they enjoyed the math I taught and did quite well. I expected African-American students to do well in math and I know I communicated this to my classes. If there was any difference, it was that the students were active rather than passive. Mathematics was not treated as a spectator sport.

Did I note any performance difference between the African-American students I had taught and the white students I had taught? I never expected any differences. While I never did any analysis of student performance, I cannot remember any instances of surprise at student difficulties or talents. There are two related instances that come to mind. I taught a trigonometry class frequently and really enjoyed it. The classes went very well. In fact one class of students at FAMU received all A's and B's (this has happened only twice in my teaching career). I also had a practice where students who had an "A" average going into the final did not have to take the final. One young man was perfect at everything in trigonometry *except* proving identities. He could not do it. He could not memorize the proofs. The identities test prevented him from having an "A" average. I told him I would write a final with only 10 percent of the grade based on identities. If he did everything else perfectly, he would get his "A." He did everything else perfectly. He got a 90 percent. Several years later he ran up to me on the street to tell me he had graduated and how much he enjoyed the class. "You know," he said, "I still can't do identities." In contrast, in my last term teaching, I had another white student in class who was from Florida State University. She was good, but not outstanding. At the last class before finals week she came up to say good-by, after I passed out papers indicating who would not have to take the final. She had a "B" average. In our conversation, I explained that she would then receive a "D" for the course if she skipped the final. She complained that some of the other students did not have to take the exam. She expected to be better than the other students in the class whether or not she earned it. I explained that she would be excused too if she had an "A" average. She took the final.

Were there any differences in my teaching style? I had changed in the past from high school teacher, where time for seat work was the norm, to college teaching assistant. There I lectured and answered questions. There were never any questions during my lectures. I structured carefully developed expositions on the day's topics, asked if there were any questions on homework assignments, answered the few questions that arose and considered it a successful class. FAMU students changed my style. I never could complete a lecture without at least one question, frequently asked without raising a hand. It might be considered rude in some circles but it did approach the points of misunderstanding directly and immediately. I found it helpful and exciting to try to answer the questions. Other students would add their points of question and clarification. I became much more flexible in my approach to mathematics and successful teaching. Control of teaching and learning was balanced between me and the students. It was an exciting dynamic. This is not the cooperative learning model because I did not set groups or ask questions leading to the construction of knowledge. The students questioned and added commentary. I supplied the answers most often, but others in the class could do so too, and I acknowledged and applauded the commentary. I had classes from twenty-five to sixty-four students. This is not an approach I could use with 150 students. I would characterize the style as interactive.

What occurred at FAMU, in teaching my classes, had to be taught to students at other institutions. Today, in addressing a theoretical question to a group, I have to wait long enough for the students to realize it is not rhetorical, and I am not going to answer it. I find that it is a matter of getting students to start talking about mathematics in class, encouraging them, and rejoicing when we reach dialogue.

In the classes at Florida A&M the students helped one another, talked about mathematics, shared calculators (they were quite expensive at the time), and did experiments together in the math lab (the lab manager complained about the noise of rolling dice in a metal pan—a plastic container kept the peace). During an exam in one trigonometry class where scientific calculators had started to make an appearance, there were four student calculators plus mine in a class of thirty. The students asked if they could share. I threw mine into the available resources and the exam proceeded successfully. Everyone was careful to pass the calculator on as quickly as possible. Uri Treisman (1992) at UC-Berkeley found that African-American students did much better in mathematics when connected in groups. It was not a problem at FAMU; it was a given.

Florida A&M University was also the first institution where I encountered a student who experienced an impasse at a certain level of mathematical abstraction. The student took my college algebra class three times. We talked about his problems and worked together outside of class, but come test time his work was not up to standard. He was not freezing on the tests, rather his work was disjointed. He did not seem to be able to make mathematical connections. When he signed up for the third time I asked him why he wanted this course. He wanted to be a doctor. College algebra was required for the pre-med program. I suggested that he should try another instructor. He responded that he had taken the course with other instructors and I was better for him. I wish I could report a success, but it did not happen. The frustration was there for both of us. It was discalculia (a dyslexia for mathematics) at a higher level. I have encountered only one other student later in my career who could not grasp basic algebra. Discalculia is rare, but it does happen. I was surprised at the level of the student's function otherwise. I also learned that I could not teach everyone. It was my first failure with someone who truly wanted to learn. I learned to better appreciate student struggles.

My last two years at Florida A&M University were spent working with the Upward Bound/Special Services Program, a federally funded program designed to support "at risk" high school and college students. I was the curriculum coordinator and math instructor. I oversaw the tutorial program, learning lab, and supervised the science and English teachers and peer tutors. I was also responsible for program statistics and block scheduling for the college students. It was in this capacity that I was asked to study the relationship between several testing programs (Florida 12th grade test, SAT, and ACT) and student performance. In my analysis I found that the only statistically significant correlation was a weak correspondence between the Florida 12th-grade test and student first term college grades. For program students the usual entrance test scores were poor predictors of performance. It calls into question for me concern over low scores reported for African-American college entrants. If the use of high school exit exams, such as the Florida 12th-grade test or college entrance exams, are used to bar students from postsecondary education despite high school performance, then potentially successful students will be lost.

The Upward Bound/Special Services Program also afforded me the opportunity to work with different curriculum materials. I selected a series of worksheets and workbooks for an individualized math development program. I later used the same materials for a virtually all white Veteran's Upward Bound program. In both places the students liked the materials and did well with them. A good development of mathematical ideas easily translates across cultural lines. I was reminded of this when I came across my copy of "Selected Papers from the Annual Special Programs Regional Conferences, 1973-1977." This also was an indicator of the most major change in my work style. I became an attendee of conferences, a writer, a speaker, and a supporter of professional participation and development.

When I started working at FAMU I was warned that prejudice was not restricted to white people. I can honestly say that I did not see any covert prejudice among my colleagues or students. When I worked with the grant program, we often traveled in mixed groups on student tours and to conferences. Mostly, we did not encounter any problems. The director was very careful to arrange seating in white establishments so that the white staff sat together and the African-American staff sat together. In African-American establishments, it was unimportant. There was, however, a McDonald's in southern Georgia which took forty-five minutes to produce four hamburgers. One of my colleagues who was very light complexioned spoke of her move from the North to Tallahassee, Florida. She was originally from the South and knew the "rules." While she was asleep her husband stopped at a "whites only" roadside restaurant. She was terrified when she awoke and saw where they were, although there was no incident. My students often spoke about moving to the North where life would be easier. I always had to warn them that prejudice was alive and well in the North. Ghettos are much more a northern phenomenon and race-based violence was not uncommon.

Most of my memories of the program students were the fun times—ice skating in Atlanta, Disneyworld, dances, chatting with tutors and students. One of the most uplifting experiences I had was taking a group of high school students on a tour of the Ringling Art Museum. We looked at paintings from the Middle Ages and early Renaissance. We looked at the art and exchanged perspectives. They were enthralled by the religious themes, and I could share with them the technical problems the artists were trying to solve. We left knowing more about one another as well as art.

The really notable thing about living in many areas of the country is that you really get to see the irony of local prejudices. There are cultural differences that influence the style of learning and teaching, but there is nothing better or worse about any approach as long as communication is possible. My students taught me how to teach them. My work at FAMU equipped me with a teaching style that was flexible and responsive to different teaching styles and teaching needs. Curiously today, many institutions of higher education in the country are grappling with how to infuse such flexibility and responsiveness into the teaching process. I was aided in perfecting the practice of responsive teaching early on during my tenure at FAMU. It was expected. A major barrier to learning is expectations, both on the part of the teacher and the student. Randy Swartz, (1997) observed that "conscious or unconscious teacher expectations of students' performance exert a large influence on their success or failure. There is a tendency for us to shape the students we expect to do well into successes and to shape the students we expect to do poorly into failure" (p.6).

Whether mathematics is a cultural artifact is an irrelevant question. I believed the students at FAMU would succeed and they did. I remember following a group of students up the stairs to class. They did not know I was there. I overheard one student say to another, "Her class is really easy. All you have to do is go to class and do the homework." She expected to pass and knew what to do. She was right. The completion and success rates were good. It is teaching and learning that matters. I owe a great debt to my students at Florida A&M University. They helped me develop a teaching style that has served me well for over twenty years. I hope the mathematics they learned and their encounter with a white teacher has served them well.

References

Jacobs, H.R. (1970). *Mathematics, a human endeavor.* San Francisco: W.H. Freeman and Company.

Swartz, R. (August, 1997). Students with learning disabilities. *Focus,* 17(4), 4-8.

Treisman, U. (November, 1992). Studying students studying calculus: A look at the lives of minority students in college. *College Mathematics,* 23(5), 362-372.

Part Two _____

*Academic Careers at Historically Black
Colleges and Universities*

Chapter 7 _____

Exploration and Identity: Thirty Years of Transformation at HBCUs

Barbara Stein Frankle

"Choose five words to describe yourself." So begins a popular icebreaker for diversity workshops (and college classes on multiculturalism). In the southern city I have now inhabited for twenty-seven years, almost everyone identifies themselves by race. Ensuing discussion on the icebreaker reveals that here there is an assumption that race has always, and everywhere, been a central self-descriptor; that it is not a category relative to time and place. After more than three decades in the South and in African-American colleges, I, too, place "white" or European American on the list. I can honestly say, however, that for the first twenty years of my life, race was not an element in my own self-characterization. Female, Jewish, American, family, and student (including where and what classification) would have made my list.

It was, I now recognize, a position of privilege that enabled me to ignore race in my earlier life. I grew up as a middle-class child in a small northern seaside city with a population defined largely by religion, one-third Roman Catholic (split into Italian and Irish churches), one-third Jewish, one-third Protestant. The white community did not consciously segregate or ignore the tiny African-American minority, and I can honestly say that I did actively socialize and work with a few African Americans, but those few were themselves children of professionals. In effect, we subsumed incipient and unexamined racism in the class discrimination that ran rampant in the town.

From my sheltered home environment, I moved on to Mount Holyoke College, a small women's college in rural western Massachusetts. Now the college is a leader in diversity, but at that time there was only one African-American student who was a regular enrollee, and she left before her first semester ended. We did have an exchange program with a historically black college for women, Bennett College, in North Carolina, but the impact of that exchange tended to be limited to the few who were directly involved, and I was not one of them. I spent the early 1960s as a graduate student at the politically active University of Wisconsin, Madison, but during the early years of the decade those radical energies focused on economic injustice and the war. The huge history graduate program of over 300 had, to my knowledge, only one African-American student and no African-American faculty. Then I went abroad to do research in English history, only learning and reading from afar about the later sixties' freedom rides and protests at home. By this time, however, I was becoming aware of my own ignorance about the problem, though I know I was not conscious of the depth of my naivete. Therefore, when I headed south in 1968 to engage the realities of racism, it was to confront what I had succeeded in evading.

As I looked at America from across the Atlantic in the years of the 1960s, I was energized by the multiple cries for social justice that echoed everywhere. The clearest and most profound voices were those of African Americans, whose demands most penetratingly pierced obvious perversions of the American creed of "liberty and justice for all." If anywhere there were lessons to be learned about social activism, it was from these 20th-century liberators who were transforming the American South.

As a European-American female (though in 1968 that was not how I would have described myself), I was naïve but drawn to the vitality of the African-American movement in the late 1960s. It was, therefore, purposefully that my husband and I became Woodrow Wilson interns in 1968 at Morehouse College, the nation's only historically black, all-male college, in Atlanta, Georgia. Little did I then expect that, with only two brief breaks, I was immersing myself in a thirty-year career at historically black colleges (HBCUs). I anticipated that I would learn to understand more about African-American activism, but I did not realize I would myself be transformed and that my metamorphosis would lead me to a new vision of education.

The plunge into the ferment of the Atlanta University (now Clark-Atlanta University) complex in 1968 was quite a new experience for me. The candor of that time led students to immediately express their reactions. What were we, as white faculty, doing there? Our roles as interns increased the suspicion—were we merely there until we finished our dissertations, then to move on to "bigger things"? This was hardly an unreasonable question. Our responses, that we wanted to understand the South, the Movement and realities of African-American life, and our readiness to discuss the issues openly, generally won us student acceptance. We were young and, since both my husband and I were on the same campus and in the same department, we entered fully into college life. We got to know many of our students well, chatting with them, eating with them, debating with them. There were, we quickly learned, certain barriers. There were certain things we could not say, certain assumptions we could not challenge openly in all venues. My husband was once asked to leave a student meeting when they started discussing the role of whites at the school. One of our European-American colleagues, a pioneer in African-American studies, was the center of a furor when Stokely Carmichael demanded he leave a forum, and some students angrily defended his right to stay. I, on the other hand, was welcomed when I was the only faculty member who attended a student rally immediately after the Jackson State shootings. We were plunged into a time of fluid but not always comfortable alliances and alignments.

If there were questions about student relationships, there were even more questions about our role as faculty. Socially, we were subtly constrained in a small circle of young whites—the younger African-American faculty members were on the whole not hostile, but detached. Many of the older faculty looked on us with distrust, even viewing us as left wing radicals. I was startled by this view of myself since in graduate school at Marxist Madison, Wisconsin, I was considered a right wing reactionary. We were even criticized for growing too close to students, and some black faculty looked askance at our inviting students home to dinner, a practice common in my own undergraduate and graduate experience. It was clear that we were in their minds purely temporary sojourners who would have to move on when our two-year internship ended, and they would be relieved when we did.

My husband and I did indeed change towns and campuses. I located for one year in a tiny women's college in Memphis, Tennessee, which closed, and then after a one-year hiatus, I returned to an HBCU, LeMoyne-Owen College in Memphis, this time for what has turned out to be a lifetime commitment. I had made contacts there during my first year in that city. The new environment was distinctly different, dispelling any illusions about homogeneity in the African-American community and offering another perspective on my journey of discovery. The deep south, urban campus of LeMoyne-Owen College consists primarily of commuter students, was much more circumspect, less radical, less overtly political. Far from demanding explanations from me, students were deferential in manner and circled nervously about any discussions of race. I was able to make friends of many students, some of which last to this day, but the charged racial discussions were much more muted in the new environment.

Faculty tensions were another matter. As in Atlanta, the older faculty harbored deep distrust, which was now more personally disconcerting because I had not applied for this post but had been sought for and urged to accept it, and once I had signed on, I felt that I was a full-fledged player, not just a temporary intern. It turned out that the institution needed a director for a new grant program, and much of what I saw as general acceptance of me as a colleague was in reality a resigned acquiescence to the realities of grantsmanship.

The divisions at LeMoyne-Owen College were not just racial, but generational. A multiracial core of younger faculty formed a circle both social and professional, and we tended to seek innovation and change in the classroom and campus. I had in fact been hired to direct a "reformed" curriculum, and quickly learned a lesson now useful that new hires, especially young minority ones, should never be expected to drive change, as only those steeped in the campus culture can negotiate the nuances necessary for innovation. We probably were young turks challenging a conservative old guard. The situation was exacerbated when an ideologically driven white priest was named dean, and he bullishly roared through the academic program, dropping requirements and revising long term academic standards. He may have been reading the portents appropriately, as the talented students who in segregation had only the choice of an HBCU now were opting to go to larger white institutions and some accommodation to the new constituencies and to the more freedom conscious curricular trends of the 1970s was probably necessary. Internally, however, the dean figured you were either for him or against him, hardening the divisions that already existed. He, however, after only a brief tenure in office, one day got up from his desk and never came back, leaving the rest of us shaken and divided, somewhat uneasily tossing the hot ball he had created. Many of the younger faculty, black and white, followed his example and left, while those of us who quietly hung on quieted down, gradually gaining respect, sometimes grudgingly given, for commitment and perseverance. We, for our part, had learned an object lesson in courtesy and discretion—the larger than life "take-no-prisoners" dean had presented us with an uncomfortable model of how not to behave. We, I think, learned to listen and to move with greater deliberation. I know I came to realize that cooperation, no competition, is much more effective, as well as more pleasant, in organizing change. This may be as much a lesson of maturity as minority/majority or racial understanding, but the backdrop of cultural gulfs made the message clearer.

People still ask me if I have any trouble teaching at a black college. After more than twenty-five years, I can grin and say I have become like a piece of furniture. Certainly I feel comfortable, respected, and truly accepted. At the same time, I have learned and even in some cases internalized a sensitivity to the subtle nuances of 1990s racism, which helps me react to slights against African Americans as my students and black colleagues do. I also know that there may be times when I am uncomfortable. It unnerves me when speakers on campus make assumptions based on Jewish stereotypes, sometimes believing they are being positive. "We should learn lessons from the Jews, who make money and buy from each other," makes me seethe. On a less directly personal level, the homophobia that makes it very difficult to integrate sexual preference into the diversity discourse is also chilling. A hostility of some to address feminism and gender studies because the history of African-American women does not coincide with that of European-American women seems to me short sighted at best. I also know that as close as I become to many students, many will be more reluctant to reveal their personal problems to me than to my African-American colleagues.

Nonetheless, working at HBCUs has been a rich experience that not only transformed my understanding of race and diversity, but has helped me reformulate an idea of what higher education should be doing in the 1990s. I honestly do not believe that I would have been able to remain at LeMoyne-Owen College all this time if the deeper cultural qualities that drive HBCUs had not resonated in me. Naïve though I may have been, I did come from a background that encouraged racial understanding and conciliation. My father was a civil liberties attorney whose funeral, on a snowy February day, was packed by the membership of a local African-American church he had represented over the years, an unusual mixed attendance in the hometown I described above. Thus I came from a background that prepared me to be receptive and open when I was in a situation of cultural encounter.

I have found in the HBCUs a commitment to teaching that resonated with me. I entered higher education as much with a dedication to teaching as to high powered research, and with as much an interest in the creativity of curriculum development as with discipline related scholarship. As I experienced the ambiance of the HBCU, I came to realize the messages it had for academe in general. The concentration of the HBCU on the needs of students, and on the delivery of instruction to their population, have lessons and implications for all higher education. The traditional understanding of the importance of diversity education also carries messages for the national discourse. From the vantage point of a faculty member who is "diverse," I think I have learned lessons about the nature of HBCUs that can be applied at majority campuses to great effect.

After thirty years, the social and educational worlds in America have changed, and many of the agendas of the 1990s are reactions of the 1960s. When I first came south, public places were integrated by law if not by custom. The worst legal abuses had been attacked, and the worst inequalities addressed, if not resolved. America's legalized apartheid is no longer in place. Professional and social interaction has increased, and there is greater economic opportunity for minorities. We are all aware, however, that deep and painful fissures remain, and these more subtle and unseen barriers are in many ways more difficult to obliterate. Economic and educational equity still does not exist. De facto ghettoization still separates communities. Glass ceilings limit upward advancement. Successful attacks on affirmative action erode gains and cast a cloud on the vision of our shared commitment to a just society. The lesson of Reconstruction, that legal protections are fragile, looms over us in an age of backlash, but many seem oblivious to that message.

Through all these changes, the historically black colleges and universities have consistently moved forward in their mission of educating African Americans for civic leadership, professional attainment, economic viability, and personal fulfillment. The social changes have not left them untouched, however. With increased educational opportunities for minorities, the HBCUs have been able to increase the proportion of doctorate-holding African Americans on their faculties, lessening their dependence on white instructors. I have, with pleasure, seen the number of terminally degreed African Americans increase dramatically at my institution, and the percentage of white faculty decrease concomitantly. There is disparity in disciplines, however, as in most colleges. We are woefully short of African Americans in our science program, which draws from an international faculty whom students too often view as impenetrable aliens rather than as resources for cultural growth.

The student body has changed, as well. When majority institutions opened doors and coffers to minority students, the traditional constituents of HBCUs changed. Many of the high academic achievers, and many middle-class students with strong and knowledgeable parental support, now choose other options. Accordingly, the HBCUs draw many first generation students who have not always been academically focused or are high achievers, and whose resources are limited. With myriad demands on their time and energies, they may not be able to make school their highest priority. Young single parents and/or key contributors to an extended family economy, these students may withdraw, return, withdraw, return, establishing an institutional retention rate that appears problematic to the unquestioning critic. Certainly the HBCUs are not alone in facing a student body that needs new approaches and assistance—faculty members throughout the country bewail the lack of preparation of their students, grumbling about the lack of writing and computational skills, the apparently scant frames of reference and knowledge bases students possess.

The HBCUs have by no means made perfect adjustments to the contemporary educational dilemma, and they are grappling with the need to find new ways to embrace and reach their current populations. What I find significant, however, is their readiness to adapt. They do not dig in their heels and blame the students. They are ready and prepared to help vulnerable young people live out the American dream of accessible higher education. They are willing to accept the tentative student, to draw out the potential in every individual. Their ability to meet this challenge and their track record in producing leaders make them a resource for the national academic community.

Equally important is the HBCU role as a special purpose institution. Even with wider choices available, many African Americans elect the nurturing environment of the HBCU. This is not just an attempt to find a cocoon, but a positive effort for meaningful growth. Traditional college age students are in the process of finding and shaping their identity, of seeking ways to exercise and expand their talents and leadership capacities. With curricula infused with the African-American experience and student activities shaped to meet their needs and interests, the HBCUs provide an invigorating setting for personal and intellectual growth. Not marginal but central to the institution's purpose, the African-American student gains validation.

The validation breeds a confidence that enables the HBCU graduate to feel assured in confronting the world beyond the campus. I can equate my own experience as a woman entering college in the 1950s, feeling tentative about my role, nervous about a woman's prospects for achievement and fearing the lack of acceptance I felt in high school if I were too aggressive or too "serious" a student. Sixties feminism had not been born, but I was inarticulately reaching for its goals and found in a women's college the validation I sought, which enabled me to persevere when I encountered hostility in graduate school. Sexism was not a term then in coinage, but my experience at a woman's college gave me the capacity to recognize it even without the active vocabulary to express it, and I was thus better tooled to negotiate it. So the African-American college prepares its students to better operate in an often challenging environment. As one of our students aptly said recently, "I can go to another place and feel comfortable because I know that if I saw something that was different I wouldn't be scared of it or angry at it because it was different."

The majority institutions may not be able to recreate the experience of the small special population college, but they can learn the lessons those colleges represent. Students need validation and support. Majority institutions need to offer their minority students the chance to develop self-knowledge and understanding. They need to provide venues of comfortable self-segregation, which may be less a rejection of others than the human need for the nurturing of our own villages. The colleges need to recognize the importance of support groups, self-exploration, and identity reinforcement and offer positive reinforcement rather than knee-jerk suspicion.

The social and extracurricular life of the student is not the only arena in which the HBCU relates to the African-American student. Consciousness of the African-American identity permeates the curriculum, and provides the fulcrum for intellectual life. The disciplined exploration of the impact of racism, prejudice, and stereotyping is central to the educational mission of HBCUs, who must, and do, equip their students to negotiate in a world where discrimination exists.

There is then a healthy saturation in issues of social justice, a critical, ongoing appraisal of how African Americans are positioned in the community, in their disciplines, in the academic world, and in professions. This cannot remain confined to "appropriate areas" of the social sciences or humanities, but infuses all areas of study. The questions students ask, the concerns they raise, the ways they learn, inevitably return to their basic identity, a racial identity that is real even if it is a social construct externally imposed. For the white (or Hispanic or Asian) faculty member, this saturation is the most dramatic and potentially transformative element of an HBCU career. Inescapably, we are drawn into engagement with the racism in American life, and this brings us into direct confrontation with our own values, perceptions, assumptions, and predispositions. Personally, we become sensitized to the subtle but insidious incursions of prejudice into daily life, to the struggles of students avoiding threats of drugs and violence, to the necessity of students working 40+ hours per week and then sleeping in class. When we urge opportunities for foreign travel, we have to recognize the instilled uncertainty of unknowns-perceived-as-dangerous because the "other" has been at best insensitive.

The sensitivity to student concerns is accompanied by an awareness of the institutional position as well. How often in settings both academic and social have I bristled at misperceptions or inequities derived from a lack of understanding about HBCUs and their students. Even colleagues I trust from our sister majority institutions often fail to realize subtle realities and say things based on faulty assumptions that impact HBCUs negatively. These range from the query of "Why should black colleges exist when students can go to the state universities?" to much more subtle threats. When granting agencies disregard the scholarship of HBCU faculties and try to impose consultants and experts from majority institutions, I bristle. When majority institutions draft our faculty to collaborate on grants, then swallow all the indirect costs and paid grant opportunities, I bristle. When coalitions develop elaborate technological link-ups that ignore the under-equipped (which I need to add now does not include my institution), I bristle. When well-meaning colleagues question the worth of HBCUs because their retention rates are low, I resent their lack of awareness of the realities of our students' lives.

These issues are against a pattern of backlash that makes them potentially dangerous, and dims the messages HBCUs have for the nation today. The drum beats for change in the 1990s may be softer, and America is still clearly fraught with issues of disparity and justice, but there is, nonetheless, some genuine appreciation for diversity and citizens look to higher education for leadership. The attacks on affirmative action are balanced by deep and genuine concern that America come to terms with the complex differences in our society. A national poll for the Ford Foundation in the autumn of 1998 by the Daniel Yankelovich Group (DYG, Inc.) revealed that 94 percent agree that "America's growing diversity makes it more important than ever for all of us to understand people who are different than ourselves." The poll further indicated that more than two-thirds of Americans believe a primary function of higher education is to prepare people to function in a more diverse society and workforce. At the same time, a majority of Americans (58 percent) worry that "America is growing apart."

Given the fear that society is fragmenting, Americans are turning to higher education to help the nation reconstruct our multicultural puzzle. They look to college campuses to lead the way to this refigured social order. Despite the media attention when things go awry, when racism erupts at drunken fraternity parties or in dorm fracases, nonetheless, the public recognizes that more fruitful encounters with diversity do occur in academe.

As higher education shoulders that responsibility, HBCUs, with their history and missions, are in a special position to be national resources on diversity education. Since their inception, they have provided curricula that educated their students in their own heritage, while preparing them to operate successfully in the wider American context. HBCUs have thus grounded students in the American and western traditions deemed central to the education of a U.S. citizen. However, the melting pot has never been an option for the African American; consequently, HBCUs historically have approached diversity through another prism, cherishing their identity but not ignoring others. They have taught about the interaction of different groups, recognizing the importance of mutual differences and of mutual understanding. This realization is ingrained in the faculty as well as the students, and has helped this writer to contribute actively to the current discourse in higher education. Our HBCU institutions need to more aggressively assert our capacities in this area, and to make our voices more authoritative in the national diversity discussion.

As repositories of scholarship, artistic creations and archives about the African-American experience, HBCUs again have much to offer to the new awakening of the richness of America's multicultural heritage. The significant art collections of Hampton and Fisk universities, the dedicated library collections at Fisk University, Clark-Atlanta University, and LeMoyne-Owen College, the civil rights collections at Tougaloo College and Jackson State University, all provide rich materials for the student of American life. An awakening to the richness of these holdings has been a revelation to me, one I would not have enjoyed had I followed the route for which I seemed more destined thirty years ago. There is a strong current movement to carry diversity incentives beyond the classrooms into the community. The extensive efforts by the Ford Foundation and its affiliate organizations such as the Association of American Colleges and Universities (AAC&U), the Western Interstate Commission on Higher Education (WICHE), the Great Lakes Association (GLA), and others have led in this direction. Again, the HBCUs are uniquely placed to serve as national models.

In educationally segregated southern states, the HBCUs were cases of reconciliation and interracial cooperation in deserts of segregation. Faculties, staff and administration historically included African and European Americans in a mutual effort to educate future leaders, and were clear examples of how such collaboration could indeed work. The campuses were often the one site in towns and cities where mixed groups could meet for serious discussion, share and pursue knowledge, and socially interact. The campuses frequently served as the focal point for the civil rights movement of the 1960s. Given their history of courageous diversity, the HBCUs can stand as obvious models for the new initiatives of the 1990s and for the beginning millennium.

As citizens grow increasingly interested in what happens on the nation's campuses, HBCUs have further important lessons for American higher education. Long standing centers of their communities, the HBCUs have a rich tradition of service and outreach to their local environs. During segregation, colleges shared with churches the role of providing African Americans cultural and spiritual leadership. They were frequently even havens for travelers whose options for places to stay were few indeed. Serving a constituency circumscribed by legal and economic restrictions, HBCUs strove holistically to advance not just the students, but their communities. It was only natural that the sit-ins, marches, and protests that heralded the end of segregation frequently emerged from these same colleges and churches.

Now as academics bemoan the civic apathy of students and as colleges seek ways to instill the ethic of service, they can learn from the still socially active

HBCUs. Generally located in some of the most economically limited areas of town, HBCUs have not built metaphysical fences to separate them from their neighbors. Rather they engage with them in community building, running development centers, mentoring youth, offering health services and counseling, housing Upward Bound and other juvenile-centered programs, and inviting neighbors to use their facilities. After 3 P.M. the library on my campus is as alive with middle schoolers doing homework as with our own students, who often find themselves aiding the young children.

With such a tradition, HBCUs are natural leaders in the current service learning movement. Historically the educators of African-American political and spiritual leaders, HBCUs are still committed to capacity building within their communities. The combination of outreach and civic education that service learning offers meshes perfectly with the historic roles of the HBCUs.

The creativity and energy of outreach and service learning at HBCUs is reflected in the highly successful programs and networks they have established. The Ford/UNCF sponsored Community Service Partnership Project (CSPP) linked ten campuses who combined coherent strategies for community development with carefully structured field opportunities for college students. The experiential learning is supplemented by related academic exploration and reflection. Further, the colleges are pledged to working directly with the schools in their communities to help the K-12 sector develop service projects and to improve the opportunities for youth to enter colleges. The CSPP offers a rich array of programs that may include mentoring and tutorial partnerships with schools and communities, family literacy projects, formation of children's choirs, environmental justice initiatives, or many other innovative approaches to neighborhood development. My own institution itself has supported a wide variety of incentives. We are currently assisting our neighborhood elementary school establish a family resource center. As part of our general education social science curriculum, approximately 200 of our students annually go to elementary classrooms teaching junior achievement units. Students assisted our neighborhood with a needs assessment for community development. For the past four years, we have provided after-school and summer enrichment programs for neighborhood children.

This deep community involvement is more than just a laundry list of activities; it resonates with the civic commitment that permeates the HBCU. Such integral town-grown interaction leaves its strong imprint on the faculty members who are drawn into not just the campus but the community life. The white professors cannot simply teach classes, spend a few cloistered office hours, and then retreat. During segregation they made a choice too often enforced by the racist environment; once they opted to be part of the African-American community, they were relegated to it. The legal strictures are gone, but the immersion in the African-American experience still is an essential part of life at an HBCU. This affects social life, and, in this age of possible movement through and across communities, helps the white faculty member serve as a voice in the wider community.

My own transformation was crystallized for me during a recent trip to South Africa, when I participated in a public forum at Fort Hare, the oldest of the universities for black Africans. During the presentation part of the event, a young African law professor educated in the U.S.A. gave a trenchant talk on the need for reforming universities in the new order to incorporate traditional law into their classrooms and, by implication, into the legal system. I know that I would not have so readily grasped the heart of his message, nor so strongly (if silently) agreed, had my life at an HBCU not shaped my vision.

The formal speakers sat down after their talks and open discourse began. The law professor sat in the row ahead of mine, with his back to me. The ensuing discussion erupted into a tense debate about service learning, exacerbated when a white South African from one of the European universities said eagerly, but not too delicately, that he would be delighted to have his political science students gather data in the townships. I know he was sincere about desegregation, but my stomach still tightened as I felt that wearied sense of the rhetoric of academic colonialism grip me. I could not refrain from commenting that the whole point of service learning was pedagogical transformation, drawing students into direct and equal engagement with the communities. The African law professor turned and stared at me, shook his head, and scribbled furiously. He shoved me a scrawled note, which I opened with trepidation, but glowed when I read it. I brought it back from Africa with me, so I can remember the exchange. He asked: "Where did you come from? You sound like a sister from Southside Chicago!" My return note reflects what this essay is all about: "I have been teaching at HBCUs for almost 30 years." He smiled and shook his head, and I am still shaking mine.

References

Yankelovich, Daniel (DYG, Inc.) (1998). *The Ford foundation Diversity initiative: National survey of voters.* Unpublished Manuscript.

Chapter 8 _____

Breaking through Stereotypes in Mississippi

Stephen L. Rozman

My only contact with Mississippi prior to my move from Nebraska was when I was a twenty-year-old student between my sophomore and junior years at the University of Minnesota. I crossed the Magnolia State from east to west by train on the way to New Orleans in the summer of 1960, and south to north on my way back. I had been minoring in Spanish, while majoring in political science, at the University of Minnesota, and learned about an opportunity to take classes at the University of San Carlos summer school in Guatemala City. Two classmates were going and invited me to join them. Having grown up in Minneapolis, and our family having confined its travels to places like Chicago and Cleveland, where we had relatives, I had never been near a Spanish-speaking country and had not even visited the South.

Once the Burlington Zephyr reached Chicago, it was all new territory for me. The Illinois Central Railroad took me through Illinois, then through Kentucky, Tennessee, Alabama, and even to the tip of the Florida panhandle. I hadn't realized we would be touching Florida, and excitedly searched in vain for palm trees (which I had never yet seen). We then crossed the Mississippi Gulf Coast. There was something about Mississippi that gave me an uneasy feeling. Firmly impressed in my mind was the image of backward white racists, the lowest of the low; the type that sowed fear and terror in the hearts of blacks to keep them down, and organized into lynch mobs to teach a lesson to those who did not know their place. This was the Gulf Coast prior to today's gambling boom and rows of glittering casinos. When I saw a white man urinating in the direction of our passing train, the stereotype of backward ignorance seemed confirmed.

In Guatemala, I saw my first mountains, had a few romantic moments with a young lady from a wealthy Guatemalan coffee family who had been studying at Boston University, and had some discussions in the Las Vegas restaurant— where I went for hamburgers in pre-vegetarian days—with Cuban exiles. I had some positive feelings about Fidel Castro, but was not about to share them with people who had been hurt by the Cuban Revolution and were so emotionally involved. Besides, this was a good opportunity to practice my Spanish and enhance my listening skills.

Fidel had been one of my Spanish teachers. Our family had an old 1938 Philco upright radio, which had AM and shortwave. Radio Havana came in loud and clear, and I would doze off listening to Castro's speeches. I kept my dictionary handy and looked up the English translation of unfamiliar words (like "stooges," "sellouts," etc.). I had flirted a bit with Marxist ideas back then, and even today I have mixed emotions about Castro. Although I find him to be fanatical in support of his illusions, I identify with his health and education programs directed toward the masses. So many Latin American countries are the preserve of the wealthy that I find it difficult to give Fidel a blanket condemnation in comparison to some other regimes.

My return trip from Guatemala took me from New Orleans straight north through Jackson, Mississippi, the state's capital city. Jackson seemed to conform to my stereotype during the half-hour stop in the train depot. The whites I saw looked like "white trash," the blacks looked beaten down and submissive. A white teenager approached me and asked whether I was headed north or south. When I said "north," he walked away without saying another word—which confirmed my stereotype of the southern rebel waving the confederate flag.

Although I returned to the North and the University of Minnesota to complete my undergraduate work, I would soon be back in the South to enter graduate school at the University of Florida in Gainesville. Northern Florida, though racially segregated, did not have the negative image of Mississippi.

It was at the University of Florida in 1964 where I began my opposition to the Vietnam War—before the growing U.S. involvement in Vietnam had even been referred to as a "war." I also participated in the picketing of restaurants and movie theaters that excluded African Americans. The civil rights movement and anti-war movements coalesced, at one point, in a march down University Avenue where some of us carried signs denouncing segregation, while others carried signs denouncing U.S. involvement in Vietnam.

Teaching and Protesting

I was not a leader in the Florida protests, nor was I a leader at the University of Nebraska, where I got my first teaching job in 1967. However, in the latter case, I happened to become overly visible and conspicuous at a delicate time, and as a vulnerable, untenured assistant professor, did not have my annual contract renewed. In early May 1970, following President Nixon's expansion of the Vietnam War into Cambodia and the murder of the Kent State students, the outrage of students and faculty alike was channeled into a town hall meeting followed by a peaceful sit-in in the ROTC building at the university—all student-led. The administration came into the building, met with us, and agreed to our staying the night, up to the time of another scheduled town hall meeting at 9 A.M. the next day. Sometime after midnight, they returned, saying we had to leave, since the ROTC people needed to use the large "pit" area where we were assembled early in the morning. (It appeared as though they were responding to pressure from higher levels.) Although the number of faculty present was quite small, and student leaders were directing the protest action, my open identification with the student position of remaining until the town hall meeting cast me in the light of leadership. A special "blue-ribbon" committee appointed by the Nebraska State Legislature to investigate the events of that evening singled me out for "inappropriate action," and my destiny was sealed.

A campus protest on my behalf led the board of trustees to appoint a faculty committee to review the evidence, but even after that committee cleared me of all charges, the board voted to terminate my employment at the end of the contractual period. At the urging of faculty colleagues, I then sued the University of Nebraska in federal court, but my untenured status weakened my case and both the court's decision and that of the appellate court sided with the university. The fact that I sued the university, more than the fact I had lost my position for anti-war activities, undermined my search for employment at other institutions. Why should they take the risk of hiring someone who turns to the courts when his employment is terminated? However, my image as a rabble-rousing professor who stirred up students likewise contributed to my difficulty in finding a job. Even the University of the Americas, in Puebla, Mexico, canceled a job offer they had extended to me once they learned about the circumstances of my leaving Nebraska. What did they think I would do—start the second Mexican Revolution?

I had never heard of Tougaloo College, and knew very little about the network of historically black colleges and universities, until the spring of 1972. An Iranian professor who was teaching psychology at nearby Doane College in Crete, Nebraska, had previously established contact with me, coming to my office and referring to me as his "hero." He had been reading about my anti-war activities and my lawsuit—a series of articles had appeared in Lincoln's morning and evening newspapers—and he wanted to meet me. He even invited me down to Crete to meet with one of his classes.

In early 1972, he told me that his job had ended at Doane College and that he was being hired by Tougaloo College, a historically black institution on the outskirts of Jackson, Mississippi, starting in the fall. He added that a job was open in political science, if I was interested. I telephoned the chair of the department and had my credentials sent down, together with letters of reference. The most important supporting letter came from the dean of the College of Arts and Sciences, stating that I was a good teacher and that my role in the Nebraska anti-war movement had been exaggerated.

My wife of seven years had a negative reaction to the prospect of moving to Mississippi. I had "dragged" her to Nebraska, and she was not going to be dragged to another (expletive deleted) . . . unless she, too, could find employment. (She had a master's degree in geography.) My interview at Tougaloo went well, and a history professor there put her in touch with an official at Jackson State University—another historically black institution just across town—who responded favorably, since they needed a geographer.

My Iranian friend in Nebraska reinforced my Mississippi stereotype prior to my Tougaloo job interview when he gave me some background on Tougaloo College faculty, based on his recent job interview. "The faculty all live on campus," he said. "The whites hate Tougaloo College on account of the role it played in the sixties during the civil rights period. You can't live next door to them and tell them you teach at Tougaloo." When I had my interview in April 1972, I learned that this pattern had started to break down; that some white faculty were living in Jackson, had white neighbors, and were getting along fine.

On to Mississippi

When Nancy and I moved to Jackson, Mississippi, we wanted to buy a house right away. We had rented a house in Nebraska and she wasn't about to move into an apartment. We found one in a transitional neighborhood, with a growing African-American majority. Neither of us were concerned about the racial composition because we did not feel prejudiced and, besides, we were each about to start work at a black college. As fate would have it, our neighbor right across the street was (the Reverend) Ed King, the key white leader in the Mississippi civil rights movement. Ed provided us with most of our early education about the Mississippi civil rights period, both in sidewalk chats and in seminars at the Unitarian Church. He was one of the major figures in the Mississippi Freedom Democratic party, which challenged the all-white "regular" Democrats at the 1964 National Democratic Convention. He also ran for lieutenant governor on the Freedom Democratic party ticket, with black leader Aaron Henry running for governor. The ballot was symbolic as the Mississippi power structure neither recognized the legality of the Freedom Democrats nor granted voting rights to African Americans. Ed had been severely injured and disfigured when he was run off the road by white racists. They had a particular hatred for this southern boy from Vicksburg who had "betrayed" his race. Ed had served as Tougaloo College chaplain until 1967, when the black power/black identity movement led to demands for a black chaplain and Ed was forced out. In recent times, he has been teaching medical sociology at the University of Mississippi Medical Center, and has captured public attention by using the courts to block release of the Mississippi Sovereignty Commission files.

Shortly after the Supreme Court's 1954 *Brown* v. *Board of Education* decision, which outlawed racial segregation in public schools, the state legislature, to protect the "sovereign" state of Mississippi against threats to its "way of life," created the Sovereignty Commission to serve as a watchdog by observing the activities of civil rights activists and sympathizers, keeping files on them, spreading lies and half-truths to discredit them, and causing the environment to resemble that of a police state. It is difficult to determine how many people lost jobs, were denied loans, were evicted from rental property, or suffered physical, emotional, or verbal abuse due to the actions of the Sovereignty Commission. Although the Sovereignty Commission was not formally abolished until 1974, its activities had greatly wound down by the time I arrived in 1972. However, I wondered whether they had a file on me and toyed with the idea of checking it out. Perhaps my reputation had followed me down from Nebraska. Even if it hadn't, some men standing by a car had photographed a group I was with (in 1972 or 1973), demonstrating outside a segregated church. (I recently learned that I had no file.)

In his losing battle to keep the files sealed, Ed claimed that their release would add to the damage and suffering the Sovereignty Commission's victims had already endured. Even if a person's file contained nothing but lies, people reading the files might not dismiss them out of hand. However, some people were concerned that the files might contain factual information that would be embarrassing to people involved in the civil rights movement. The American Civil Liberties Union and others identified with the public's right to know and with the historical value of this rich reservoir of information—or misinformation.

Another important figure I had met was Ernst Borinski, who had been present at my job interview in April 1972. Dr. Borinski related well to me—perhaps due in part to our common Jewish heritage—and we established a strong friendship that lasted until his death in 1983. A refugee from Hitler's holocaust in Germany, Dr. Borinski received his Ph.D. in sociology at the University of Pittsburgh and then sought out a black college for employment, joining the Tougaloo faculty in 1948 and serving as the chairman of the Social Science Division for many years thereafter.

Dr. Borinski is featured in a book about Jewish refugees from Germany who rendered outstanding service at black colleges, and his memory is cherished by blacks and whites alike. During the late 1950s, he held social science forums at his "social science lab" where Tougaloo students and faculty were joined by students and faculty from nearby Millsaps College, a segregated white institution. Although such gatherings violated state segregation policies, they continued to take place—though highway patrol officers parked outside the Tougaloo gate and took down license numbers.

Dr. Borinski, a trained lawyer and judge in pre-Hitler Germany, taught constitutional law courses in addition to his sociology offerings. Many of the top black lawyers in Mississippi today were his students, a period when Tougaloo attracted the state's top black students. Jackson State lacked the image of quality that Tougaloo boasted, and the historically white institutions (Ole Miss, Mississippi State, and Southern Mississippi) were still off limits to African Americans.

As Dr. Borinski and I became good friends, he became "Ernst" and we reserved Tuesday as our day to "eat Chinese" together at the Golden Dragon restaurant—the only Chinese restaurant in town. In traditional Mississippi, a Chinese restaurant almost seemed to be an anomaly. I remember hearing a man who, upon leaving the Golden Dragon, say to his companion, "I can't see how they can serve all those dishes with so little meat." Chinese restaurants are a barometer of change here in Jackson. Today, we must have close to twenty, plus some Japanese restaurants, a Thai restaurant, some Italian and Greek restaurants, and now, even an Indian restaurant.

Getting Acclimated

Just as Ed was my mentor on the civil rights front, Ernst was my mentor in acclimating to Tougaloo College. He referred to himself as an "inside outsider," pointedly suggesting that a white could not expect to be fully accepted as family. Although he had become an icon and the most positively regarded white person in memory, he had no illusions about the role he could play. Always the diplomat, he carefully established relationships and acted skillfully to avoid offending the key people at the institution. He was likeable, with a personality that tended to embrace rather than push away.

Ernst also referred to teaching at Tougaloo College as a "twenty-four-hour" job, allowing that the needs of the students demanded an around-the-clock response. Indeed, he lived on campus during his first two decades of service and in the dorms with the students much of this time. He was there for them, sometimes providing financial assistance and dedicating himself completely to the institution. He also saw his major mission as one of teaching "social literacy," making the students more aware of the society around them, at the local, national, and global levels. He established on campus a repository for

United Nations documents, brought in well-known speakers for "social science forums," and did all he could to equip Tougaloo students for success in the outside world. I have heard many of Dr. Borinski's former students—including those who have become nationally known—credit him for the success they have attained.

The years of Tuesday lunches and discussions at the Golden Dragon also served as a barometer for my own change. I came to Tougaloo College as a transplanted hippy, with long hair and love beads. At the University of Nebraska I had undergone a transformation from a fairly formal and conventional professor to a more informal and unconventional one. In 1968, I decided to grow a beard and have maintained one ever since. Now, for a college professor, that's quite conventional, and it blended well with my coat and tie and formal classroom lectures. As the Vietnam War deepened and our students were being sent off to fight and die in it, the counterculture started to take root—spreading into Nebraska from more avant-garde areas of the country. My mild Marxist tendencies blended well into New Left culture, and I became active in the campus New Party movement. As my anti-establishment attitudes intensified—especially after Richard Nixon became president—I loosened up in the classroom. The necktie bit the dust, as did the formal lecture—replaced by discussion questions and a more active student role. Following the ROTC sit-in and subsequent action by the Nebraska Board of Regents, I let me hair grow down my shoulders, started to wear love beads, and began to fraternize more with students—attending their parties, even smoking a joint or two (until my asthma reacted with a vengeance). My office walls at Nebraska came to be covered with anti-establishment posters, including one of Che Guevara and one demeaning President Nixon.

When I moved to Mississippi to begin my relationship with Tougaloo College, it was difficult to switch gears. I had become disillusioned by the brutality of my government's war against a people 10,000 miles away and its growing brutality against its own people—exemplified by Kent State. The action against me in Nebraska deepened that disillusionment. In my mind, I had been made a convenient scapegoat for an event that was blown way out of proportion. However, conservative Nebraska, unlike many other parts of the country, was unaccustomed to such anti-establishment protests—peaceful as they may have been.

Now I was moving to another conservative area. A colleague at Nebraska looked at me incredulously when he found out I was heading for Mississippi. "You're moving to Jackson, Mississippi?" he blurted out, then he erupted in uncontrolled laughter. However, I felt reassured by the fact I would be teaching at a black college. After all, I would feel much in common with blacks—the oppressed. I could join them in their struggle against white racism and continue to use the classroom as a forum for exposing injustice at home and abroad and for discussing strategies to promote a more humane society. I hadn't realized how liberating my move to Mississippi would be, how much it would contribute both to my academic growth and personal development.

During my job interview at Tougaloo College, a liberal-leaning, white faculty member attempted to explain the campus political environment by saying, "The president is conservative, but fair in hiring good faculty members and respecting their freedom in the classroom." This was evident from the large number of white liberals on the faculty—a number that had been decreasing prior to my arrival and would continue to decline. As the glamour of the civil rights days wore off, being in Mississippi as part of a struggle for justice no longer had the attraction to offset Tougaloo's low salaries. I later learned that this president was Tougaloo College's first black leader, having been selected in 1963 during the civil rights turmoil. The white president had been very liberal, identifying with the civil rights movement and promoting a climate of solidarity with the struggle. Although rumors are hard to separate from fact, the Mississippi state legislature apparently threatened to revoke the Tougaloo College charter unless changes took place. An arrangement was made to replace the white president with the college's business manager, thus giving the college its first black president and one whom the white power structure felt would be less threatening.

The aforementioned white instructor had long hair and was involved in progressive political causes. He wore the dress of the Woodstock generation— multicolored slacks and tie-dyed shirts. His wife was to become my colleague in the Department of Political Science. With my Ph.D., I immediately became department chair, and have held that position to the present time. Two years later, in 1974, the three of us, plus other faculty and students, caravanned to the Mississippi Coliseum to stage a protest against visiting President Nixon, who was under siege for Watergate. Bearing placards calling for his impeachment, we tried to show him that even in this pro-Nixon state, a core of people wanted him out of office. Our demonstration reminded me of one against General Westmoreland—commander of U.S. forces in Vietnam—in Nebraska. He had come for the Nebraska versus Army football game and seemed genuinely startled when he exited his taxicab at the Cornhusker Hotel and was confronted by a throng of angry, shouting, anti-war protesters waving placards. Could this be happening in conservative Nebraska?

My first encounters with my stereotype of white Mississippi came in the summer of 1972, even before I had begun my teaching duties at Tougaloo College. Some Tougaloo students, faculty and blacks from the local community had been active in registering local black citizens to vote. Although the Voting Rights Act had become law in 1965, many blacks were not yet registered, and we targeted those in outlying Madison County. Tougaloo College was located just on the Madison County side of County Line Road, with Hinds County and the city of Jackson located on the south side. (Several years ago, Jackson annexed the area that includes the college.) We drove up to the Magnolia

Heights subdivision in the town of Flora and picked up people who had previously indicated a desire to go to Canton (the county seat) to register to vote, but lacked transportation.

When we entered the Madison County courthouse to get the people registered, we were confronted by Foote Campbell, the elderly county clerk who dated back to the days when blacks were denied their voting rights for failure to interpret the Mississippi Constitution to the liking of the voting registrar. I introduced myself to Mr. Campbell, extending my hand, telling him I was on the Tougaloo College faculty, and mentioning that I had brought some people to him to register to vote. I didn't think he received a bonus check for registering additional voters, nor did I expect a thank you, but I was a bit startled by the hostility in his response: "I don't want to shake your hand," he snapped, recoiling as though a venomous snake were about to strike. However, the people were duly registered and then driven back to their homes.

The presidential campaign was by now in full swing, and George McGovern had nailed down the Democratic nomination. Sporting my showy "McGovern for President" bumper sticker, I drove down a rural road to reach some unregistered black residents who lived on a plantation. The black community leader who accompanied me had heard there were several black workers who lived and worked there. Although a sign said "No Trespassing," we decided that the only way to reach those workers was to drive through. We encountered a young black woman, told her we were there to take her to register, and were met by a response laden with fear. She admitted that she was unregistered, but said she didn't want any trouble—which not only meant that she would not accompany us to see Foote Campbell, but that she didn't want us hanging around any longer.

We realized that this was a losing proposition and began to fear for our own safety. Just after we left the plantation property and headed toward the main highway, a pickup truck approached from behind with a rifle mounted on the rear window. I accelerated, reaching the highway and making my right turn. The pickup truck came to a halt and started to turn back. Mississippi's past was not about to dissolve by the stroke of Lyndon Johnson's pen. I kept the McGovern bumper sticker on the car until well after his crushing defeat, just to make a statement, though a white man with that bumper sticker must have looked awfully strange in this conservative, pro-Nixon state. If the number of students who had signed up for one of my classes had equaled the number of Mississippi whites who had voted for McGovern, the class would have been canceled for lack of enrollment.

Turning back to my experience with the black woman on the plantation, one more example of black fear in the face of apparent white power stands out in my mind. In the mid-1970s, during the nationwide grape boycott on behalf of striking grape pickers in California, I was out on a picket line at a Sunflower supermarket, urging would-be shoppers to turn away and patronize supermarkets that refused to carry grapes from non-unionized producers. Many of the shoppers were African American, including a frail, elderly woman whom I met with my placard as she approached the store. "Please don't shop here," I said. "They are hurting the farm workers by selling grapes from producers who won't let their workers join the union." As she turned away, I at first felt a sense of victory that she had related well to my message. But suddenly it dawned on me that she had left trembling, probably due to fear of me as a white authority figure. Here I was trying to show my solidarity with African Americans, to bond with them in their just cause, and I had just taken on the image of the white oppressor who had probably caused this woman untold anguish during her lengthy life. I had come to realize that the color of my skin would be a barrier to such bonding, given the personal and collective experience of blacks in this state. Dr. Borinski's reference to being an "inside outsider" would come to mind on numerous occasions.

Starting My New Teaching Career

When I started my teaching at the end of August 1972, the Tougaloo College environment was under the influence of a number of conflicting forces. There was the lingering influence of the civil rights period, with the push toward registering more voters, promoting the candidacies of African Americans for public office, teaching about the movement's history and heroic figures, and organizing poll watchers to expose violations of black voting rights on election day. During that first year, I made several trips to Madison County with other faculty members to meet with black leaders and plan strategies for getting blacks elected to office in this majority black county. At the time, all key government offices were held by whites—though this would change over time.

There was also the influence of the black power movement, one that had apparently reached its peak in the late 1960s and was now starting to decline. A white colleague of mine in the Economics Department told me about a meeting of a black power group on campus one summer, and of his being confronted and roughed up by a man in attendance who wondered what a white man was doing on this black campus. Stokely Carmichael (Kwame Toure) had been a leading black power figure, had spoken at Tougaloo College during the civil rights struggle, and returned to Tougaloo College periodically to spread his message. Although most faculty had come to ignore his visits, I had always welcomed his interaction with my students and had invited him to my classes. I recall such a visit in the mid-1980s. He was discussing movement history and had asked those in attendance whether they had heard of a particular leader (whose name now escapes me). The only hand raised was my own, as I had shared that historical knowledge with our visitor, together with the positive feelings for the role that individual had played in advancing the struggle. When our guest saw my hand raised, he gave a knowing nod and blurted out "Of course," suggesting that a white faculty member at a college such a Tougaloo would no doubt be knowledgeable in this area. It dawned on me that Stokely/Kwame and I, in some important respects, had more in common than he had with my students, though he was making great efforts to get them to see themselves as "Africans" (not African Americans) sharing that common identity with him—and having a duty to serve their African community.

A third influence—one that was growing rapidly to the detriment of the other two—was the pull of the job market, postgraduate education, and material well-being. African Americans in Mississippi were getting more and more opportunities as the barriers to their advancement were breaking down. By the late 1960s, Tougaloo College had sent the first black students—male and female—to the Ole Miss law school, and job opportunities were starting to open up. Little did I know in the early 1970s how great the change would come to be for my students.

One of my duties as a political science instructor was to arrange internships for the students. The three academic credits and experience with a community agency (including law-related agencies for our large number of pre-law students) provided a good incentive. However, very few students had cars, and we had to arrange transportation with our maintenance department and confront the problem of vehicles not showing up on schedule. With the advent of credit cards and their purveyors on campus during the 1990s, nearly all students seem to have cars—most far newer than my 1988 Toyota Corolla—and I no longer bother to ask whether a student needs transportation to get to an internship. Their material lifestyles have advanced markedly and their grades often suffer on account of the twenty to forty hours per week they have to work to pay off the credit cards and perhaps expand their satisfaction of material desires. But I'm getting ahead of myself.

As a white liberal, I assumed that I would establish an easy rapport with my students. After all, northern white liberals and Mississippi African Americans had worked together in successfully challenging racial segregation. Reflecting on my Jewish background, I recalled the solidarity of Schwerner, Goodwin, and Chaney—two Jews and one black—in the civil rights struggle and their martyrdom at the hands of white racists. However, as a non-practicing Jew, I had never emphasized my religious background, though it has occasionally come up over the course of twenty-six years.

I quickly learned that the students did not fit any simple stereotype. Some were quite liberal in their views, while others were conservative on a number of issues (e.g., prayer in the schools, abortion, women's rights, capital punishment, welfare, and even affirmative action). Some were friendly toward whites, while others were wary and sometimes even hostile, given Mississippi's lengthy history of racial oppression and continuing experiences of students, their families, and their peers with racist whites. Indeed, racial segregation had only been outlawed seven years prior to my arrival.

Mississippi whites, likewise, did not fit the stereotype in my mind. Many of those I met seemed genuine in their claim that they wanted to clear the past and relate to blacks as equals. As the years passed, it became less and less a rarity to see racially mixed couples out on a date. Although I detected some awkwardness and perhaps some negativity on the part of white observers during the early years, such couples came to attract less and less attention.

Stereotypes, however, do not fade easily. On several occasions, I have gone to the airport to pick up African-American visitors to Tougaloo College, and have found them to be very uneasy about coming to Mississippi. It was their first time in the state and they were worried about their safety. In their minds, the Klan was still strong and threatening, and blacks were always vulnerable to attack. My response in reassuring them was to say that African-American students and colleagues who had lived in the North had told me that they felt safer in Mississippi than up north, and that Klan-based violence had virtually disappeared. Blacks and whites freely interacted, professionally and socially, with no negative consequences.

After I had lived in Mississippi for several years, I received a telephone call from a old friend from my Minneapolis school days. Still living in Minneapolis, Harvey was a public parks official on his way to a conference in New Orleans. Although he was on the northern outskirts of Jackson, he did not have time to stop in Jackson to see me, but called to get my answer to an urgent question. A black female colleague was accompanying him, and he wondered whether he should ask her to sit in the back seat while he drove through Jackson. I almost felt like laughing, as the situation seemed so comical. But after a moment of reflection, I realized that the two travelers must be genuinely fearful, given the image Mississippi continued to have in the minds of northerners, and that I might have felt the same as he, had our roles been reversed. I assured him that nobody would pay any attention to the two of them in the front seat, and that I had driven around town with black females in my front seat, too. The continued production of films such as *Mississippi Burning* and *A Time to Kill* unfortunately reinforces the old image of Mississippi.

Although the Mississippi of the 1960s no longer exists, racial division and suspicion remain. Shortly after I began my teaching career at Tougaloo College, I became aware of how easily a campus issue became a racial issue. The majority of vocal faculty at the monthly faculty meeting—we do not have a faculty senate, but a general faculty meeting to discuss problems and vote on proposals—have normally been a combination of whites and foreigners. During the 1970s, when the percentage of white faculty was higher than it is today, white faculty were particularly active at these meetings. I did not keep "racial score" and may not have paid much attention to the race of those introducing proposals or making comments except for the fact that some of the African-American faculty seemed to be bothered by the high profile of white faculty.

Until the 1980s, the college president presided over the faculty meetings, a situation which probably contributed to some negative feelings. When white faculty took issue with the president's position on some issue, whatever the issue was became secondary in the eyes of some black faculty to the issue of white faculty challenging a black president. On one occasion, an African-American faculty member proclaimed, "I smell a rat," alluding to a white conspiracy against the black leader. One could not readily determine how many black faculty identified with that position since it would have been rather awkward for a dissenting African American to openly challenge his colleague for injecting race into the picture. However, our greatest challenge in working together as a faculty would not take place until the late 1980s and early 1990s, when an administration with an openly racial agenda was in command.

The major issue in the 1970s that assumed a racial overtone was ROTC. The president had communicated with officials in the Jackson State University ROTC program to work toward establishing a similar program at Tougaloo College. With the Vietnam War barely history, many faculty opposed ROTC, saying that it would prepare our students to be used as tools for questionable U.S. military action abroad. An ad hoc coalition of concerned faculty and students (including the student body president) held meetings to plan a strategy to challenge the ROTC initiative. Unfortunately, most of the faculty involved— including myself—were white. Many of the black faculty—perhaps most—were more pragmatic in their assessment of ROTC, seeing it as a career option for Tougaloo students. Why should the ideological leanings of some faculty deprive our students of an opportunity to become military officers? As the issue took on racial tones, with the implication that white faculty were manipulating black students, the student/faculty coalition broke down. The student body president became cool and distant toward the white faculty involved, and a subsequent faculty vote endorsed the adoption of ROTC.

Prior to the vote, the president met with students in the chapel, in a town hall setting. A student opponent of ROTC asked the president to consider the situation a black ROTC graduate would find himself in if he was sent to South Africa to come to the rescue of the white separatist government under siege from black opponents. The president answered that, as an American soldier, he should follow orders, even in that context. In my twenty-six years at Tougaloo College, I have encountered perhaps three students from my hometown of Minneapolis, and Michelle was one of them. She approached me in class the next day, quite agitated by the president's stance. "How could he give that type of answer and tell blacks to sacrifice their lives for a white racist government?" I identified with her position and told her that I could not support the president's position.

Although that president and I had a good working relationship and I have positive feelings about him, we had openly disagreed on another issue: the Freshman Social Science Seminar. This interdisciplinary, two-semester course focused on the black experience: one semester on the African experience, the other on the African-American experience. The president was troubled by ethnic studies courses such as this one, claiming that it reinforced feelings of separation rather than promoting an awareness of unity as Americans. I found it ironic that I was sitting there in his office, arguing for the ethnic studies courses, while he was arguing against them. The apparent decline of idealism on campus also disturbed some of our students. I recall one of our political science majors who, after experiencing one or two semesters at Tougaloo College, approached me one day with a sense of anguish. He had come to Tougaloo College because of its civil rights reputation, thinking that the college would still be in the vanguard of the struggle for racial justice. His experiences had made him totally disillusioned and disheartened and his academic work was suffering. He dropped out of school and later became the mayor of a small town in northern Mississippi.

Student activism, however, had not totally disappeared from the college. During the final weeks of every spring semester, around the beginning of May, disgruntled students would call a strike—with many students boycotting their classes and holding rallies to voice complaints. The student strike was an annual occurrence during my first few years on the faculty. Students protested against the food service, dorm conditions, treatment by various campus units, etcetera.

In 1974, with the student body president leading the strike, the president decided to take a firm stand. He ordered seven students he saw as ringleaders to leave the campus and reserved rooms for them at the nearby Holiday Inn. The students refused to go and continued to hold rallies to challenge the administration. I had just finished teaching a class in Beard Hall late one morning and arrived just in time to see the Madison County sheriff and his deputies—black and white—approach a group of students who were holding a rally in front of Beard Hall. The student body president was speaking into a microphone as the law enforcement officers came to arrest him. As some of the students showed signs of resistance, a white deputy drew his gun and seemed ready to shoot. A black deputy then took out a can of mace and sprayed it on one student while he used his club on another student. A white exchange student from Germany who had identified with the student protest tried to block the officers from making their arrest and was, himself, arrested.

I had never experienced this type of confrontation and felt the anger well up in me, not anger at the student protesters, but anger at the president and the Madison County law officers. The sheriff had a reputation of being quick to use his gun, particularly against African Americans, and I could not imagine the need for bringing him on campus to resolve our differences. I still find it ironic that my only experience with the use of police force in Mississippi to break up a demonstration was one on the Tougaloo College campus, brought about at the invitation of the college president. The image I had long associated with white racist Mississippi had been manifested under totally unexpected circumstances.

Three faculty members, two white (including myself) and one black, spoke out against the action of the president in calling the Madison County authorities onto campus. A strong parental backlash to the president's action also took place, leading to a special weekend meeting. Under enormous pressure, the president finally agreed to allow the students back to campus and to their classes. No student strike occurred during the following year, nor in subsequent years.

I have often reflected on Dr. Borinski's reference to himself as an "inside outsider." Although he was highly regarded and still revered in memory, his style was to proceed with caution and play the role of diplomatic negotiator when feasible. He avoided direct confrontation, either because he did not feel he had the right to do so, or because he felt it would be counterproductive. Other white faculty, including myself, have felt that as part of the Tougaloo College community, we had the right to engage openly in discussion to promote our positions, the same as our African-American colleagues. However, not all whites have felt this way or have attempted to be actively involved in dialogue. I recall a colleague in psychology, who left Tougaloo after no more than two years of teaching, who argued that this was a black college, that white faculty should see themselves more in the role of guests than the role of leaders and that they should keep a low profile.

I feel certain that some black faculty would have agreed with him; that this was their college and that whites should not try to "take over." However, I also believe that a number of black faculty accept non-black faculty as colleagues with equal rights and duties to partake in faculty governance and to make their voices heard. Since the mid-1980s, faculty have been in charge of the monthly faculty meeting, with non-black faculty (including myself) presiding during some of these years.

It seems to me that when negative feelings from black faculty toward white faculty at Tougaloo College have been manifested, they have been directed toward the natural science faculty and Kincheloe Hall—the science building. Disproportionate numbers of our most talented students have come to Tougaloo College to major in the health sciences, with the goal of becoming a physician or other health care professional. Disproportionate resources have often gone to natural science faculty, as outside grant money has generally been more available to science faculty than to the faculty in general. However, these faculty have often been more active in proposal writing to secure grants than the overall faculty.

The fact that the large majority of natural science faculty are non-black (white and Indian, for the most part) has fed whatever resentment exists. Such resentment has also been fed by the high failure rate in beginning science courses (particularly biology courses). An image has developed in some minds that the faculty are insensitive and have poor teaching styles, otherwise they would be able to reach more students and have more students succeed in their courses. Yet, the Natural Science Division has received high acclaim for the number of its students who have entered medical school and have later become practicing physicians.

The image has persisted that the natural sciences have functioned separately from the college and have not been responsive to the black administration, an image which has led some black faculty to refer to "Kincheloe College." The creation of this image was due in part to some friction that developed between science faculty and our president during the 1970s and early 1980s. Some of the science faculty felt the president was insensitive to the needs of the Natural Science Division; that they were bringing in most of the outside funding; that their programs were attracting the most capable students; and that strengthening the sciences was the key to Tougaloo's future survival. So strong were these feelings that science faculty communicated directly with the board of trustees to argue their cause. Although some science faculty have admitted to me that this contact with the board was a mistake and that they are more appreciative of the president today than they previously were, the image of their unwillingness to accept black leadership still prevails in the minds of some black faculty.

Expanding the Scope of My Work and My Life

During the time I served on the faculty at the University of Nebraska, I saw my role as that of instructor and researcher. I taught three courses each semester—in areas of international relations and Latin American politics—and was expected to publish in my field. While at Nebraska, I wrote an article on the Peruvian military for the *Journal of Inter-American Studies*, a chapter on the Latin American military for a text edited by Nebraska scholars on Latin American scholarship, and another chapter on conservative and liberal party leadership in the Cauca Valley of Colombia—based on my doctoral dissertation research in Cali, Colombia—for a book printed in Spanish and marketed to a primarily Colombian audience.

When I started my employment at Tougaloo College, I continued to be influenced by my Nebraska mind-set. However, I felt somewhat out of my element with regard to research. Tougaloo prided itself on being a teaching institution, and faculty members taught twelve hours of courses each week. The environment did not seem conducive to my undertaking research projects on Latin America, and neither my academic background nor current interests inspired me to do research on local Mississippi topics. My negative experiences at Nebraska apparently weighed upon me more than I was willing to admit and may have blocked my creative urges. It was not until the early 1980s that I became involved in research again, inspired by three years of funding from the Urban Institute of Washington, D.C. to undertake a research project on the role of the private nonprofit sector in the Jackson and Vicksburg, Mississippi, areas.

Two publications resulted from this study, which was part of a project conducted in sixteen geographical areas across the nation.

I was thrust into the role of chair of the Department of Political Science. The department chair who hired me had a master's degree and felt it only proper that I, with my Ph.D., assume leadership of the department. In this capacity, I learned budget management, slowly learned about strategic planning, and started to develop a more bureaucratic approach to academic work—something I had been sheltered from at Nebraska. Although my leadership skills were slow to develop, I was propelled into a position of greater responsibility with my appointment as Social Science Division chair. This came about on the departure of the existing chairman and the reluctance of other faculty to assume the position. My colleagues prevailed upon me to accept this role and the administration ratified their decision.

I now was responsible for leading a fifteen-faculty division encompassing the economics, history, political science, psychology, and sociology departments. My style, however, was rather laissez-faire. Rather than provide much direction, I tended to respond to situations as they developed, seeing myself basically as a problem solver. Although no other faculty in my division aspired to the job, dissatisfaction with my performance reached the level that I felt compelled to resign. Ironically, the colleague who assumed the chairmanship was also quite laissez-faire in his approach and saw himself primarily as a caretaker. When he resigned from the college for a faculty position up north, the division faculty again turned to me. Initially, a semi-collective rule was established, with me as the head of a five-faculty council—one representative per department. After one year of this arrangement, I was put on my own to run the division. By this time, I had learned from earlier mistakes and provided more direction. I had also developed a few skills in proposal writing, although my talents in this area remained quite limited. In response to the urging of a new and dynamic academic dean, I wrote a proposal for a National Science Foundation Student Science Training Program in the social sciences, a four-week summer program to be held on the Tougaloo College campus for high ability eleventh grade high school students. My proposal was funded, the program was a positive experience, and I submitted a new proposal for the following summer. This, too, was funded, as was a third proposal for the summer of 1980.

Nebraska also left me with a certain sense of malaise that was slow to disappear. My marriage was in the process of dissolving, my Latin American research focus was derailed, and I felt stressful and irritable. I was quite open to ideas related to stress reduction and positive thinking. During the early 1970s, transcendental meditation was enjoying national popularity as an easy method for eliminating stress and for enjoying life to the fullest. I had actually attended a TM lecture at the University of Nebraska, but had not been ready to take up the practice of meditation. Now, in early December 1972, a public lecture in downtown Jackson was advertised and was attended by both my wife and myself.

Nancy and I started the practice of TM, but feeling no benefits, she soon stopped. I continued to do my twenty minutes of meditation in the morning and twenty minutes in the evening—a practice I still continue—and came to feel a steadily decreasing level of stress and an increasing sense of well-being. Within a year, I began to attend weekly meetings of the local TM group, started to read spiritually oriented literature, and increasingly adopted a vegetarian diet (as my body was responding less favorably to meat). This change of lifestyle contributed to the disintegration of my marriage, and in 1974 Nancy and I separated (with our divorce following two years later).

Meditation seemed to affect my performance at Tougaloo College in two ways: (1) it helped to relax me and to create a reservoir of positive feeling, which generally enabled me to handle problems and challenges without losing my balance; and (2) it sometimes "spaced me out" to the point where I seemed too much within myself and too detached from my surrounding environment. In this condition, I did not project myself as a leader, which contributed to the dissatisfaction of my division colleagues and my resignation as division chair. I could feel the effects the meditation was having on me, but felt that the positive effects far outweighed the negative ones and that I would overcome the "spaciness" and attain a more positive balance—a conclusion which, I believe, has proven to be accurate.

Meditation also brought me together with my new wife, in a relationship which has strengthened with the passing years. As chair, I hired Jeanne to be our new Social Science Division secretary in 1978. At that time, I was not only practicing TM, but had joined a meditation group—which practiced a type of group meditation and met Wednesday and Sunday nights in my apartment. Jeanne was seeking a new approach to life and asked if she could attend our meditation meetings. The group experience led her into transcendental meditation, to spiritual readings, and to a vegetarian diet. She has become an excellent vegetarian cook, and our lifestyles reinforce each other. She has since completed an undergraduate degree in sociology and a master's degree in social work and holds a professional position as a social worker.

During the late 1970s and early 1980s, I promoted meditation on campus. I arranged for the visit of two African-American leaders of transcendental meditation who gave introductory lectures at both Tougaloo College and Jackson State University. Several Tougaloo students, faculty, and staff began the practice of TM. (The visitors had such an interest in initiating African Americans into the practice of TM that they charged only a small fraction of the normal fee to people who felt unable to pay the going rate.) Although I have been unable to monitor whether most of those who started TM are still practicing it, I have maintained periodic contact with an African-American faculty colleague who left Tougaloo nearly twenty years ago, and he continues to practice TM and feels the benefits of doing so. I also promoted meditation on campus by organizing a group that met weekly (in one of the campus classrooms) to do a meditation. Those who had not learned TM did a type of visualization. As the national interest in TM and meditation began to fade, and as the students I had been meeting with graduated, I shifted my attention to other activities and the group dissolved.

As I look back on the last twenty years, I feel a deep sense of gratitude that meditation was available for me, for it has strengthened my capacity for meeting some major challenges. In the mid-1980s, change came to Tougaloo College as the president retired after serving for more than twenty years. He was a man of dignity who was recognized as such by the board of trustees, who have named our new health and wellness center after him and his wife.

Changing Administrations

The change of administration in 1984 opened the door to my first major challenge at Tougaloo College. Our new president was a man who had been raised in New York and had managed an innovative college program in California. He wanted to be called by his first name, dressed casually, and mingled freely with faculty to engage in intellectual discussion. I responded positively to his style, as did many other faculty. The problem was that non-black faculty related better to him than black faculty did, even though our new president was black. In the eyes of some of our African-American faculty, he apparently did not fit the image of a black college president.

Almost immediately, opposition to his leadership developed, led by a senior black faculty member. The president's academic credentials came under question and gossip was spread related to his wife and one of his personal assistants. The two key staff he had brought with him were both white, which seemingly fed an image of him as being insensitive to the campus community and as an outsider who would not fit in. The president's style was non-combative, which perhaps contributed to his being viewed as a vulnerable target. To many of the non-black faculty, the senior black professor was engaged in an unwarranted personal vendetta against the president and was disrupting faculty meetings with vitriolic personal attacks on him. The faculty became divided between supporters and opponents of the president. Supporters urged the president to take action against the senior professor, since they felt that his frequent written statements and spoken comments had crossed the line into libel and slander.

I was seated in my office one day when a faculty colleague approached me with a petition to the board of trustees to terminate the employment of the senior professor. I read the list of faculty who had already signed the petition and was concerned that all were non-black. I had mixed feelings about signing, but finally did so as I believed that the senior professor had gone beyond the bounds of propriety. The president would not endorse this initiative and the board did not act. However, the petition became public and had a negative effect on relations between black and white faculty, especially given the fact that the senior professor was one of the more productive faculty in terms of grant writing and in administration of innovative programs. This professor also coordinated our accreditation Self-Study to a successful conclusion at a time when the college seemed vulnerable to negative action by the accrediting team. In retrospect, I regret that the petition drive was undertaken.

The president's support deteriorated, due mainly to deteriorating conditions on campus. Student enrollment was declining, with the residual effect being a budget crisis. To growing numbers of faculty, the president did not have the administrative skills needed to manage the institution and to address the growing crisis. My support for him began to waver, and I finally joined the forces of faculty who wanted him out. Informal meetings took place between faculty and members of the board of trustees to argue for a change in the presidency. As concerned faculty held strategy meetings, a black female colleague warned about the possible consequences of forcing the president out. She alluded to the type of president in charge of most historically black colleges and universities, claiming that most were highly dictatorial and abusive of their power, and that such a president would be worse than our current one. This argument did not impress me since Tougaloo College had not had a history of heavy-handed, abusive leadership. I was confident that our tradition of relatively open, liberal administration, with respect for faculty rights, would prevail. My colleague's message would soon come back to haunt me, though I believe the board of trustees acted properly when they terminated the president.

Another Change in Administration

After a short caretaker administration under an acting president, our new president took office in 1988. He was very young for a college president (early 30s), but energetic and dynamic, and won my confidence. I looked forward to positive and productive leadership. Under his leadership enrollment went up, reaching record levels and contributing to a cash flow that erased our budget deficits and whittled down our accumulated debt.

The positive feelings seemed reciprocal as he responded well to me and my initiatives. The regional utility company—which supplied electricity to Mississippi, Alabama, and Louisiana—had sent out a request for proposals to conduct a summer program for high ability high school students. As chair of the Social Science Division, I took charge of writing the proposal, bringing together colleagues in economics, history, and sociology to provide their input and to take part in our proposed program. Our proposal was accepted and we received major funding that provided a sizable amount of summer money for each of us. My colleagues were pleased with my leadership role as was the president, who attended the "graduation" dinner for our students and addressed the group on behalf of Tougaloo College.

The program, however, was not a totally positive experience. Prior to the signing of the contract that awarded the program to Tougaloo College, our president met with a high official of the utility company, a meeting attended by me and by a female representative of the electric company who served as my counterpart in operationalizing the summer program. The president had initially voiced opposition to having the program on another campus—Piney Woods Country School, nearly thirty miles south of Tougaloo College—a decision made by the company, which concluded that Tougaloo facilities were inadequate.

At the meeting, the president assumed a racially oriented posture, one which put the white utility company executive on the defensive and offended him. The president's approach both surprised and disturbed me. The next day, my counterpart from the utility company telephoned me to say, "Your president almost blew it," with his offensive approach. The president also phoned me, apparently feeling vulnerable from his interaction with the utility company executive and wanting some reassurance from me. "Steve, you understood what I was trying to say, didn't you?" he asked. I gave him a reassuring answer, implying that I had heard nothing inappropriate and hiding my true feelings.

I was looking forward to the continuation of our positive relationship and did not connect his comments to the executive with a posture that could prove problematic in the times ahead. Indeed, our relationship seemed to strengthen as the president named me the Tougaloo College recipient of the Headway Award, an annual award given by the Mississippi state legislature to the outstanding faculty member at each of the colleges and universities in the state.

Racial miscommunication during the summer program itself created a problem that turned out to be more serious and even threatened to terminate activities ahead of schedule. Over half of the high school students were African American and the program was held on an African-American campus. The Tougaloo faculty were racially mixed, but the counselors were all African American. Frankly, I did not anticipate any racial problems since I had assumed the students who were applying to the program, and who were recommended by their high school principals and counselors would be flexible and adaptable to new situations.

My assumption held true for the male students. They got along fine. However, some of the female students felt more vulnerable, and one incident set off a chain reaction. A white female student from Louisiana had been unaccustomed to living in a predominantly black environment and recorded her thoughts in her notebook: "Blacks all around, everywhere, ugh!" She unthinkingly lent the notebook to a black classmate, who wanted to review her notes from one of our classroom sessions. The classmate came across the negative reference to blacks, took offense, and confronted the white student with the admonition to "Watch your back!" This response terrified the white student, along with a group of white females from northern Arkansas—which has a relatively small black population. When I became aware of the confrontation, I assembled the students, asked them to be forgiving of one another, and asked the counselors to work closely with the group to resolve remaining differences.

The mistrust, however, could not be easily cleared, and negative feelings remained just below the surface, seemingly waiting to be released. Some of the white female students felt that the two female counselors were identifying racially with the black females, which contributed to their feelings of vulnerability. Nonetheless, the program seemed to be moving forward successfully. The days passed by, and we were entering our fourth and final week. Suddenly, an incident occurred on a field trip that created a crisis. A blonde from northern Arkansas had her ponytail pulled by a black female student. She became highly emotional, phoned her parents, and wanted to leave the program. Some of the black females claimed that she had been antagonizing them with insensitive remarks, and that the pulling of her hair was in response to the insensitivity.

I received an angry telephone call from the blonde girl's father, who also telephoned the utility company. The next day, four utility company executives flew up from their New Orleans headquarters to engage in damage control. They feared a lawsuit by angry parents and told white female students who feared the onset of a race war that the company would fly them to their hometowns on the company jet. Four of these students accepted the offer and left the program. The remaining twenty students stayed for the duration and we had a good "graduation" ceremony. The argument had been made after the first incident that I should have sent the two offending students home, that this would have set a no-nonsense tone that would have precluded further incidents. To this day, I believe such a move would have backfired since the white student had not meant to offend anyone with her foolish remarks and the black student was just expressing her hurt at the racist statement in the notebook. An overreaction on my part might have polarized the group racially to the point where the program could have been jeopardized at an early date.

If these experiences were somehow designed to prepare me for dealing with a racially charged atmosphere, I did not have long to wait for further tests. Indeed, my high point with the president in receiving the Headway Award was "soiled" by an ominous experience. My wife, Jeanne, was invited to accompany me to the ceremony at the state capitol and we drove down with the Tougaloo student who was named recipient of the student Headway Award. At one point, I was rushing back to the car to fetch an item, taking a shortcut down a grassy hill. I suddenly stepped on a slick spot and fell into a muddy area, coating my slacks and sport coat with mud. Fortunately, I had time to drive back home, change my clothes, and return prior to the start of the ceremony. Jeanne and I had our photograph taken with the president and the day ended happily. Only later did I see an ill omen in my spill.

Several months after the president took office, a search began for a new vice president for academic affairs (an upgrading of the academic dean position). The president had appointed me to head the search committee, which seemed a further indicator of his positive feelings toward me. I convened our meetings, coordinated the review of candidates, and worked with the committee to select three candidates for the president's final review and decision (as per his request).

Several of the candidates had impressive academic credentials, but few had significant administrative experience, the type of background the search committee felt was necessary for the position. We selected our three candidates, invited them to campus for interviews, and telephoned administrators at their respective institutions to get additional assessments of strengths and weaknesses. Concerns about two of the candidates led us to recommend the third candidate, a Tougaloo alumna. The president, in meeting with the search committee, told us that he concurred with our recommendation and that she would be offered the position.

I seemed to start things off well with our new vice president for academic affairs. She would be traveling to Brazil for a conference just prior to taking her position at the college, so I told her about my background in Portuguese and lent her my book on Brazilian Portuguese phrases. During the year, I headed our Faculty Steering Committee—which had functioned effectively under the previous president in providing a vehicle for faculty governance, but had also served as a vehicle for communicating with the board of trustees and encouraging the board to replace the former president. As head of this committee, I ran the faculty meetings, including our pre-school conference. One of my roles was to prepare the meeting agenda, which included comments by the president and the vice president for academic affairs.

Storm Clouds on the Horizon

Although my relationship with the president remained positive, my relations with the vice president began to deteriorate. She had brought the assistant dean of students over to her office in the capacity of assistant vice president for academic affairs and seemed to be making decisions for the academic program mainly as a result of input from her new colleague. Division chairs felt increasingly excluded from the decision-making process—contrary to the Tougaloo tradition of considerable input. Some of the chairs also found difficulty in gaining access to the vice president to discuss important concerns, as meetings were often difficult to schedule.

Two of the division chairs resigned due to these concerns, but I decided to remain in my position, with the hope that I would have some meaningful input.

At the meetings of division chairs called by the vice president, I found myself questioning decisions she had made in the absence of input from the chairs. Such questions seemed to alienate her, and our relationship, unfortunately, became increasingly adversarial. At one meeting, she made a critical comment related to something I said and then asked her secretary to put the comment in the minutes of the meeting. I responded and asked the secretary to include my response in the minutes. The vice president reacted by advising the secretary to include her comment but to exclude mine. I recognized that our relationship was unlikely to improve, but felt that I needed to remain in my position to represent the interests of the faculty in my division.

One of my early conflicts with the vice president resulted from my attempts to represent these interests. We had hired several new faculty in the Social Science Division for the 1989-90 academic year and had informed them that they would be teaching four courses for a total of twelve credit hours. Just prior to the beginning of classes, the new faculty came to me to complain that the vice president had assigned them a section of our two-credit freshman seminar course, with no additional pay. I sent her a memo in which I communicated the concerns of my faculty and asked her why such an assignment had been made without any input from me. The tone of her response was unfriendly, with the message that this was her prerogative and that I should be more supportive. I recall that at one meeting of the division chairs she responded to one of my concerns about lack of division chair input by saying, "Why don't you just ask what you can do to help," rather than question the action that has been taken.

Although my administrative role as Social Science Division chair was becoming less rewarding due to my deteriorating relationship with the vice president for academic affairs, another dimension of my academic experience was receiving an important boost. The Southwestern International Studies Consortium (SISCO), headquartered at Grambling State University in Louisiana, a sister African-American institution, had invited Tougaloo College to become a member. I prepared our formal response and the vice president signed the agreement. We would be receiving three years of mini-grants in exchange for committing ourselves to internationalizing our curriculum and attending an orientation conference at the host institution. As project director, I coordinated the formation of our planning team, following the grant guidelines. Our six-member team then prepared to attend the mid-October conference at Grambling.

A scheduling conflict provoked an unfortunate confrontation with the vice president that further undermined our relationship. The previous year, she had presented a positive initiative, the convocation of a "Faculty Awards Ceremony" in appreciation of faculty achievement. The event was favorably received and was then scheduled as an annual activity. However, the second year's ceremony was to take place at the very time our group needed to be in Louisiana.

As the time approached for our trip, I informed the vice president, who reacted negatively to our missing the awards ceremony. She had previously been invited to meet with the Social Science Division faculty at a regularly scheduled meeting and took the opportunity to tell us that we could not go to the SISCO meeting since the awards ceremony was more important. (Five of the six faculty scheduled to go were from the social sciences.) I responded by reminding her that the agreement she had signed committed our faculty to attend the meeting, and that the orientation session was very important for our administering the mini-grant. When I discussed the problem with the SISCO director, he emphasized the need for our attendance and reminded us of our institutional commitment.

I then scheduled a meeting with the president to explain the situation and to invite his intervention to resolve it. By his very action of signing the paperwork to release the money—from the mini-grant—to pay for our travel and lodging, he seemed to be giving us his implicit support. However, our group left under a cloud, given the disapproval of the vice president. Upon our return from the productive meeting of delegations from many historically black colleges and universities (HBCUs), the vice president chastised me and remarked that I would have been fired from other institutions for having defied authority. I then asked her whether she would have approved the travel had I been going to a prestigious conference to deliver a scholarly paper. Her response was that the campus activity had priority, regardless of competing professional demands. This was not the Tougaloo College I had been accustomed to serving, and I was unwilling to bend to arbitrary authority. In spite of this early confrontation, our work under the SISCO grant proceeded smoothly. Our group attended the remaining meetings without further incidents. New internationally oriented courses were designed, and three of us were funded by SISCO to take a seventeen-day cultural study trip to Mexico during a winter holiday break.

Another boost to my professional growth came from an opportunity presented by the Bush Foundation of St. Paul, Minnesota. Tougaloo College had previously received a one-year faculty development planning grant from this foundation and had been invited to write a proposal for a three-year program grant. However, nobody seemed willing to take the lead in developing the proposal. When the assistant vice president for academic affairs brought this opportunity to my attention, I responded affirmatively, took charge of developing the proposal, and became director of the grant we received. Nine years later, I am still managing faculty development projects with Bush Foundation funding. I had no idea, at that time, that the Bush Foundation would be opening the door to developments and accomplishments well beyond my expectations.

I also had not realized, in early 1990, that my most serious altercation with the vice president was still to come and that it would severely test my relationship with the president. During the first months of the year, the vice president had informed me, as division chair, that she would not be recommending to the president the reappointment of two of our first-year faculty. I was informing the two faculty of the situation, to cushion the impact of a non-reappointment letter, when one of them responded, "If I get that kind of letter, I'm going to tell you something that will blow the lid off this place." For a moment, I was a bit stunned, but I quickly made sense out of his comment. At the very beginning of the academic year, a longtime member of our Social Science Division faculty came to my office to inform me that two new members of our division faculty—including the one who had made the cryptic remark—had been circulating a petition to remove me as division chair. They were only approaching black faculty and had succeeded in gaining only one signature other than their own—that of another new faculty member.

Rather than confront my new colleagues after their petition campaign had fizzled out, I sought to ignore the challenge to my authority and attempted to bond with them. However, I remained perplexed that new faculty, vulnerable to my authority as division chair, would engage in such a bold action. I defined the problems in racial terms—concluding that they felt offended at having a white person as their chair—and felt they would come to accept me in my role after we got to know each other better. I was not about to conclude that someone in a higher position than mine had encouraged their action: not until the warning was made to the impending termination of employment.

The "lid blower" entered my office to inform me that he had received his notice of termination. I responded by saying, "Now, let me tell you what your bombshell is. The vice president for academic affairs was behind your petition drive last fall." He answered with the word "bingo," and added that, "We thought you would figure that out." He went on to say that she had painted a negative picture of my competency and commitment to the institution and students and had asked him and the other new faculty member to lead a campaign to get me removed as division chair. When the president gave me the Headway Award and I was named "Outstanding Academic Administrator" at the faculty awards ceremony, my colleague, in his words, realized, "We had been had." The two new faculty members had been used as instruments of a personal vendetta against me. The vice president denied that she had played any role in the petition drive.

The terminated faculty member agreed to describe what had transpired in writing and to meet with me and the president to inform him about the experience. I felt confident as I telephoned the president's office to set up an "emergency" meeting. The president's secretary made room in his busy schedule to accommodate the colleague and myself, given the sense of urgency I conveyed. An hour prior to the scheduled meeting time, I received a phone call from the president, with the vice president on the other line. His message was that he did not want to meet with the accusing professor, but just with me. I had become the problem by informing the two pink slip recipients ahead of time that they might be receiving non-reappointment notices. By violating proper procedure, I had committed a grave offense.

I felt betrayed by the president and sensed a hidden agenda. Our relationship had taken a negative turn, one which would not be reversed prior to his departure. However, a very positive moment of interaction between us was to take place, though not before the administration orchestrated a change in the faculty handbook that facilitated my removal as Social Science Division chair.

Although my relationship with the president had remained positive prior to the sudden downturn, events had already taken place that had caused me deep concern. At a closed door meeting of people in high administrative and academic positions—including the division chairs—the president announced a new "paradigm shift" away from a "Eurocentric" focus to an "Afrocentric" focus. He went on to suggest that European culture and development were due to European contact with African culture and that the analytical, scientific approach imposed by Europeans was detrimental to African Americans. I had no problem with a more Afrocentric focus, since I was well aware of the important contributions of past African civilizations, having taught about them in the old freshman seminar course. The problem was in the president's message, which seemed to be combating white ethnocentrism with a version of black ethnocentrism. The discussion became so racially focused that the African-American librarian asked the white chair of the Natural Science Division whether he felt awkward being white.

During the next two years, speakers promoting Afrocentrism were brought to campus. The keynote speaker at a faculty awards ceremony, introduced as a longtime friend of both the president and vice president, harangued the faculty about the "aliens" who are teaching our students, telling us that we needed to become Afrocentric to play a positive teaching role. The racial approach stirred up submerged racial feelings and created an awkwardness in relations between black and white faculty. Some black faculty reacted positively to the president's approach, seeing it as an expression of racial pride, and seeing him as being a strong black leader who was finally putting the white faculty in their place. Those faculty who were unwilling to accept the president's leadership style were seen by some black faculty as racists who were unwilling to accept strong black leadership. The president and vice president, on more than one occasion, made this insinuation.

The increasing racially oriented agenda and authoritarian style of the administration created an awkwardness at faculty meetings. African-American faculty—even those who privately expressed their concerns about the administration to non-black colleagues—were reluctant to break ranks and openly take issue with the administration. When non-black faculty were the only ones to speak out, it seemed to aggravate racial division. When job openings came available, the administration seemed to seek out African-American replacements rather than support an open search.

In February 1991, four senior faculty members, including myself, signed a letter to the chairman of the Education Policy Committee of the Tougaloo College Board of Trustees asking for an investigation of the condition of faculty and academic governance at the college. We alluded to a "grave" situation where the administration was "needlessly" combative in its interaction with faculty, and argued that "the rights of individual faculty have been undermined." Although no action by the board immediately followed, the vice president later left the college for another position and the president was replaced by the board under circumstances that have not yet been clarified. Unfortunately, the president's racially oriented agenda offended the local white business community just as it was beginning to embrace Tougaloo College and brought about some renewed alienation. Our current president has reversed the direction of his predecessor, with an apparently positive response from the business community.

A Positive Assessment

My years under that administration were the most difficult ones for me in my twenty-six years at Tougaloo College. However, my professional growth continued to accelerate, which helped balance the negative experiences. With Bush Grant funding for faculty development, our coordinating team helped promote a variety of teaching innovations. Faculty adopted approaches to address diverse learning styles, team-teaching projects were undertaken, and courses were revised to promote the college's new set of expected student outcomes.

My relationship with students has remained positive during my tenure at Tougaloo College. Although I have been characterized as a demanding instructor, my student evaluations have been high and political science majors who have gone on to law school and graduate school have reported back to me that my essay exams were very helpful in preparing them for post-Tougaloo academic demands. Even the promotion of Afrocentrism had little if any impact on my interaction with students.

In writing a proposal to the Bush Foundation for renewal of our grant, our coordinating team requested funding for a faculty development conference here in Jackson, Mississippi, for faculty from HBCUs. Many HBCUs had been receiving Bush grants, and faculty from these institutions were eligible for travel grants to attend the semi-annual conferences and summer institutes of the Minnesota-based Collaboration for the Advancement of College Teaching and Learning, which was funded by the Bush Foundation. Several Tougaloo faculty, including myself, had attended some of these conferences, were impressed with their high quality, and had a strong desire to hold our own conference in the South, where a large majority of our institutions are located.

Following a positive response from the Bush Foundation, the First National HBCU Faculty Development Symposium was held (in early autumn in 1994). It was a great success, attended by some seventy-five faculty from over thirty different institutions. To help make it a success, I called the director of the Collaboration to get the names of people she considered to be the most dynamic faculty development directors at HBCUs who had been actively involved in collaboration activities. I phoned the five faculty on her list, invited them to become members of a new steering committee that would take responsibility for planning and running the symposium, and received positive responses from each one.

Although my relationship with the president and vice president had remained negative, I invited him to serve on a panel and her to give welcoming remarks. When the president saw the number of people in attendance, he reacted positively. He was particularly impressed with our success in attracting representatives from four major foundations—Bush, Mellon, Lilly, and Kellogg—and shook my hand vigorously, claiming that it was a major achievement to get that number together at a conference such as ours. I felt particularly moved by his show of support, given our past interaction.

Our steering committee has remained in place—with some changes in personnel—and has since completed the work for the subsequent (five total) HBCU Faculty Development Symposiums, changing the venue from Jackson to Charlotte, North Carolina, to Memphis, Tennessee, to Atlanta, Georgia, and to Miami, Florida. As this chapter is being written, we are preparing for the Sixth National HBCU Faculty Development Symposium in Houston, Texas, in October 1999.

Following the success of our initial conferences, the Bush Foundation responded favorably to our request for a three-year grant to fund a new HBCU Faculty Development Network, but asked that we find another sponsor who would match their financial support. I contacted several foundations, receiving a positive response from the Ford Foundation. The Bush Foundation has since renewed our grant for a second three-year period. I remain co-director of the HBCU Faculty Development Network, together with the female faculty development director from Johnson C. Smith University in Charlotte, North Carolina.

In addition to my professional growth related to the aforementioned grant activities, I have managed an International Studies grant from the College Fund/UNCF Institute for International Public Policy to design an International Studies emphasis at Tougaloo College. The emphasis was approved by a most supportive vice president for academic affairs, the president, our board of trustees, and the planning committee of the social science and foreign language departments. The faculty have since implemented it. At the time of this writing, I am co-teaching our interdisciplinary capstone Seminar in International Studies course.

My major areas of concentration in graduate school were international relations and Latin American studies, as was my major teaching focus at the University of Nebraska. At Tougaloo College, with our two- to three-person political science faculty, I have been compelled to teach a wide variety of courses. This has expanded my horizons and versatility as a teacher. The creation of the Mississippi Consortium for International Development (MCID), an organization composed of three Mississippi-based HBCUs—Tougaloo College, Jackson State University, and Alcorn State University—has enabled me to utilize my Latin American and Spanish language backgrounds. MCID's participant training programs (funded by USAID) have brought groups from many Spanish countries for training in community development, democratization, and other skills. With my fluency in Spanish, I have conducted sessions for many of these groups. I have also traveled to Costa Rica, Brazil, and Guyana, with my initial trip to Brazil in 1994 being in the capacity as director of a Fulbright-Hays Study Abroad grant.

Oh, yes, I have regained my position as chair of the Social Science Division, with the upgraded title of Dean of Social Sciences. I have learned a lot from my experiences—both those I have viewed as good and those I have viewed as bad. I have made some mistakes, and am working hard to avoid repeating them. Perhaps I am really an "inside outsider," as Dr. Borinski might say, but I refuse to accommodate myself to the notion of being an outsider. I have made my commitment over twenty-six years, paid my dues, and feel that I belong. I try to be sensitive to racial factors, but feel most comfortable seeing people as individuals—with strengths and weaknesses—and try to avoid stereotypes, which have the effect of dividing and destroying.

Chapter 9 _____

The Academic Road Less Traveled: Challenges and Opportunities

Jesse Silverglate

Life for me ain't been no crystal stair.

Langston Hughes (1979)

Do not follow where the path may lead . . . Go instead where there is no path and leave a trail.

Robert Frost (1928)

Teaching at a historically black institution for nearly three decades has provided me with numerous challenges and opportunities. In this chapter I will discuss a number of them. One of my recent opportunities occurred when I was challenged to find a way to motivate my group dynamics class. Group dynamics is one of my favorite courses. It allows me to combine theory and practice. Students study the concepts that inform the group process: perception, communication, membership, norms, goals, and leadership. Then they have to lead the class in experiential exercises that demonstrate these concepts. Students enjoy the experiential activities; they struggle with the more abstract concepts that the exercises demonstrate. Each semester I have to find ways of getting the class to learn the concepts that underpin the activities they experience so naturally. Some groups are easy to teach; others are a real challenge. My spring 1998 class at Florida Memorial College (FMC) in Miami, Florida, is proving to be one of the most difficult groups I have had to teach.

After a very poor showing by most of the class on my mid-term exam, I found myself trying to connect the concrete exercises with the abstract principles we have been studying. I used the example of the difference between left brain and right brain activity. Most of the students enjoy the creative and interactive excitement of the right brain inspired exercises. They balk at analyzing, synthesizing, and organizing the results of what we have been doing. They find the textbook dull and my lectures on the concepts of group process boring.

The exam results confirmed what I had expected. The students who had been coming to class on time, who had been doing the textbook reading, and who had been participating in the lecture discussion had done well on the mid-term. The students who came to class late, who did not take notes or ask questions had done poorly. I suspected that this latter group of students did not organize their class involvement, a left brain activity. I tried to point out that critical thinking requires use of the left brain skills of analysis, synthesis, and organization. I told them that I favored my right brain. I have always enjoyed using my right brain more than my left, but my college experiences taught me that comprehension and mastery required using the whole brain. In order to see if my message had reached them, I advised the class that students with grades below 70 would have the opportunity to do a make-up exam after spring break.

Educational Transformation: Scholar, Teacher, and Facilitator

> The curriculum should have a direct relationship to the students for whom it is intended and the times in which it is taught—emphasis should be placed on "cultivation of curiosity, on development of critical ability, on wider perspectives on self and on culture, on ways to approach knowledge."
> Carnegie Commission on Higher Education (1972)

As I headed home from class that Wednesday night, I hoped that everyone would make it through the semester. I also reflected on how I came to be teaching group dynamics at Florida Memorial College. I have a Ph.D. in European history from the University of Wisconsin. My dissertation was on modern German history. However, I have never taught a course in German history or even in modern European history. When I received my Ph.D. in 1969 the job market in higher education was shrinking rapidly. As a ROTC officer I had to fulfill a military obligation before beginning my teaching career. By the time I left the army in 1970 the bottom had fallen out of the college job market.

I had few job opportunities at the college level and they were all at historically black colleges and universities (HBCUs). I came to Florida Memorial, a small college that had relocated from St Augustine, Florida, to Miami, Florida, in 1968. I was recruited to teach in an interdisciplinary program that combined the humanities and the social sciences. I would teach the western civilization portion of the freshman core curriculum. Because I had been a teaching assistant in the western civilization program at Wisconsin, this seemed like an easy transition. I was in for a rude awakening.

Most of the students in my western civilization sections at Wisconsin had high school courses in European history. They came to my classes with basic facts and concepts upon which I could expand. Most of the students in my classes at Florida Memorial had never had more than an American history course in high school. They often complained that it had been a boring course that consisted primarily of memorizing names and dates. Thus, the students came to my class historically tabula rasa. They had no basic core of background historical information upon which I could build. Moreover, the western civilization textbook that we used at Florida Memorial focused exclusively on European history. There was nothing in the text that related to African or other non-Western cultures. I did not think having them learn a list of popes and kings would spark their historical curiosity.

I felt that if I could add some African, Asian, and Latin American components to the course, I might spark greater interest in the students. Unfortunately, I had not had any graduate course work in non-European history, so I had to educate myself before I could revise the course. After several semesters of intensive reading, I felt comfortable shifting the text from a western to a world civilization focus. I also added a supplemental paperback, Margaret Shinnie's *Ancient African Kingdoms.*

While I saw some improvement in student performance, the improvement was minimal. Therefore, I began to look outside of the course content for the source of my problems. Most of the students in my classes had reading and writing skills that were far below college standards. Florida Memorial had an open enrollment policy. The tradition at many HBCUs was to take students from where they were academically and bring them up to college standards. Most of the students had ineffective study skills and habits. Consequently, I had the task of trying to teach content to large numbers of students who did not have the basic skills needed to read and comprehend the text, write exams, or complete reports in standard English. This lack of basic skills often compounded the difficulties of the teaching and learning process because it led to a lack of student interest in the subject that often translated into student comments of "history is boring."

My graduate training had not provided me with any teaching instruction in dealing with basic skills deficiencies, nor had it taught me anything about alternative teaching or learning styles. I had a one-size-fits-all teaching style. I assigned readings from the text and presented lectures on the topics. Then I tested students on the material and assigned grades. After several semesters of large numbers of failing grades, I began to doubt my teaching abilities.

I had assumed that broadening the content of the western civilization survey would solve the problem. I had devoted many hours to expanding my historical knowledge base in order to make the course more interesting and relevant to my students. However, all this effort had given me little time for pursuing my research interests. In spite of my efforts, my students did not seem to be learning. I thought that perhaps I was not cut out to be a teacher.

In 1976 I had the opportunity to participate in the 13 College Curriculum Program. This program offered summer workshops that centered on developing teaching methods and curriculum materials that would be effective in the teaching and learning process for students with skills deficiencies. However, the academic content of the program focused on an interdisciplinary social science curriculum. It had no western or world civilization component. If I were to participate in this program, I would have to expand my academic base from history to the sister social sciences of psychology, sociology, anthropology, political science, and economics. What little time I may have had for concentrated research in German history would be effectively eliminated. Without continued research and publication in my specialized area of graduate training, all possibility of advancement in the history profession was removed.

I decided to participate in the program and also continue to teach world civilization. In addition, I worked on several articles based upon my dissertation. During my third year in the 13 College Curriculum program I came down with bleeding ulcers. To pay my medical bills I also taught two summer courses at Florida International University in Miami, Florida, and then went to the 13 College Curriculum summer workshop that was held at Dillard University in New Orleans, Louisiana, during the summer of 1976. I was still taking medication for my ulcers and could hardly function. Many of the faculty members from sister HBCUs who had known me from previous summer workshops were shocked at my physical deterioration. Grady, an older math instructor, called me aside and asked what would happen at Florida Memorial College if I died. I told him the college would go on. He then told me I could push myself until I expired and Florida Memorial College would remain, or I could set some priorities and limitations on my career and I could be there to see the college grow. Of course, I wanted to survive, and now I realized I would have to make some difficult decisions. On the one hand, I understood that I had little hope of pursuing a research career at Florida Memorial College. I had a heavy teaching load; I had no teaching or research assistants, and the college did not offer sabbaticals. I had no library or archive resources available on campus or in Miami for my specialized research. The longer I stayed at Florida Memorial College the less likely it would be for me to find employment at a college or university that would allow me to continue research in German history. On the other hand, I realized that I really enjoyed working with interdisciplinary materials. Teaching at Florida Memorial College allowed me to teach across academic disciplines. I would not be able to do this if I were at a research institution. In truth, I really enjoyed teaching more than I did research. Unfortunately, I also grasped that I did not have the teaching skills that I needed to be effective in the classroom.

I decided to pursue a master's degree in education at the University of Miami. I had a few years left to use or lose my veteran's educational benefits. I thought working on the education degree might provide me with the teaching skills I lacked. I had done draft counseling during the Vietnam War and enjoyed that, so I decided to focus my coursework in the school of education on community counseling. My thinking was that if I could not make it in the classroom, I would switch careers and move into social work or counseling.

My internships and practicums in the master of education program convinced me that I did not have the temperament to pursue a career in counseling. However, I did learn a great deal about motivating individuals and working with their problems. I realized much of this could be used in the classroom to motivate students and help them with their learning. From my counseling experience, I learned that in order to be effective in the classroom I had to find ways to facilitate the learning process. No matter how much content information I provided or how effectively I lectured, I would not maximize student performance until I mastered methods of facilitating self-motivation and learning among the students. I began to offer students a variety of options for them to demonstrate their mastery of the course materials. In addition to traditional examinations, I offered book reports, oral reports, and group projects. I also decided to develop a grade contract. This would allow students the opportunity to select the grade they wished to work toward and would reduce my frustration at trying to get all students to do the same quantity of work. I found that under these conditions most students who came to class regularly and turned in the assigned work would be able to pass the course. Those who had greater motivation and did more work would earn higher grades, and even students with limited skills were able to demonstrate enough mastery to pass the course.

Service to Community: An HBCU Norm

We, the members of Du Bois's Talented Tenth, must accept our historical responsibility and live King's credo that none of us is free until each of us is free.

Henry Louis Gates, Jr. and Cornel West (1996)

Several years ago, I decided to expand my teaching to include courses in group dynamics and community psychology. These were courses I had enjoyed during my master of education degree program. Moreover, these courses allow me to work with upper division social science majors who are being educated for careers that involve community service. All the students majoring in one of the social sciences have to participate in an internship at a community agency. This emphasis on service to the community is part of the historical mission of black colleges. J.C. Brazzell (1996) notes that most HBCUs were founded on "principles centered around the belief that Black students must be educated both to assume leadership and service roles in the Black community and to succeed in the larger community" (p.50).

My own experiences as a college student in the 1960s had provided me with a strong commitment to social intervention and social change. Both as an undergraduate at Rutgers and as a graduate at Wisconsin, I had been active in civil rights and antiwar activities. As a teaching assistant at Wisconsin, I had been active in trying to organize the TA's into a union. I also participated in the Big Brother program in Madison. In addition, I had taught for several years at the Florida Memorial College Prison Outreach Program that attempted to provide prisoners at the Dade County Correctional Facility with an opportunity to earn a college degree. These experiences as well as my internships and practicums at both a drug rehabilitation center and a family services counseling center convinced me of the importance of community involvement. I find the most effective learning experience is one that balances theory with practice.

In my community psychology classes students are required to provide reports on the activities of various community agencies in the South Florida area. Many of the students report on agencies for which they are working or at which they have worked. Adhering to the philosophy of community psychology, students are encouraged to explore how their agencies show a respect for diversity and the empowerment of the agency's clients. Students are also asked to focus on how the agencies are working toward planned social change that will prevent problems rather than solely treat serious crises. Recently, a student who worked as a counselor in a Miami agency told me that she was often frustrated when she went into the homes of either older Jewish or Hispanic clients. She also indicated that the agency had not offered her any training in the culture of these client groups. I suggested that, during the initial home visit, she ask the agency to team her up with another social worker who had familiarity with the culture of her clients. This class discussion made me realize that as more African Americans become professionals delivering services to non-black clients that my students would need additional cross-cultural and multicultural course content and internship experiences.

Currently, Florida Memorial College is exploring two programs that involve community involvement: Service Learning and American Humanics. Service Learning has become very popular at sister HBCUs. I learned about this educational emphasis that combines teaching, research, and service integrated around community problems from a colleague at LeMoyne-Owen College in Memphis, Tennessee, one of the HBCUs that pioneered the concept. Barbara Frankle noted:

> LeMoyne-Owen's service learning program has taken more than 200 students per year into different environments, fostering student awareness of social issues, of the importance of their civic participation, and of the potential for self fulfillment that service provides. A good example of service learning at LeMoyne-Owen College is the Junior Achievement program where students in the required social science Core Curriculum classes each year present units on the neighborhood and community to children in third and fourth grade classes in Memphis, Tennessee, and Shelby County. Nervous and skittish at first, students come up with many excuses not to participate—"My car broke down," "I have to work all day," "I can't find that school." Once convinced that a passing grade rides on the involvement, however, the students make the necessary effort, and are surprised at how much the school children enjoy their visits, and relish their contributions. The students enter a variety of settings, and realize they have much to say to all the youngsters of whatever race or ethnic group or class. The self-esteem of the college students rises while they inspire the children to think about their own college potential. Many of the LeMoyne-Owen students go back to visit "their class" even after the project has been completed. Thus, service learning advances their leadership potential, their sense of self worth, and their understanding of diversity. They are also able to combine experience in the community with the theory they are learning in the social science classes. (Barbara Stein Frankle, personal communication, May 1997)

American Humanics is an alliance of colleges, universities, and nonprofit community service organizations preparing undergraduates for careers with youth and human service organizations. The chair of the FMC social science division recently attended an American Humanics national conference in order to investigate the possibilities of establishing a Humanics program at Florida Memorial College. At a recent faculty meeting, the vice president for academic affairs discussed a survey of incoming FMC freshman that showed many of them had participated in community service programs while in high school. He encouraged the faculty to look for ways of expanding our current community service based offerings to include students from all majors, not just those from the social science division. Hopefully, formal programs like service learning and American Humanics can provide guidelines for expanding the college's long tradition of student service to the community.

Race, Culture, Class, and Religion:
Challenges and Responses

To understand what happened to me . . . one has to drop the simple model of
each ethnic and racial group interacting singly on a one-to-one basis with the
central Anglo American culture. . . . [I]n an ethnically diverse society cultural
models abounded and one had choices and influences far more numerous than
many of the theorizers of assimilation and acculturation recognized.

Lawrence W. Levine (1996)

During the early years of my tenure at Florida Memorial friends would often
ask, "Why are you teaching at Florida Memorial?" I often thought what they
really meant was, "What's a white, middle-class Jew with a Ph.D. from
Wisconsin doing at a black, Christian college?" The simple answer I would give
was, "That's where I was offered a job."

As for dealing with the subtext of the question, I have never felt uncomfortable with people of different races or cultures. I attended an integrated high
school and was active in civil rights issues in college. While a student in
Munich, Germany, under a German government fellowship, I lived in an
international dormitory. I roomed with a German and a Kurd. I also became
friendly with an Indian student. I remember walking with him through Munich's
beautiful English Garden one sunny, spring morning. He asked why all the
Germans had taken their shirts off. I told him they were trying to get a tan. He
looked at me and said, "I was born with a tan and it has never made me very
popular." We both laughed.

I remember a great chess rivalry that developed in the international dorm
between a Turkish medical student and a Greek law student. They played
monumental matches that would begin after dinner and run late into the night.
Then one day they suddenly stopped playing. In fact, they stopped speaking to
each other, because war had broken out on Cyprus between the Greek and
Turkish Cypriots. That experience impressed upon me the potential consequences of ethnocentrism. Whenever I read about the genocide in Bosnia, I
reflect back on my two chess-playing friends in Munich, and I also wonder what
can educational institutions do to insure that a multiracial, multiethnic,
multicultural America will survive into the 21st century. One of the central units
in my Introduction to Social Sciences class at Florida Memorial deals with
culture. Together with readings, lectures, and discussions about ethnocentrism
and cultural relativity, students are required to read a book about a culture or
subculture different from their own and to write a report about the elements of
that culture.

Strange as it may seem, in nearly three decades of teaching at Florida
Memorial, I have only had one significant racial incident. It occurred early in
my career. I was teaching a world civilization course and I had given a student a

failing mid-term report. He came to my office and told me I was failing him because I was a racist. I told him I was failing him because he had failed the mid-term and because he was not coming to class or turning in his assignments. I told him he could still pass the course if he improved his attendance and did his work. He dropped the course.

My tenure at Florida Memorial has allowed me to gain a great deal of insight into African-American history and culture. I have had the opportunity to attend many lectures, recitals, and presentations by outstanding African-American artists and scholars. While being exposed to the high culture of the African-American experience has been intellectually stimulating, I think I would have gotten a lot of that exposure had I been teaching at a large research university. African-American culture has become very popular since the 1960s. What I would not have gained by teaching at a predominantly white college or university was exposure to the popular culture that came from the professional and social contacts I have had with colleagues and students at Florida Memorial. During the past thirty years, I have been to parties, weddings, and funerals of colleagues, students, and neighbors. Attending the wedding of my neighbor's daughter, I met the chair of the FMC board of trustees who was among Florida's first post-reconstruction black federal judges. It turned out that my neighbor's daughter was his niece. His wife and my neighbor were half sisters.

One of the most moving experiences of my life was a funeral service held at the college's religious center for a colleague. I had hired Sarah to teach in the Social Science Division in 1972. She had expanded her duties to include that of foreign student advisor. When she passed away in 1991, the students held the largest memorial service I have ever attended.

I also remember attending a sensitivity training weekend in Overtown; this was an opportunity to spend a weekend in one of Miami's largest black communities. In reality Overtown was a ghetto and analogous to the European Jewish communities of my ancestors where the term originated and first came into widespread use. The Miami Community Action Agency sponsored the weekend in an attempt to allow white faculty teaching in Miami schools and colleges to experience black culture firsthand. I stayed in a motel and visited homes, businesses, and churches. I learned that Overtown had once been an important center of black culture in Miami. Famous black entertainers had lived in the motel where I was staying when Miami Beach was segregated. The Baptist church was still the center of the community, but many of its most affluent members had moved out of the ghetto to the suburbs. They still came to worship and supported the church's community outreach programs and day-care center. While I have lived in an integrated neighborhood since coming to Miami—my neighbors are middle-class, black professionals—I had always been nervous about going into the ghetto areas, especially on my own. After that weekend in Overtown, I have felt more comfortable going into Liberty City and Overtown by myself.

Class and religion have always been more problematic issues with me than race or culture. I come from a working-class background. Neither of my parents went to college and my brother just made it through high school. To graduate from college I had to work hard. If I wanted to make it from the working class to the middle class, I knew I would have to be an overachiever and work twice as hard as students from prep schools. Therefore, while I can identify with some of the concerns, anxieties, and academic deficiencies of first generation college students, I cannot identify with students who do not seem willing to put out the extra effort to make up for past mistakes.

I find myself torn between understanding the source of student problems and pressing for performance rather than excuses. I understand that I was fortunate to have attended elementary and high schools that prepared me academically for college, while a number of the students who come to Florida Memorial do not have adequate academic preparation. They come to college not only without basic reading, writing, and computational skills, but also not knowing how to be effective students. I also understand that I have been fortunate in having a mother who encouraged my academic interests, even though she had not been to college. I know that many of my students come to college because their mothers want them to get ahead. Thus, I feel a strong obligation to help any student who puts forth an effort. I have an equally strong feeling that I should not allow excuses to substitute for performance.

Since my teaching assistant days at Wisconsin, I have had a policy of lowering students' grades if they turn in assignments late. From time to time I would wonder if I were being too inflexible about not accepting excuses. But, I reasoned that part of a student adjusting to the demands of the real world was to learn how to follow rules or suffer the consequences. Moreover, how was I to figure out what was an acceptable excuse and what was an unacceptable excuse. This policy is spelled out on my course syllabus and over the years I have heard dozens of excuses. I would sometimes feel guilty about not accepting a particularly moving or creative plea. However, I felt that fairness required me to treat all students equally: a rule is a rule.

About a dozen years ago an incident occurred that made me more flexible. One of my best students turned in a book report late. She did not offer any excuse for her action. Since she had a perfect attendance record and had never before turned in a late assignment, I reminded her of my penalty for late work and asked why she, of all people, had not gotten the report in on time. She told me that while she was typing her report shooting had broken out in her neighborhood and her mother had told her to get down on the floor. By the time she was allowed to return to her typing, it was too late to finish the report and turn it in the next day. She then apologized for the work being late and said it would not happen again. I decided at that moment that I needed to temper my hard and fast rule with some common sense.

What I hope is that Florida Memorial's first generation college students will not only provide their children with the skills and support needed for them to move to higher academic levels of performance, but also will help the children of the working class and unemployed poor by becoming mentors and tutors to other first generation college students. Moreover, I hope they will not forget what it was like before they became part of the "Black Bourgeoisie."

I realize that prejudice and discrimination exist. I have seen the results of racism and I have experienced the pain of anti-Semitism. Nonetheless, I choose not to see others or myself as helpless victims. I prefer to adhere to the aphorism that states if life provides you with a bowl of cherries, bake a pie, but if life gives you lemons, make lemonade.

Working at a religious institution was my greatest fear when coming to Florida Memorial. I had always attended secular academic institutions and I believed that colleges with a religious affiliation would stifle the free exchange of ideas. As with most stereotypes, my prejudices were proved wrong. While Florida Memorial has strong ties with the Baptist church and students are required to take an introduction to religion course, I have never been asked about my own religious beliefs, nor have I ever had my course content or teaching methods questioned on religious grounds. Moreover, I have found the black church's advocacy of racial and social justice to be similar to my own values. In fact, it was the writings and actions of Dr. Martin Luther King, Jr. that significantly influenced my civil rights activities and my successful petition for a discharge from the military as a conscientious objector.

Innovative Programs: Meeting the Needs of the Underprepared Learner

As I choose to work with younger children, it is important to consider the goals of community psychology: empowerment, emphasis on strengths of client, and respect for diversity . . . my school would be designed so that the students' strengths would be their key . . . conventional teaching was not utilized in this class. All avenues were used [producing] an outstanding learning experience. If this technique is captured by me, my learning center would be a tremendous success.

Mia Brooks (1998)

One of the major contributions of the HBCUs to higher education has been their constant effort to find programs and methods that would meet the needs of underprepared learners who matriculate at open enrollment colleges. During my tenure at Florida Memorial, I have participated in a number of innovative and creative programs. In addition, I helped write a faculty development grant that was funded by the Bush Foundation.

As I have already pointed out, when I first arrived at Florida Memorial, the traditional western civilization program did not meet the needs of the students. The course content and texts were Eurocentric. The reading levels of the texts were well above the mastery of most incoming freshmen, and the course was taught in a large lecture format. Fortunately, during my fourth year at the college, Florida Memorial became part of the 13 College Curriculum Program.

As I mentioned above, the 13 College Curriculum program was an attempt to allow faculty from historically black colleges to meet together at a summer institute to share effective teaching methods and to develop course materials that would meet the learning needs of students matriculating at HBCUs. The program ran for more than a decade. I participated in the final three years of the program. During the three summer institutes I met faculty and staff who expanded my understanding of effective teaching. I also had the opportunity to build an integrated social science curriculum that included materials that focused on African-American history and culture. As I began teaching the broader concepts of psychology, sociology, anthropology, political science, and economics, I found it easier to relate them to the interests and experiences of my students. Although the experiences of the 13 College Curriculum program strengthened and broadened my teaching skills, I still found myself unable to meet the needs of students who lacked basic learning skills.

The introduction of the text *Becoming a Master Student* into the freshman core curriculum has aided me by providing all freshmen with a solid foundation on how to develop and master the skills needed to become an effective learner. The course materials address all of the major adjustments students need to make when coming to college. The information is particularly useful for first generation college students with poor study habits and basic skill deficiencies. The material is presented in an interactive manner that requires students to actively practice what they learn. Students explore such valuable information as different learning styles, how to manage their time effectively, and how to enhance their memory and critical thinking skills. In addition, students practice methods for improving their reading, writing, and test-taking skills. The course also examines issues of diversity and social relationships. This last element of the course is important because while the majority of students at Florida Memorial are African American, the college enrolls large numbers of blacks from a variety of Caribbean cultures including the Bahamas, Jamaica, Trinidad, and Haiti. In addition, Florida Memorial has a sizable number of Hispanic students, primarily in its outreach centers.

In addition to the aforementioned programs, the college has received funding for two major faculty development efforts from the Lilly and Bush Foundations. Under the current Lilly grant faculty meet to share teaching and learning methods that work in our classrooms. Faculty may apply for grants to develop projects that enhance the teaching and learning process. Priority is given to cross-discipline projects that involve faculty teams teaching in the core curriculum and in developmental education. Moreover, funds are available that allow faculty to present results of their projects at professional conferences on teaching and learning.

Nearly a decade ago I was involved in writing a faculty development proposal for the Bush Foundation. The proposal was funded and I became the program director. Over the course of several years the Bush Faculty Development Program at Florida Memorial supported a number of campus-wide reading, writing, and computing activities across the curriculum workshops. In addition, the grant supported divisional conferences that allowed faculty to have workshops specifically related to their academic disciplines. One of the highlights of the Bush proposal was the creation of funds for mini-grants that provided faculty funding for individual projects, including the funding of three issues of a faculty academic review that allowed faculty to publish research related to both disciplinary scholarship and innovative teaching methods. To maximize faculty participation, grant awards were made by a twelve-person steering committee that had representatives from all the academic divisions of the college.

Technological Change: Director of Academic Computing

> I'm eager to learn more about this modest new trend toward . . . Centers for Teaching and Learning—in which the resources of librarians, technologists, and faculty development specialists are combined and focused.
>
> Steve Gilbert (1998, April)

One of the challenges of working at a private HBCU is limited resources. Initially, I was frustrated by the insufficient library holdings that limited my research. As my interests shifted more from specialized scholarly pursuits to more general disciplinary content and effective teaching techniques, I found the library had more to offer; however, its holdings were still insufficient. I began to look for ways of overcoming the library's limitations. The growth of the Internet offered a possible solution. While pursuing my master's degree in education, I opened a dial-up account with the University of Miami and began to learn how to search for information on-line. In the early days, there were no graphical user interfaces and it was difficult to find materials. As I struggled with the arcane UNIX and VMS text based user interfaces, I realized the Internet offered a way of leveling the academic playing field for small, resources starved colleges such as Florida Memorial. Unfortunately, Florida Memorial lacked the computing capabilities to take advantage of the Internet's potential. About a decade ago we got a new president who had worked in the North Carolina Department of Education and had strong contacts with IBM. He understood the potential of computing and wanted Florida Memorial to move forward technologically. Since he knew that I had a strong interest in the academic uses of computing, he asked me to take on the role of director of academic computing.

During the past decade, Florida Memorial has developed a comprehensive technological base. Under our current vice president for academic affairs we have built a campus-wide high speed T-1 connection to the Internet. All faculty members have computers at their desks and students have access to the Internet via terminals in the library, in their dorms, and in several computer labs around the campus. Faculty and students have e-mail accounts that provide them with access to colleagues around the world. All students are required to take an introduction to computing class, and for the past three years I have been conducting hands-on workshops and training sessions to help faculty develop methods for incorporating the resources of the World Wide Web into their classroom teaching.

Networking: Creating an HBCU
Faculty Development Network

The HBCU Faculty Development Network is . . . committed to promoting effective teaching and student learning through a variety of collaborative activities that focus on faculty enhancement. These collaborative activities are designed to make a connection between teaching, research and service.

HBCU Faculty Development Network Mission Statement (1997)

One of the demands of working at a small HBCU is the need to wear many hats. In my case, along with my teaching duties, I have been the chair of the Social Sciences Division, project director for the Bush Faculty Development Grant and director of academic computing. These duties have always been in addition to my teaching responsibilities. While my heavy teaching and administrative duties have limited my time for research, they have often provided opportunities for growth that I might not have had if I had been narrowly focused on specialized research. One example of this was the opportunity I had to help found the HBCU Faculty Development Network. The HBCU Faculty Development Network is a network of historically black colleges and universities dedicated to the sharing and dissemination of innovative instructional techniques. It sponsors an annual symposium that brings together representatives from sister HBCUs and other interested parties for the purpose of sharing methods used to advance the teaching and learning process. It also encourages collaborative efforts between HBCUs, including the sharing of teaching innovations and the writing of proposals for outside funding. I have been a member of the Network Steering Committee since the Network's founding. Presentations featured at the annual

HBCU symposium include: collaborative models, teaching and learning styles, curriculum design and revision, instructional strategies and techniques, diversity and globalization, learning across the curriculum, educational technology, evaluation and assessment of learning, outcome based assessment, and community service/ service learning. For additional information on the HBCU Network and its annual conference visit its web site at http://www.fmc.edu/ ~silvergl/Hbcu/.

The ability to network with colleagues from sister HBCUs has been one of the most rewarding aspects of my tenure at Florida Memorial. Given the limited resources of small, private HBCUs, it is often difficult to find the stimulation and support needed to deal with the academic and administrative challenges and pressures one faces on a daily basis. The HBCU network provides rich sources of intellectual stimulation and support through its annual conference and ongoing exchanges via e-mail.

Administrative Challenges: Autocratic Leadership to Shared Governance

> There are two images or theories of how to lead. In the first . . . people are seen as having little ambition, a reluctance to work, and a desire to avoid responsibility . . . . The leader operating under these conditions must motivate, organize, control and coerce . . . . Another theory . . . holds that people are motivated by a hierarchy of needs . . . . Each of us has a desire to use our potential, to have responsibility, to actualize ourselves . . . the leader creates challenge and an opportunity for subordinates to use their abilities to a greater extent.
>
> Rodney W. Napier and Matti K. Gershendfeld (1993)

My greatest challenge during my first two decades at Florida Memorial was creatively engaging what I perceived to be the autocratic leadership style of the college's presidents. As a product of the 1960s I had been raised on a strong diet of autonomous behavior. Adjusting to an environment where decisions were made from the top down was difficult for me. For most of the 1970s and 1980s the faculty at Florida Memorial had no real voice in the governance of the college. From time to time a faculty senate would be constituted in order to pass the visits of a Southern Association of Colleges and Schools (SACS) accreditation team, but in reality faculty had little or no say in the governance of the college. The college had no tenure or sabbatical programs. Faculty were often required to teach five courses per semester and there were no limits on class size, even in the freshmen programs. There was no standardized salary scale. The board of trustees was predominantly handpicked supporters of the president. Even more frustrating than these difficult conditions of employment was the marginalization of faculty suggestions for the improvement of the teaching and learning environment at FMC. All of this contributed to significant faculty turnover and to a great deal of apathy and cynicism among remaining faculty members. Perhaps the most critical clash between faculty and administration came when the college president fired faculty from an entire division without the concurrence of the division chair. This unilateral decision led to a unionization movement that resulted in the creation of a faculty union affiliated with the National Education Association in the 1980s. The administration was eventually able to decertify the union. However, during the years of the union's existence, many of the faculty were not only able to have their voices heard for the first time at Florida Memorial, but they were able to have some substantive changes adopted by the college's administration.

I thought that the authoritarian leadership style might be unique to Florida Memorial, but my contacts and discussions with colleagues from sister HBCUs led me to understand that similar administrative structures were common to many HBCUs. While common to many HBCUs, the power struggle between administration and faculty was not unique to HBCUs. It also existed at predominantly white institutions, particularly at the community colleges and newer four-year colleges that emerged in the 1970s and 1980s in Florida. I had the opportunity to learn more about these power struggles when I served as the Florida Independent Colleges representative to the steering committee of the United Faculty of Florida National Education Association between 1986-1988. Presidents at the Florida community colleges and newly created four-year colleges opposed the unionization movement that threatened their power and authority. At United Faculty of Florida steering committee meetings we shared tales of faculty grievances, often viewed as threats by college presidents, as we collectively sought to find ways to empower faculty at our respective colleges.

Fortunately, in the 1990s college presidents have adopted more democratic, collegial styles of governance at Florida Memorial and many sister HBCUs. In a recent discussion with a scholar of higher education about why this shift from an adversarial to a collegial relationship has occurred, he suggested that in the past many presidents of private HBCUs were fighting for the survival of their institutions. Perhaps they perceived faculty attempts at seeking more power as yet another threat to their colleges' survival. I know that there were many months during the 1970s when the college could not meet the payroll and had to be bailed out by borrowing and donations. Raising money to keep the college's doors open was almost the singular pursuit of the college's president. I suspect having to deal with the demands of a critical faculty only added to the problems of leadership. A colleague, who had been on the faculty union bargaining committee with me, recently reminded me that during the 1970s and 1980s many outside forces hostile to the survival of HBCUs tried to use internal college conflicts as a sign that administrators at HBCUs were not competent at maintaining viable academic institutions. In fact, many hostile critics of HBCUs used internal conflicts as a reason for trying to close or integrate them with established predominantly white colleges and universities that did not share the historic mission or expertise of HBCUs. During this decade the faculty has developed a more collegial relationship with the present administration that has encouraged faculty to take an active part in contributing to the governance of the college. Today, it is easier, given our current sound fiscal situation, for the administration to make long range projections that include "wish list" inputs from the faculty. It is challenging and rewarding to participate in the growth and development of Florida Memorial. In the past decade I have begun to see the college move toward the academic potential I first saw nearly thirty years ago.

As I reflect about why I have remained at Florida Memorial, I think it was my desire to teach. Most of the job offers I had would have moved me out of the classroom into research. I was also fortunate enough to work with some very talented and dedicated colleagues who offered me support when my spirits were flagging. The missing ingredient was a progressive, academically oriented administration that would empower faculty to meet the academic and social needs of the students. The current administration seems oriented in that direction, and I feel optimistic that increased student learning will be the main beneficiary of faculty and administration cooperation.

References

Brazzell, J.C. (1996). Diversification of postsecondary institutions. In S.R. Komives, D.B. Woodard, Jr., & Associates (eds.). *Student services: A handbook for the profession*, third edition (pp.43-63). San Francisco: Jossey-Bass Publishers, Inc.

Brooks, M. (1998). Excerpt from student examination at Florida Memorial College, Miami, Florida.

Carnegie Commission on Higher Education (1972). *Reform on campus: Changing students, changing academic programs.* New York: McGraw-Hill.

Ellis, D. (1994). *Becoming a master student.* Boston: Houghton Mifflin.

Frost, R. (1928). The road not taken. *Selected poems.* New York: Henry Holt and Company.

Gates, H.L., & C. West (1996). *The future of the race.* New York: Vintage Books.

Gilbert, S. (1998). Promotions and tenure and institutional change at IUPUI. In *AAHESGIT #78* [On-line]. Available: gopher://list.cren.net:70/OR56288-65200-/archives/aahesgit/log9804

HBCU Faculty Development Network (1997). *Mission statement* [On-line]. Available: *http://lions.fmc.edu/~silvergl/Hbcu/hbcumission.html*

Hughes, L. (1979). Mother to son. *Selected poems of Langston Hughes.* New York: Alfred A. Knopf.

Levine, L. (1996). *The opening of the American mind: Canons, culture and history.* Boston: Beacon Press.

Napier, R.W., & M.K. Gershendfeld (1993). *Groups theory and experience.* Boston: Houghton Mifflin Company.

Shinnie, Margaret (1966). *Ancient African kingdoms.* New York: St. Martin's Press.

Chapter 10 _____

Taking up a Professorial Line at FAMU

Frederick P. Frank

Hey, You! Yeah, I Mean You!

I was walking across the center of the Florida A&M University (FAMU) campus—the quad—feeling good. The scene was pleasing. The white light of the late morning sun reflected off the buildings, greenery, and people. On that quiet morning amidst historic buildings, many named after great African Americans, with people going to and from class, I was aware that the quad at FAM (as FAMU is called by those of us who call this place home) is a place not only of great beauty but of great tradition. It was early summer—a very warm day—a day to count one's blessings. There were lots of reasons for me to be proud to be here. I had been at FAM a year and a half. To my mind, I was lucky to be doing work in an important program with students who deserved my best efforts. I had worked at more prominent universities prior to coming to FAM, but by my personal standards, FAM has the most noteworthy record of achievement by far. From all I could read, FAM had accomplished more with less resources than most institutions of higher education could possibly have done. During its century of achievement, FAM had survived (listing from bad-to-worse) benign neglect, deliberate neglect, and pernicious attack, sometimes all at the same time, by all manner of persons for all manner of reasons. These sometimes difficult circumstances for FAM had been and are still rooted mostly in the negative effects of the dominant white culture's confusion about race. There is a very long complicated story to the "Agricultural and Mechanical" in FAM's name. And in the midst of this constant struggle, FAM had grown to become one of the United States' distinguished institutions of higher education and one of the country's most distinguished historically black colleges and universities (HBCUs). It seems to me, looking at the beauty of this campus, that anyone who understands higher education in the U.S. and who possesses any sense of generosity whatsoever could see that over the century FAM, like so many HBCUs, had delivered ten dollars worth of graduates for every six dollars of budget. The institution had kept to a high level of productivity primarily by following three paths: (1) underpaying faculty and staff, (2) overworking and underinvesting in faculty, and (3) deferring maintenance on campus infra- structure and buildings. Even today, faculty at public HBCUs are often paid significantly less than faculty at other public institutions and carry a higher teaching load to help make ends meet—all to the purpose of helping as many young people as possible to acquire a college education. Even today, FAM's capital facilities are underdeveloped. In recent years the most fuss has been about inadequate technology infrastructure and equipment, but FAM also (and most HBCUs) needs roofs and plumbing, more dorms, labs, and teaching space. FAM has an awesome record of service to young people, but it comes as no surprise that these compromises show from time to time as reduced scholarly productivity and structural inefficiency. A century long tradition, born of desperate necessity, of robbing Peter to pay Paul has its long term costs; even those who are committed to a noble cause get tired. At some point they return to being ordinary mortals and must cope with the everyday reality of being overworked.

In the midst of this reverie and reflection, my bubble of equanimity was suddenly and unpleasantly burst. She, the source of my instant disquietude, was approaching me from the other direction—her eyes flashing an "anger-laser" that I was fearful from the very first instant was aimed directly and only at me. I was held captive by her anger as she approached me—partly by the surprise of it and partly because there was no appropriate response possible. I could see her face very clearly as she walked toward me into that late morning sun. Despite my best hopes that she would be flashing only a momentary anger-laser and that she would abandon it when she had gotten my attention, she persisted as she came closer. Responding as though hypnotized by her anger-laser, I behaved like an animal caught in the headlights of an oncoming car, confused and compelled to maintain visual contact with the light.

As we approach each other, I am acutely aware of the contrasts between us—contrasts born of everyday life but made more important by the setting—

ordinary stuff turned into sharp-edged differences in the face of her anger. No question. In this HBCU setting, at this moment, the contrasts between us are significant. She is black; I am white. She is tall, regal, a striking physical presence who would be noticed and admired in any crowd; I am short, male, overweight, and easily lost in any crowd. She is young, in her early twenties. Her life is mostly ahead; I am fifty-nine with a life mostly spent. She is as undaunted by me as we approach each other as I am daunted by her high dudgeon. I don't want this to happen. She is determined to make it happen. Our steps bring us closer to each other's intimate space as must happen when people pass in public. But now the proximity is charged with additional meaning. At this distance she is close enough to hit me. I don't think she will do that. Now at even closer range, her eyes continue to shoot an "anger-laser" directly at me and the sense of force increases. Her laser hits my chest like a powerful fist—poom! I almost stop walking forward from the force of her look, but I catch myself beginning to hesitate and urge myself to keep on walking lest my stopping in mid-stride be perceived as aggression. I say "Hello" as she comes within easy earshot and smile my best, pleasant, nonintrusive "I don't want to be in your face" smile. She did not look away, she did not smile back, she did not speak, and she did not withdraw one photon of power from her anger-laser. I remained ensnared in the grip of her look even though I looked away for those last few feet. With her anger-laser easily outshining the white, early summer sun, we are now parallel to each other. For an instant I also feel the power of her personal energy field. Finally, finally, we pass each other. The brief but commanding episode is over. I do not turn around. I do not believe she engaged once she had passed me by. She had done her best to express her anger. She had succeeded. I would remember.

"It Could Be a Good Thing," said Dr. Pangloss

It had happened to me before at FAM. Each time it happened to me, I felt targeted and traumatized. I was pushed, squeezed, and pummeled down into a psychological place where self-doubt and questions about my purpose and role here held sway. Despite these episodes, my basic sense of equanimity prevailed because I had some confidence that I belonged here at FAM, and because I believe that the anger-lasers flashed my way at FAM are partly right.

The reasons why that young woman was at least partly right and why I am partly right, too, to be here at FAM taking up a professorial line are important to me. These reasons, I believe, are worthy of further explication. In part, I present a defense of who I am and why I am here. I don't think I am particularly unique but I make no pretense of speaking for anyone but myself. I suppose I will hear from those who read this piece about how unique I am or am not.

There are always good things to be gained from any experience. If nothing else, my own personal awareness of what it means to be targeted was renewed. I had been targeted before in my life but my memory of the experiences had paled. At FAM I was learning again, in a more complete measure, what it meant to be targeted for reasons unspecified, except for race. I suppose there is a very small possibility that I was being targeted at FAM because I am a male, or because I am short, but I don't think so. I have been targeted because I am a white guy. No matter how unprepossessing I may appear in most settings, I do stand out on this campus. I have learned anew that the pain of being targeted takes an edge when there is unfairness in it. Oh, sure, I've been around long enough, and I'm experienced enough to have a resilient personal framework with which to receive misplaced anger, but it still hurts. I have a rekindled sense of what happens to a precious minority child who is treated with disrespect early and often.

To put another good face on it, it is a good thing for me to more fully understand what it feels like to be targeted in this way because I can identify more easily with those who are angry enough to target me. To start, I believe they are good at it because it has been so often done to them; they know the laser look from deep personal experience. I believe that I spend time with people every day at FAM who have been traumatized by anger-lasers, no, hate-lasers, cast at them by white people on a far greater number of occasions than could possibly have happened to me. I know, too, that I am probably targeted less often at FAM than a young black person would be targeted on a predominantly white campus, especially a black male. In that sense, even my updated "in-my-gut," earthy sense of what it means to be targeted is still a mere shadow of the trauma surely experienced by those who target me here.

In a larger context, these difficult incidents constitute an exception to my overall feeling of well-being at FAM. For the most part, I have been welcomed and accepted with generosity and friendship by colleagues, students, and workers who have treated me with courtesy and respect. In comparison, I well remember that black doctoral students at Northern Illinois University, located in DeKalb, Illinois, and sixty miles due west of Chicago, where I spent twenty-one years as a professor, would often be hesitant to come on campus. Black students would ask to meet with me for tutorials in a restaurant off-campus rather than at my campus office to avoid the ugly treatment they knew could happen on campus. All this occurred at an institution that, from all I could see, loudly, piously, and continually declared itself free of institutional racism. And even then, having retreated to a public restaurant to minimize mistreatment, we were sometimes not served promptly by the wait-persons in small town, mostly white, DeKalb. Later I learned to always ask individual black students where they preferred to meet rather than put the onus on them to request an off-campus venue for a meeting. Invariably, they knew where to meet, where they would be treated with respect. And during the brief time I worked as a department chair at Georgia State University in downtown Atlanta, Georgia, in the mid-nineties, I was acutely aware that our black students (and black faculty) were routinely treated badly by other faculty and staff. At Georgia State University, for instance, two decades of affirmative action had produced a trifling twenty-nine black faculty members in tenure lines out of eight hundred lines at the university. Yet, the white faculty expressed continued frustration with the oppressive nature of affirmative action as though affirmative action was actually working—in my opinion, an effort to create a faux cause célèbre by those who sought to minimize the number of minority persons in academe. I know from personal experience, then, that it is not uncommon for black students to be treated badly by white faculty and staff on predominantly white campuses. I also know from personal experience that those who speak up about those awful practices bring down the wrath of frightened, belligerent, and bellicose spokespersons for the status quo. I've been there.

Maybe it served an important positive purpose for that proud young woman to radiate hostility toward me, the job stealer, the white guy who doesn't fit, the symbol of oppression. Maybe on this campus, where her behavior would be endorsed by some and protected by all, being free to be enraged at me and to be so openly expressive about it could be developmental—a release that healed some hurt or righted some wrong. Maybe being able to declare her rage at me with relative impunity, to "go after" the outnumbered, unprepossessing, "surely not gonna fight back, out of his element, plump, short white guy in a power outfit on a black campus" was not only a good thing for her, but a good thing for others to witness. Maybe when I received her anger-laser, she was discharging a great deal of anger she had built up and then stored over an extended period of time—be it an hour, a day, a week, a month, or a lifetime. This could be a healthy thing. When she sent that rage out like a blast—poom!—she completed a process of personal affirmation.

I fully believe that for every angry glare she has proffered, she has received ten such glares herself on prior occasions. What's more, I believe that those occasions when she was the recipient of reciprocal anger-lasers were far more potentially dangerous for her than this particular occasion was for me. It doesn't cost me all that much to receive the blow—maybe it costs me less to receive it that it costs her to emit it. Doing hurt is a very strenuous thing for people who are otherwise caring individuals.

But I remember the hurt. And I remember the other times this has happened, too, because, trauma sometimes leaves an indelible mark. One remembers each and every time one is targeted, and one is never absolutely sure when it will be called into consciousness to fuel an ungenerous purpose. Maybe this chapter is one of those occasions for me. I wondered how many of those laser exchanges had been built up in the aggregate capacitors of FAM's family. There would be good reason for lots and lots of anger to have been stored up here. The amazing thing to me is how few people display the anger they hold inside. Even more amazing and instructive to me is how many good and wise people at FAM have shed the anger and reached a point of equanimity about the patterned unfairness they have experienced in their lives. Almost everyone here has a friend or loved one who has been damaged or destroyed by the norms of the majority culture and then blamed for their failure to "measure-up" to the challenge.

Another trigger to the anger-laser that morning might have been my dress. I had discovered on past occasions that a white guy all "done up" in formal clothing tended to induce more anger on the FAM campus than my more typical jeans and sport shirt. That morning I was "done up" in a properly professorial "grade-six" dark suit, white shirt and tie and wing tips—a "power person" uniform. I theorize that the "power outfit" tends to flag me as a person taking a high status job in a world that rations high status jobs to black people. As a result, I had learned to avoid wearing power clothing on campus. I didn't mind dressing down because I am inclined to be an informal person anyway and actually prefer more casual clothing. I simply told my professorial colleagues who might interpret my casual dress as inappropriate, or even disrespectful, that I had gained a lot of weight of late and my good clothes fit a person twenty pounds lighter.

I was on my way to a meeting of faculty at the faculty dining room across the quad from the College of Education building. Formal dress was de rigueur. That's how I happened to be out there that day in what I knew to be my "higher-risk" outfit, the power outfit, the one that says, "I am somebody important on this campus." If that young woman was keying to that aspect of "me," she was mostly right. It is very clear to me in ways I did not fully understand before I joined the family at FAM. FAM is not just a place of solace and excellence for black students and faculty; it is a sanctioned repository of good jobs to the black community. From grounds keepers to president, FAM is a place where each and every job is a blessing and is deeply cherished. Each job is a resource to be guarded and appreciated—doled out and schemed for with all the care and messy complications typically attached to conserving a scarce and valued resource. I knew this on an intellectual basis when I arrived but I know it differently now. For many here at FAM, there is no apology for nor hesitation about fighting for, guarding, shepherding, or protecting each and every job. Lives are at stake. Children, parents, and family are to be cared for. Individual actions based on self-interest have an appropriately respected place among those whose lives have been marginalized by the consequences of inequity. Anger at the white guy taking a "black job" has some genesis in bitter experience. Not only are good jobs routinely given to the "non-black" candidate regardless of qualifications but, to recall the sometimes puerile environment at Georgia State, the twenty-nine courageous black faculty out of eight hundred tenured professors there were often treated as undeserving interlopers—believe it or not—treated as black persons who were taking "white" jobs. Pay back also has an honored history among those who have been treated badly.

Nevertheless, the costs to the black community of my holding this position are real. I have taken a senior professorship here at an HBCU. These are rare and important positions. I would guess that the position I hold is one of less than seventy-five in the entire country. More importantly, I have come here to help start a brand new, very important, high profile, controversial program that is meeting a repressed need for advanced training in educational leadership in the educational enterprise.

Like that young woman who had stored up her anger and whose quick trigger stayed ready to fire, all those who had stored up anger would be at least partly right if they pounded me with a laser blast. From males and females, young and old, students, faculty, and university support people there came an infrequent but noted stream of anger-lasers as I worked on campus. Again, this happened significantly more often when I was dressed up than when I was dressed down. Expressions of undifferentiated anger toward me as a white guy didn't always come from peoples' eyes alone. I had heard anger-lasers in the form of words that amounted to almost the same thing. From time to time I have heard the following from faculty:

"You want to turn FAM into a 'white school,'" or

"There's no way you can understand FAM's culture."

As a way to tell me that I had spoken as though I belonged at FAM when it was not welcomed, I've heard, "Why are you speaking up for FAM? Is it that we pay you?" Sometimes when these verbal weapons are employed to discount my input to FAM, especially when nineteen out of twenty reasonable persons would assess my input as good sense for FAM or for any graduate program anywhere, I am momentarily stupefied and silent—a response would be as inappropriate and inadequate as words would have been to the young anger-laser woman on campus. Importantly, I find these verbal lasers from faculty more difficult to be generous about than the comparatively innocent anger of a student walking across the quad.

What I Bring Could Be Okay

The details of my life don't matter much to those who are bold enough to act on their anger. That the details of my life that might tend to attenuate their anger doesn't matter all that much when these incidents occur. The instance of confrontation is not the time to shout out a defense of who I am and why I am here and why, on balance, I have a contribution to make that is positive. But who I am and why I am here does matter. I am grateful to be here at FAM, and I am grateful for this opportunity to tell my story. I wouldn't expect that my story will stop "the anger that is a good bit right." That is not necessary for me to be able to make my contribution here and be appreciated. I am contributing and I am appreciated.

I have a lot in common with the anger in that young woman and in all those who find my presence at FAM discomforting on its face. There was a time in my life when my own capacitors had stored a good bit of rage, too. And some of the reasons for the anger in my life resemble those of my colleagues here at FAM. The hurt I brought to my adult life is under better control now than it was when I was younger, but it is not gone. I have salvaged a productive life from a shaky, long-odds beginning, and still the undifferentiated anger, the legacy of anger from a dangerous childhood, is there to be drawn on for comfort and for expressive satisfaction. I know how to shoot the anger-laser, too. These days a lot of my anger has been assuaged by a congenial life, but I can still bring the anger to the surface in a flash when I work on physical projects that require repair of some sort. To my shame, it is a tic I may never be able to fix. Most of the time I am alone when this happens, and this fact minimizes the damage to others. Of course, the tone of this piece, the very inclination to write it, to engage in these issues, is based in those old hurts somehow—a much disguised and "wrapped up in a lot of words" anger-laser of my own.

But there is one aspect of my life that the young woman and I and all those who find my presence here discomforting do not have in common. And it is a very, very, big difference. I'm a white guy who has had far more numerous and more generous chances to recover from a childhood that was not always kind. I have less good reason to give vent to stored but unexpressed anger than many people I meet here at FAM because I have had so many opportunities to recover from the imprudence of others. While I worked like a Trojan to earn my way in this life, I, nevertheless, assert that a good measure of my success as an educator is the result of a constant, deep, and abiding affirmative action for white males. For all of us white guys who are honest enough to admit it, we know in our heart that we have been blessed by birth to have had options not available to those who are not white and not male. This sounds a bit obvious once one faces up to it, but I meet white males every day who don't have a clue (or pretend they don't have a clue) about how much they have benefited from privilege they didn't earn. Further, not only don't they know it, they get fightin' mad as soon as they hear the idea. I've gotten my share of rage-lasers from those guys—and those white guys who get fightin' mad at any question about their right to be who they are—those white males who have always had it their way—are often dangerous when they are challenged. In short, I believe that I've gotten lots of breaks just by showing up. I try to be grateful.

My choice to come to FAM was not philanthropy. I was committed to the idea of doing good work in the new doctoral degree program at FAM, and I was excited about the chance to work with wonderful students, but coming here served my personal as well as my professional interests. I wanted to get back to full-time teaching after years of working as a department level university administrator. Further, I wanted to get warm and stay warm somewhere in the sun belt near the water after living my entire adult life in cold climates away from the sea. From the day I left Bayonne, New Jersey, as a teenager to attend Syracuse University I had wanted to return to a warm coast. I had moved from Syracuse to Buffalo, New York, to do doctoral work, and then to Columbus, Ohio, to work at Ohio State University, and then to DeKalb, Illinois, to work at Northern Illinois University. Except for Columbus, Ohio, these were pretty cold places. I had moved from DeKalb, Illinois, to Atlanta, Georgia, to work as a department chair at Georgia State University, in part, to get warm.

My move from Georgia State University (GSU) to FAM was a timely opportunity for me because I didn't like the environment at GSU. At Georgia State, I found that my personal values about equity, access, and developmental instruction in graduate education were in direct conflict with the prevailing norms (not majority norms) of those who controlled the College of Education. There, as it was explained to me, I was the northern guy who didn't understand the South. I was having a hard time, I was told, accepting the intricacies of the "plantation" style of management, and until I did understand it, I couldn't be successful in the South. There I heard, "You guys from up north just don't understand the South," as a defense of practices that, to me, were egregiously stupid, dysfunctional—even venal. I quickly reached a point where I could not abide one more conversation held together by a theme I can only approximately translate as "us white guys, the intended leaders in this world, need to stick together so 'they' don't take over in our place." To me, some of the folks at the College of Education at Georgia State University were clinging to the nineteen sixties with all the passion endemic to those who are terrorized by changes in the status quo. In my opinion, the harm being done to young people, especially minority persons, was inappropriate and indefensible. I saw abundant living proof of the "rigged game" that works against minority students and that, according to Feagin and Sikes (1994), inhibits their success at white majority institutions like GSU. At GSU these abuses were often proclaimed noisily as courageous acts of those whose mission it is to maintain quality. I got out of there as quickly as I possibly could. I stayed less than two years. They were as glad to see me go as I was glad to leave. So, coming to FAM served a lot of purposes for me. I was glad to get the offer to come to FAM.

I bring a lot to the table, and I am serious about doing good work at FAM. I arrived here in January 1997, to fill one of four new professorial slots created to staff a new Ph.D. program in educational leadership, a program that has been assigned to FAM about fifteen years late. I have had the opportunity to teach at five universities in graduate programs in educational administration, a field that in more recent times tends to be called "educational leadership." Except for being a white guy, or, ironically, from time to time *because I am a white guy* (while this is not an important aspect of the actual work I am capable of doing here, it is sometimes a good thing for the program to trot out a white guy for appearances) I am a good fit at FAM. I bring the experience of almost thirty years of graduate level instruction in doctoral institutions, twelve years of which have been associated with a "cohort teaching model" (technically speaking, based on a "constructivist" instructional model), one of the cornerstones of the new Ph.D. in educational leadership at FAM. I've directed lots of doctoral dissertations to completion. I can trot out a weighty vitae, to attest in academic parlance to a long productive career as researcher, scholar, and effective, kindly teacher. I come from a culturally diverse childhood. I have taught at the K-12 and university levels in culturally diverse settings. I have done well at it. My credentials and again, ironically, "diversity" bring additional legitimacy to the staffing profile in the new program. My work with four doctoral programs prior to my arrival at FAM brings a breadth of experience important to an institution with little experience in doctoral level instruction and to a college of education with no experience at it. I'm no star, but I know my beans. I've been consistently productive, and I have national and international connections.

In a complicated set of multilayered practicalities, sensitivities, and passions about access among minority scholars to senior professorships, it is important that I will not keep this job long—probably no longer than four or five years. Not everyone, especially a senior black professor of educational leadership, would have been willing to risk coming to FAM in January of 1997 to staff a program not fully approved by the Florida Board of Regents. I found the notion of helping start a new program very intriguing and was pleased to take a chance on a new program that was still a bit of "blue sky" at the time I arrived here.

Even though the new Ph.D. program at FAM had not received final approval from the Florida Board of Regents, and FAM administrators could not guarantee that the program would be implemented, I decided to join the effort. At the time I signed on, the job might not have lasted more than six months. Though leaders at FAM believed that final approval for the new program would be given in the spring of 1997 with enough time to plan for the beginning of the program, final program approval was given by the Board of Regents just a few weeks before the first group of students was to begin classes. This circumstance would have been very, very difficult for a person worried about moving to Tallahassee, Florida, with a family in tow.

In contrast to the hectic events of the spring and summer of 1997, I believe that when I depart in a few years there will be a successful, real Ph.D. program in place, a program with a track record and a program that will not be at risk from the smoke of Florida educational and racial politics as was the FAM Law School in the not too distant past. If I were a successful black senior professor at, say, the Ohio State University, and I had fought my way through that system to be a tenured associate professor, I would be far more likely to be interested in the position at FAM once the program is in place and is stable. This is a circumstance that will allow FAM to more successfully recruit a senior professor upon my departure.

Two Real Issues

There is a legitimate question about the relevance of what I have to offer students at FAM. I think I do have plenty to offer but this assertion is not without qualification. To my mind, the central issues are about the culturally entailed nature of the content of the field of educational leadership and teaching in cross-cultural settings. Being a white professor of educational leadership at a HBCU mixes into a potentially dysfunctional soup.

The field of educational leadership is a culturally entailed field in that teaching people to run schools cannot be divorced from the messiness of everyday life nor the norms of society. Durkheim (1956) posits that the focus of education is to produce each society's image of the ideal person and that education is "the means by which it secures, in the children, the essential conditions of its own existence" (p.28). In the confusion about the "ideal person," schools reflect every vice, every bit of glory, and every bit of meanness that resides in our society at large. If society is confused about equity, the schools reflect that confusion. If society is confused about child rearing, the schools will reflect that confusion. If society is confused about notions of discipline and compliance in children, the schools will reflect that confusion. If society is confused about whether to nurture or exploit some of its children or even all of its children, the schools will reflect that confusion. Societal confusions about the purposes of schooling abound. In my view, teaching people about leadership in our schools must be mostly about equity, access, fairness, child development and, to some degree, an element of outrage that so many children are not prospering. I teach people how to run schools, how to fix schools, how to make them work better for black kids, how to make them more fair for black kids, and how to make school environments that nurture black children to full flower rather than setting out, using the words of the old South that still have powerful currency, to keep them in their place.

Teaching about educational leadership, therefore, is not about doing pristine science, a clean process disconnected in large measure from the complexities of our social world, as in, for example, teaching chemistry or engineering. There are social aspects to all graduate instruction but in educational leadership the weight of instruction centers on coping with social meaning as compared to fields like chemistry and engineering where the weight of instruction would tend to be more on content mastery and science. There is plenty of science to cover at the graduate level in educational leadership and instruction is richly embedded in it, but a great deal of the clinical applications of that content merge into belief systems and coping with everyday life.

Accountability for my work as a professor is also different. In engineering and chemistry, the social aspect of my work would focus more on fairness and respect to students in my classes. In teaching educational leadership, accountability is based not only on expressing fairness and respect during the process of instruction, but also in expressing fairness and respect to the children in the schools represented by graduate students in the program. There is a particular and proper expectation that a professor at FAM will clearly acknowledge that black children, by and large, have not been treated well, nor fared well in our nation's public schools and it is not their fault. I do bring this personal and professional platform to my work and try to act on that platform. Because this work is so socially entailed, one could argue that in a field like educational leadership FAM takes a special chance with bringing me here.

Amidst my general acceptance at FAM, some graduate students in classes I have taught since I have arrived have openly expressed cynicism at my ability to teach meaningful things here. Remarks I have heard are:

"Are you the savior we've heard was coming?"

"Are you going to teach us 'country club' school administration?"

"I just don't like white people but you're okay!"

A different face on these complex expectations is heard in:

"I was surprised that I enjoyed your course."

"I wasn't expecting much from you when I came into this course but you surprised me with the relevance of what you taught."

"You don't talk like a white person!"

"I have never talked with a white person who says the things you do!"

I believe these remarks to be both gentle compliments and rituals of acceptance, but such words reveal negative expectations at the onset. In these many ways is the societally entailed nature of work in educational leadership revealed. In my judgment, my job at FAM is far more important than that young woman knew at the time I made her so angry. Had she known the details of my work, the culturally entailed nature of my work here, she might have been even more angry and perhaps more justified.

About teaching in partial or potentially cross-cultural situations, the brilliant Lisa Delpit (1995) in her book *Other People's Children: Cultural Conflict in the Classroom*, holds that in order to teach effectively we must see the children we teach as our own children. Only then is the multilayered caring released that fuels good teaching in ways that the kids understand and respond to. Delpit (1995) says that when we decide that the children in our care are "other people's children" we are free to pull back from the kind of total commitment to their success that is the bedrock of the relationship that supports teaching and learning (in school or out). When children sense that they are somehow one of our own, they can take the risks of learning with us. Every good teacher knows that learning is very risky for the learner, and learners will tend to wall themselves against risk if they do not sense a bond with us—a bond that assures them the security of unconditional love and support. According to anthro-pologists, this is the bond that we are all "hard-wired" to offer to children and that children, in turn, are "hard-wired" to receive from us from millions of years of living in small multi-aged internally related hunting/gathering family groups.

When we bring race bias, class bias, or gender bias to our teaching, the handy "other people's children" rubric kicks in and first gives us permission to teach badly, and, then in the classic double whammy that debilitates and alienates children, gives us permission to escape our own remorse about giving the kids less than our best. We can then declare the children to be defective. When the children in our charge become "other people's children," we do not depend on them for our continued well-being; we can throw them away. That young woman of the "anger-laser" probably didn't know how important it is that I follow Lisa Delpit's admonition. I think of FAM's graduate students and the students of FAM's graduate students as my family, and a good bit of the time I succeed at it.

My FAM Friends Tell Me Black Culture Did It but I Don't Quite Buy It 'Cause I've Seen It All Before'

In my opinion, the FAM community is often too hard on itself and on FAM when things go wrong. Here's a way to frame my sense of this issue. I've seen a lot of wonderful, glorious things in my almost three decades in higher education prior to my arrival at FAM. I have had more than my share of joyful moments, moments when I know in both my heart and mind that I was doing good and that people's lives were better as a result of them being at the university. I have had many, many moments when I was proud of my colleagues and when I was affirmed in the value of our mission to help our students and make all school better places for kids. I have witnessed and admired many acts of genuine and unfailing generosity. I have watched brilliant professors who could have chosen to disengage, choose, instead, to devote their lives to teaching and learning as its own kind of life's work. I have seen all manner of graduate students at the university—those with high energy, brilliance and ambition, those with low energy, not so much brilliance, and those whose ambition is only to be minimally certified. I have participated with colleagues in helping graduate students give substance and content to the internal changes they had already felt in their bones when they knocked on our door and asked to be admitted to our programs. I have watched graduate students studying educational leadership make their own lives better and the lives of the children in their charge be better, too; I see these things at FAM, too.

On the other side of the coin, over the last thirty-one years at these other places, I have seen some really nasty people operating with comparative impunity in higher education—predators turned loose in a gentle environment who found early and often that they could bully and abuse the kindly people around them with little fear of reprisal. I have watched sexual predators operate with only conspiratorial winks as reproach. I have watched racists, sexists, elitists, pathological narcissists, and just plain old fakers make a great deal of noise day after day to camouflage their disinclination (or inability) to teach and do scholarship.

I believe the good stuff outweighs the bad by a significant margin, but there have been a significant number of bad days, especially the days when you wonder how people who are so pathologically committed to self-service can get away with so much for so long. One of the deans I worked for many years ago said to me with some vexation at my concern about faculty productivity, "Higher education is not about ideals; it is about making the system work for you so that you can get as much from it as possible, and if you teach our students in educational administration anything different, you are doing them a disservice." I walked away from that conversation then as I walk away from equivalent conversation now wondering how to function in such an environment. I grew up thinking that the function of knowledge was to help people have a better life, that generosity to others is a hallmark of a civilized society, and that with accepting power comes the responsibility to try to do good. I believed that higher education would be one of the places where there would be general agreement on these premises. Some days seem to be mostly about that kind of bad stuff and on those days, few as they may be, I feel like I just don't fit. I've seen that stuff here at FAM, too.

Here's my point—I have an "attitude" against "bad stuff" that was honed to a razor's edge during three decades of service in majority culture institutions. This is the comparison I offer to all those in the FAM family who are angry and disengaged at FAM: I have seen more nobility, more talent, more commitment to young people, more clear sense of a generous and kindly mission at FAM in the last two years than I have seen in all my previous years in higher education. I have seen more sacrifice and more personal involvement with the well-being of students at FAM than I have ever seen before. I have also seen more forgiveness from students toward faculty at FAM and more loyalty, even reverence, to FAM as a bastion of black hope and black achievement. To my mind, this is a glorious, positive difference between where I have been and where I am now.

I have found it particularly interesting that my black colleagues regularly interpret difficult or just plain dysfunctional events, practices, or patterns at FAM as a function of black culture and generalize their statement to include all HBCUs, as in, "It's a Black thing" or "It's an HBCU thing." From my point of view, however, these behaviors match those I have seen so often at predominantly white institutions, and excoriated there not as a function of "white culture" but seen as either people screwing up or an outcome of organizational arrangements that make people dysfunctional, or both. People who are afraid, feel oppressed, are disrespected or disempowered, no matter where they are, get upset, disengage, and turn their energy thermostat down. Some of those people will do mean things. My point is that nowhere in the literature about the most unproductive majority culture institution of higher education is the fault placed at the foot of "white culture." I argue that many of the frustrations of faculty and staff at FAM or any HBCU are not the inevitable artifacts of black culture as is so often expressed to me by my black colleagues. Solving problems is about working assiduously to honor people's gifts, investing in their development, and changing organizational processes and structures for the better. FAM is a very special place, a place of great achievement. I prefer to cling to the premise that the great things done here are an outcome of "Black Culture" and that the screwed-up things are a leadership issue, are not inevitable, and offer us the challenge to fix them.

Hey! You! — Back!

That young woman who made contact with me that morning on the quad was a lot right and a lot wrong. I have taken her anger seriously. I have tried to measure up to the responsibility to do good work here. That is my response to the "right" part of her anger. I may not succeed but I am reasonably aware of the gifts and limitations I bring to my work. I know very well that good intention in no way assures effectiveness here but it is an honorable starting point. I will try to do my best for as long as I am here and I hope I will play a part in adding to the distinguished record of this institution. I will try to listen and learn. I remain a short, plump, white guy with lots to offer and I will not ration or withhold what I can bring to the success of this program. I cherish without condition the success of every wonderful person who has committed years of their lives to pursue graduate study in educational leadership at FAM. This, young lady, is what I might have said after thinking about your "look" for a long time. It could be that the fates will put this piece of writing before you, whoever and wherever you are, and we will smile as we greet each other on the quad.

References

Delpit, L. (1995). *Other people's children: Cultural conflict in the classroom.* New York: The New Press.

Durkheim, E. (1956). *Education and sociology.* Toronto, Canada: Collier Macmillan Canada Limited.

Feagin, J.R. & Sikes, M.P. (1994*). Living with racism: The black middle-class experience.* Boston: Beacon Press.

Chapter 11 _____

Life from Another Heart

Roy C. DeLamotte

I first began teaching at Morristown College, a historically black college, in 1956 in Morristown, Tennessee, as a United Methodist minister whose aim was to promote racial equality. After two years of part-time work there, I transferred, in 1961, to Paine College in Augusta, Georgia, and taught there with the same purpose until my retirement in 1991. Education was to me an integral part of the social revolution; thus, I never thought of myself as an educator per se, but as a minister committed to teaching the Bible and ethics to African-American students. The following is a summary of the lessons I learned during those years.

As a thirty-eight-year-old Mississippian who had had virtually no social contact with African Americans, I had many small problems. Men wore hats in those days, and I wondered whether I should tip my hat to my African-American female colleagues. Would they think I was trying to be funny? Such a gesture had been made into a cartoon in my college paper as an unthinkable absurdity, so to solve this problem I began leaving my hat in the car. Saying "Mr." and "Mrs." also made me feel self-conscious, and the pathways of habitual speech contained many potholes: "You're free, white, and twenty-one," "This story will curl your hair," "Black as sin," and "A little white lie." In one area, however, fate was a friend, for I have always done chalk talks in teaching, and my blackboards made everyone black.

I found that this new world of black-white social contacts was also full of potholes for my students. "Yes, sir" was taboo, a relic of yesterday's subservience, which resulted in many an "Exactly!" or "Precisely!" Even smiles were a problem, for a smile had long been required by the lady of the house or the boss, or just anybody who was white. My students were a generation of young people in a new world. They had no wish to be rude, but had to create their own courtesies and find their own way, for their elders could not lead them and often dared not even follow. A jingle said it all, "Ma is scared, and pa is too, and so it's up to me and you."

It seems quite incredible to me now but, at age thirty-eight, I had never known an African American as an individual. Growing up in Mississippi had left me imagining all African Americans were the same. I can still remember grading my first set of essays and discovering to my amazement that some students were smart, some were dumb, some honest, some deceitful, and so on. For people who have never experienced separateness from a given race or religion, group identity is quite real. They think in terms of "all Jews" and "all Catholics" and "all Muslims" much as tourists on a cruise ship might see only groups of people massed on the shore of an island as the ship passes by. But in 1956 I "went ashore" for the first time in my life, and group identity vanished forever.

The first lesson I learned in teaching in a historically black college was that the social revolution then in progress was not the primary interest of most of my students. Many worked for justice, equality, and civil rights, and many endured danger and suffered hardship for doing so. But like their white counterparts, most were concerned about grades, dates, ball games, sororities and fraternities, and money.

As a fire-breathing white liberal entering the world of African Americans, I had expected to find every male a Malcolm X and every female a Sojourner Truth. Alas, as on a white campus, the devotees of Babbitt far outnumbered those of any rival god, and few students doubted that the meaningful life began in the suburbs with a split-level house and two well-dressed children in a private school. The reductio ad absurdum of this goal is the African-American athlete who has a private plane and million dollar mansion and is too timid to join the NAACP.

I had problems in attempting to critique this American Dream in a roomful of students who felt excluded from it. The original purpose of Paine College was to give students more meaningful goals in life than a house and a car, but since I had already attained both simply by being born white, how could I disparage the dream before such impassioned believers? The answer to my dilemma came from the African-American speakers who visited Paine College from time to time and poured out in tones of thunder their own doubts about the

American Dream. I soon saw that the president of a successful African-American business was armed with weapons the average college professor would never have in his arsenal. From then on I limited myself to a defense of the liberal arts and humanities. Why make enough money for a tour of Rome unless you can appreciate the Greek temple that appears in its viewfinder?

During my thirty years in Augusta, Georgia, the aims of Paine College were repeatedly affirmed as teaching liberal ideals and producing students with Christian character. The college had been founded in 1882 to educate ministers and teachers, but when I arrived in 1961 ministerial students were few, majors in education numbered a few more, and social studies boasted a large group of potential social workers. Some students were like sizzling sticks of dynamite, ready to blow injustice and poverty away and build a brave new world, but most were more like sticks of firewood, hoping someday to cast their light and warmth on the status quo.

History and change were big factors in my teaching experience. Half of my students in the 1970s had never seen a "whites only" sign, and the president of the college once took up an entire general assembly period to describe to them how Jim Crow had once ruled on busses, in movie theaters, filling station rest rooms, hotels, and public swimming pools. Such students had no historical frame from which to mount their mental images of James Meridith, Charlayne Hunter-Gault, Rap Brown, Eldridge Cleaver, and groups like the Freedom Riders. Some seemed to take their civil rights for granted and to have no idea that in their parents' day the act of voting could cause the loss of one's job, safety, or of life itself.

In the 1980s I noted a big increase in business administration majors, all of whom were required to take ethics. I had always felt that "business ethics" was an oxymoron but did my best to prepare students for graduate study in their chosen field. They were highly motivated and studied harder than any students I'd ever had, which I attributed to the fact that the combined annual incomes of a minister, a teacher, and a social worker would probably not equal the starting salary of a Harvard MBA.

One of my primary aims was to give these young people an experience of dealing face to face in perfectly ordinary situations with somebody who was white. I believe in the necessity and usefulness of black colleges, but the world our students must live in today is still largely dominated by whites. Thus, I revealed as much of myself as I could, both in word and deed, without reducing the course to rank autobiography. I used every possible excuse to tell them about my mother and father, my childhood, and my years of growing up in Mississippi. I wanted them to feel that they knew at least one white person individually from the inside. I also tried to modify black stereotypes of whites which, like similar misconceptions in white minds, can make life in the real world difficult.

In my early years at Paine College my students were products of the "separate but equal" system that continued long after the *Brown* v. *Board of Education* decision. This resulted in academic deficiencies that some white instructors were unable to cope with, especially in fields like math and chemistry. My solution was to find out where my students were, to begin at that point, and try to relate my material to their current knowledge and ability. Of course, it's easier to accept the pros and cons of student opinion in an ethics class that to split the difference with a math class over the results of an algebraic equation.

Perhaps my biggest shock came in learning that I was usually the only person in the room who had read Richard Wright or the poetry of Langston Hughes. In the days before Black Studies, my students had been taught Tennyson and Browning, but in many a class not one had read a single line of Dr. King's views on non-violence or Maya Angelou's account of her own education in *I Know Why the Caged Bird Sings*. I gave questionnaires to students as a way of getting acquainted and always included, "Name the most enjoyable book you've ever read." The answer might be *The Return of the Native*; it was never *Native Son*. I now realize that black students "educated" in white-run schools could hardly be expected to know the novelists, poets, playwrights, and social reformers who were part of their literary heritage. Nor should we take refuge in white students who have never read Hemingway or Dreiser, for no board of education denied them these treasures out of ignorance and hostility.

I am an old-fashioned "content teacher" whose aim was to convey a specific body of material in the field of scripture, ethics, or world religions. For example, in teaching Islam I taught the history of the movement, the life of its founder, the origin and content of the Koran, and gave systematic quizzes on final exams. Students who could give me back 65 percent of the material passed.

In ethics the pure content method was unworkable. There I usually gave moral puzzles like, "If it was OK for Dr. King to break the law, why wasn't it OK for the KKK to break it too?" Or I gave an exercise in freedom and determinism in which a student had to convince the one in the next row that when he stole $5.00 from her purse he had been a victim of forces that literally compelled him to commit the crime. He would then list such forces as growing up with no spending money, having a drug dealing father, being ridiculed by his peers for going to church, and so on. My usual classroom thief invariably claimed to have a mother in the hospital, though how five dollars could help solve her medical bill was seldom spelled out.

The unconscious racism of some white professors in black colleges has doubtless caused many a problem. The self-deception involved may be deeply hidden from our own awareness, but that only makes us more likely to say words or do deeds we later regret. I am always uneasy with people who protest their impartiality too much. I feel more relaxed with those who admit, "Yes, I do feel prejudice against African Americans and have to fight against it in dealing with them." Such persons will swim against the current and are surprised when it sometimes sweeps them away.

There's probably no way one can help an unconscious racist. Not many white teachers in black colleges are such, I think, but I've found that those who have had difficulties over race rarely began their accounts of a clash with, "I wonder if prejudice made me say the wrong thing today?" Their tales more often began with, "There's not a racist bone in my body!" The "bone" in these cases was usually in their heads and hence unnoticed. One battle-prone colleague of mine, a recipient of many wounds over many years, was as perennially bewildered as if he were a redheaded bullfighter, for the cause of his troubles was obvious to everyone but himself.

Being a professor in a black college gave me an entry into the African-American community, whose internal politics make Machiavelli's *Prince* sound like *Little Women*. Nevertheless, this understanding of the complexity of group relations and the helpfulness of compromise and coalition never seemed to include the contributions of white liberals. Most of the nationwide gains of our day, such as the Civil Rights Act, have been to some extent the work of white liberals. Many local triumphs in cities and states have come when a sizable African-American group found enough white liberals to give it a majority. Whites have sacrificed careers, status, money, and family and, in a few cases, life itself to be a part of such victories. Yet the most painful chore of the liberal white professor in a black college is to sit in general assemblies year after year and hear denunciations of white liberalism.

It is sadly true that many white liberals tend to leave the bus before it reaches Martyr's Square, and black denunciations of this may be mere rhetorical soul food meant for black enjoyment only. But such public vilification is a price white liberals should expect to pay if they seek employment in a black college. It may help us if we confess that we have rarely done all that we could and that few of us could endure even briefly what many African Americans endure from the day of their birth. Thus, guilt may fuel our resentment of painful home truths. I have also been helped by African-American friends who reject stereotypes of whites as well.

For a brief period some historically black colleges were beset by the view that an all-African-American college should have an all-African-American faculty. Obviously, African-American teachers could be assumed to be better qualified to teach black poetry, black art, and black history. But is there any such thing as black physics or black math? In addition, black colleges were finding it difficult to sign up desirable black professors when in competition with headhunters from white institutions of great wealth. Thus the "blacks only" movement died on the vine, but while it lasted white teachers sometimes found strange faces in their classrooms. I had an unregistered student appear in my ethics class one day who had come to find out whether my whiteness was more than dermatological. Presumably, he stamped my dossier with the cliché, "white man but has black heart," for I was never called in by the dean as were some white professors who were told, among other things, that in a black college classroom the word "boy" was an unacceptable choice of wording. Like the name of God in the Old Testament, it is never spoken aloud.

I believe that is possible for African Americans and whites to cross the color line so that they view each other as individuals, not solely as black or white. But formal lessons, discussion groups, coaching, and adroitly balanced get-togethers in idyllic country settings are of limited help. You cross the color line when you work with somebody on a project that draws both of you to itself—building the set for a musical, playing on an athletic team, researching some movement or locale. Talking about race keeps our eyes on ourselves; doing things together creates a relationship that transcends self.

Such activities brought me a number of lasting friendships over the years, and among my African-American colleagues I saw both physical and moral courage that were extraordinary. In addition to the often terrifying public conflicts of that era, African Americans also had to endure the endless little snubs and slights that marred their everyday life in the South. I especially admired one elderly colleague who bore it all with such dignity. When I asked how he could do so, he said that he simply sloughed it off, and added "I can't carry all that stuff with me every day."

Years of helpless subservience forced African Americans to study their white overlords in order to survive, to escape further suffering, and to gain advantages and preferences. Success in exploiting white weaknesses led many African Americans to conclude that they understand whites, but this is a half-truth based on their accurate perception of the white man's vices—his vanity, blindness, cruelty, hypocrisy, and fear. Thus, he could be flattered, cajoled, and (in recent decades) threatened into political acts like the passing of fairer laws. But "A man convinced against his will is of the same opinion still," and often such laws were never enforced, for real power still lay with the oppressor, and his ill will was only exacerbated by outward defeats.

Martin Luther King, Jr., actually did understand white people. In addition to being well aware of our moral failings, he credited us with positive values that most African Americans considered mere pretense. He saw the genuine religious devotion so often noted in the Deep South and usually dismissed as hypocrisy. He saw the authentic nationwide love of our flag, Constitution, and Bill of Rights, a love that to less perceptive African Americans was empty jingoism and made the American flag seem to them a symbol of the KKK. It's much harder to deal with an opponent who believes in your virtues than to deal with one who sees only your faults. King helped the entire nation to move forward because he really did understand whites in their completeness, and in the course of the struggle he enabled whites to understand blacks in their fullness as well.

Part Three _____

Transformed and Transforming at Historically Black Colleges and Universities

Chapter 12 _____

Building Conversations of Respect: The Voice of White Faculty at Black Colleges

Toni P. Anderson & Juliana S. Lancaster

It was the kind of warm, sticky day we often have in late August. Registration was going full tilt, and excited, slightly nervous freshmen were easy to pick out of the crowd. I (T. Anderson) was headed toward the Academic Affairs Office, cheerfully welcoming back those students whom I knew and greeting the newcomers to the Morris Brown College family. As I met a group of students, again I said hello and they returned the greeting. But as we passed, I overheard one say, "Why doesn't she go where she belongs?"

The statement did not shock or upset me. I had been a member of the institution for over ten years and felt quite comfortable being a minority on the campus. I had developed many true friendships with my colleagues and students, and played an active role in the life of the college. Yes, there had been moments when I was very conscious of being white, and times when my race was an issue. Yet, overall, my experience at a black college had been overwhelmingly positive, both professionally and personally. The statement, however, certainly started me thinking. What constitutes "belonging" and, more specifically, what factor(s) had made it possible for me, a white female, to feel quite at home at this historically black campus?"

I posed the question to a colleague and our discussions and reflections on the matter yielded the insights contained in this chapter. For both of us, our arrival on a black college campus marked the first time in our lives that we found ourselves a racial minority. Whereas before we may have defined ourselves in terms of gender, age, or professional interests, now race became an identifying charac-teristic. In other words, we now held the status of "the other." This new awareness of our race was disconcerting at first, but also marked the beginning of a journey that led to significant personal growth and an emerging awareness of our own voice. The concept of voice as a particularly important one grew out of our preliminary discussions for this chapter. A brief look at the existing literature on diversity in general, and the experiences of white faculty in black institutions in particular, further reinforced our understanding of the role of voice in our growing sense of belonging at an HBCU. The remainder of this chapter will clarify our common experience as white faculty at a black campus. We will provide a framework for the development of voice supported by our own stories and the commonality of our paths.

We perceive "voice" as a complex phenomenon with deep meaning that is perhaps best understood by first defining what it is not. To us, voice is not just simply talking or expressing one's own opinion. Furthermore, voice is not a matter of "rights," nor is it something given by anyone else. Rather, it is an evolving phenomenon based on relationship, built over time, and affected by situation. We use the term "voice" here as an umbrella for a complex sense of belonging, which includes the ability to be heard, respected, understood, and valued. Having an acknowledged voice in a given community leads to a sense of personal worth, empowerment, and inclusion. According to bel hooks (1989), finding one's voice is the initial step toward freedom. While this is especially true for those who have experienced oppression and exploitation, we found the concept of "voice" to be also applicable to our situation, and "finding voice" a key ingredient to our becoming a connected member of the campus family. For us, the ability to "exercise voice" was simply a way of saying, "I am a valued member of this group."

Further discussion led us to formulate a model of four developmental stages in the evolution of voice: silenced, channeled, heard, and transformed. We discovered that each of us experienced the same sequence of stages, albeit at different paces. We contributed this time incongruence, in part, to the different positions we held in the institution. T. Anderson held a faculty position and interacted mainly at the departmental level, while J. Lancaster was hired in a high-level administrative post. Lancaster's responsibilities and interaction with major power players in the institution required her to move through these stages more quickly if she were to survive and flourish in her new environment.

Time, situation, and relationship each contribute to one's capacity to exercise voice. Voice is time related because it changes in a developmental sequence. It is situational in that one may feel empowered to express herself freely in one case, but not another; on one topic, but not another; in one circumstance, but not another. Voice is relational in that one's sense of audience begins on the individual level and extends to cover an entire community. Moreover, each stage in the development of voice has an internal and external component, with the internal corresponding to one's private wrestling to find and use voice, and the external component referring to the group's ability to receive and hear "the other." Boundaries for these developmental stages are not hard and fast, for evolution of voice is a fluid process that constantly changes, sometimes even moving backwards.

In the healthiest environments, diverse communities engage in what Hill (1991) calls "conversations of respect," in which the participants dialogue freely with a clear understanding of their need for each other. Conversations of respect are characterized by much more than a mere tolerance of the other; rather, they are distinguished by intellectual reciprocity in which the participants "expect to change at least intellectually as a result of the encounter" (Hill, p.43). We found Hill's concept of "conversations of respect" to be a useful tool in describing the final stage of our experience in finding and exercising voice.

The Silenced Voice

A silenced voice, one that is neither heard nor received, can be the result of both internal and external influences. An internally silenced voice is characterized by feelings of "I don't belong in this conversation" or "I have no right to state an opinion here." A number of factors may lead to one's choosing to remain quiet. Among these are fear of rejection; concern about being misunderstood; being aware of one's own prejudices or stereotypes; and "tokenism, " or not wanting to be a spokesperson for one's race. It is important to note that these feelings are not specific to us. They are commonly reported in the literature summarizing the experiences of minority students and faculty on predominantly white campuses (Fleming, 1984; Pascarella and Terenzini, 1991; Brown, 1994; Fields, 1996). As has been the experience of other minorities, both of us recall instances of such self-silencing from early in our tenure. In retrospect, it is clear that our sensitivity to racial considerations was heightened by our status as novice members of a white minority in a black institution. Each of us can still recall instances where we chose not to enter into conversations that revolved around the college's culture, identity, or mission. In these decisions, we often were motivated by an awareness of the possible impact of our preexisting expectations and stereotypes and by a concern that our comments could be misconstrued. The choice of silence came when we weighed the potential cost, both professionally and personally, of being misunderstood. Not only were we keenly aware of the possible expense of any wrong statement, no matter how well intended or carefully considered, we also felt a degree of probationary status with our black colleagues. As has been noted, it is difficult, if not impossible, to defend oneself against a perception or charge of being racially insensitive or offensive (D'Souza, 1991).

By electing silence, we gained the time to develop a better understanding of the context and to build relationships that would support more open conversations. Generally, we found that the period of time within which we chose such silence was relatively brief. In this regard, our experiences perhaps differ from those of our minority colleagues in majority institutions who seemingly grapple with silence and isolation on an ongoing basis.

Externally imposed silence, on the other hand, can occur in a number of circumstances, such as when one is not invited to participate in decision making. For example, J. Lancaster was once asked to arrange a retreat, but purposefully given incorrect information regarding the number of participants and the budget available. This action effectively silenced her voice in decisions about an event for which she presumably held primary responsibility. A second circumstance of externally imposed silence is when language sends a message that one's input is unwelcome or inappropriate. When someone says, "This is a Black experience that you just wouldn't understand, " the door has been effectively closed on any further discussion. Third, externally imposed silence can occur when the topic being discussed is so culturally bound as to be preemptively closed. In our experience, this occurred primarily in informal settings where culturally specific references and language dominated the conversation, thus precluding a more inclusive dialogue.

We found that, as we became more integrated into the community and as we put to rest any preexisting stereotypes, we encountered fewer instances of silencing, whether internal or external. We attribute this as much to the efforts of our black colleagues and to the nurturing environment of HBCUs as to our own efforts to become valued participants in the life of the institution.

The Channeled Voice

Channeling refers to getting one's message communicated via another individual with whom one has formed a strong relationship of mutual trust and respect. While all of the stages of voice we have identified have a relational component, the success of channeling rests squarely on the quality of the relationship between the individuals. Channeling requires a friendship where there is honesty and integrity. The concerns over the cost factor associated with silencing are rendered moot under these circumstances. In such a friendship, a genuine level of intellectual reciprocity exists. The differences, racial and other, between parties have not been eliminated; rather, they are acknowledged and respected, thus making conversations of respect possible.

The importance of the message or topic drives the choice to channel one's voice rather than to silence it. For sensitive issues that needed addressing, we both recalled times where we decided it would be safer and more certain if the message was communicated by a black colleague. Each of us remembered instances when we intentionally and overtly discussed an issue with a trusted friend who then served as our voice in the public forum. We have found no reference in the literature to this pattern of communication being utilized by minorities in predominantly white institutions.

As with silencing, time comes into play as a factor. As we built more full relationships and trusting friendships, we became more comfortable speaking for ourselves on campus issues. Nevertheless, we also acknowledge that, in highly volatile situations that are racially charged, we easily reverted to using channeling as the most acceptable communication tool. The issue's level of sensitivity and the extent to which we had built an audience were factors motivating this choice.

The Heard Voice

A heard voice comes into being when the participants in a conversation are in a relationship of mutual trust and full acceptance. As noted by Hill (1991), it is under these circumstances that genuine conversations of respect occur and true intellectual reciprocity is encouraged. We found that as our sense of belonging increased, our concerns over rejection and potential misunderstanding diminished. Consequently, we found ourselves more able to speak openly, with an assurance of being heard and accepted by the full community.

Our reflections on this stage of voice revealed that this phase was inextricably bound to our growing sense of audience. In other words, as the number of individual strong relationships we formed increased, the capacity for the community at large to extend trust grew, as did our commitment to the community. As a result, we became "members of the family," fully included in all conversations, both public and private. No longer were we simply "white women"—we were now ourselves, speaking as individuals, not as tokens of our race or gender. At this point, our voices reflected our own thoughts, our own place, and our own status in the college community. The potential for misunderstanding that was costly initially had been virtually eliminated by the shared experience of relationships. Attainment of this status did not occur overnight or without mutual effort on all sides.

It is our firm belief that the nurturing environment characteristic of black college campuses is ideal for the transformational process leading to this awareness of being heard. This is entirely consistent with Willie's (1994) statement that "predominantly Black educational settings are more nurturing and inclusive than other settings" (p.155). Based on our experiences, we concur with Willie's assessment of the nurturing character of the black campus. Moreover, we both perceived from our earliest days at an HBCU that being fully integrated into the campus family was not only possible, it was welcomed. This is not to say that we never encountered then or now sensitive moments or difficult individuals during our tenure, but that we consistently felt the culture to be more supportive than antagonistic. This awareness freed us to pursue individual relationships in increasing numbers, eventually leading to a state of communal inclusion and full participation.

The Transformed Voice

A transformed voice is difficult to define, yet a real developmental stage in our experience. Like the heard voice, it comes as a result of building relationships of intellectual reciprocity that nurture its development. Yet, whereas the stage of "heard voice" is measured by the way in which it is received externally, the transformed voice is measured by internal personal changes. The transformed nature of our voices became most clear to each of us in circumstances in which we were back in majority environments and encountered attitudes or stereotypes we might not have noticed prior to our experience on a black campus. In other words, we realized that we had become sensitized to racial concerns, in both personal and professional contexts.

For T. Anderson, the realization of a transformed voice first became apparent as she interacted with colleagues at professional meetings and other venues apart from the black campus. The reaction, both in language and gesture, to the knowledge of her place of employment varied from total acceptance, to surprise, curiosity, and/or sympathy. These responses were accentuated during a time when the institution suffered a financial crisis and received negative press. She became keenly aware that, too often, the positive elements of the college received no response from her colleagues, whereas any negative press elicited a flood of editorial comments laden with racial stereotypes, both conscious and unconscious. She found herself glad to be the spokesperson for an institution in which she felt ownership, and willing to discuss frankly and honestly the issues plaguing black higher education without fear of being labeled by whites as biased, or on the other hand, by blacks as racially insensitive.

J. Lancaster had a somewhat different realization of her transformed voice. She found herself assuming that she could speak and be heard in predominantly black environments off campus without fear of reprisal or judgment. In a sense, the positive growth experience gained at Morris Brown College had empowered her voice. Moreover, rather than merely tolerating the "other" out of respect—a stance sometimes held by those who attempt to embrace diversity—she found that she had sharpened her ability to meet individuals as individuals, thus fostering conversations of respect with others.

Our ultimate awareness of our transformed voices came for each of us when we realized that a return to a majority environment would represent a significant loss to us. In other words, we had come to truly appreciate the value of working in a diverse, nurturing environment. Other scholars have noted the transformational effects of a black immersion experience upon white faculty (Willie, Grady, &

Hope, 1991). Referencing his previous research, Willie (1994) notes:

> White teachers who temporarily left their posts in Black institutions for further study toward doctoral degrees in predominantly White universities had become so sensitized by their Black immersion experiences that they usually expressed dissatisfaction with the absence of faculty diversity and the negative race relations climate in the predominantly White institutions at which they matriculated. (p.158)

Though our institution had its share of problems, it had succeeded in creating an environment that welcomed our growth into full, accepted participants of the community. By creating opportunities for conversations of respect, the institution had nurtured the process of self-transformation described by Hill (1991):

> One criterion of the genuineness of the subsequent conversations is the transformation of each participant's understanding or definition of the question— perhaps even a transformation of self-understanding. (p.43)

As our voices were heard and accepted, as our self-understanding grew, and as our transformed voices were discovered, we gradually developed a firm sense of belonging that could not be shaken by the negative comments of those few within the campus who might challenge our place.

The Components of Voice Development

Upon discovering that each of us had experienced similar "stages" in the development of our voice, we began to explore the factors that had contributed to this growth and, ultimately, to our sense of belonging. It is risky at best to infer a common process from two cases. Nevertheless, we recognized that we had both experienced the developmental stages of voice in a similar pattern, despite the differences in time required to reach the point of feeling comfortable speaking in any forum. We each had experienced the silenced voice upon our initial employment, the product of both internal and external forces. The changes that led to our sense of inclusion and freedom of voice have taken place both internally and externally as well. In this section, we identify common points of our experience and note some factors that can either "speed up" or "slide back" the developmental process.

Individual Relationships

Individual relationships are the foundation of the transition in voice described in this chapter. They form the bases upon which one moves from silenced voices to the pairing of heard and transformed voices and represent the first context in which one begins to feel comfortable addressing important issues. The relationships that contribute to developing voice are characterized from the beginning by honesty, integrity, and intellectual reciprocity. For us, it was through individual friendships that we began exploring the assumptions and stereotypes that were inhibiting our voices in the wider arena. Here, concerns over the possible cost of misunderstanding were eliminated through the process of building trust. When we elected to channel our voices through another, these friends were most often our elected spokespersons.

Building Audience

Naturally, as we formed more and more friendships, the pool of individuals with whom we felt free to speak began to grow, as did the number of circumstances in which we felt a sense of receptive audience. Consequently, it became possible to speak in group settings rather than in individual conversations alone. Eventually, the audience reached a transitional point of what is best termed "critical mass"—the point at which the balance shifts from an unreceptive audience containing a few responsive members, to a receptive audience with a few unresponsive members. Just as the cost concerns associated with silencing diminish and then vanish in personal relationships, the enlarging sense of audience on the campus leads to the eventual elimination of these concerns at the community level. For us, this marked the point at which we began to exercise our voice in more public arenas and to build a personal history of intellectual reciprocity and mutual trust on a larger scale.

The Boomerang Effect

Despite these clear benchmarks in voice development, it is important to note that there are some factors and/or circumstances that can lead to temporary reversions of voice to an earlier level. We refer to these episodes as the "boomerang effect, " so termed because they cause a retreat to an earlier state of either a silenced or channeled voice followed by a return to the heard/transformed voice. As with silencing, the boomerang effect can be instigated by either internal or external conditions. Furthermore, the effect can be triggered by either the content of a specific issue or by shifts in relationship. For example, a content triggered, internal reversion arises when an issue or situation raises anew the same concerns that led to choosing silence initially: fear of rejection, concern about being misunderstood, awareness of one's own stereotypes, and a desire to avoid "tokenism. " The situation triggering this effect may be restricted to the campus or may arise out of the larger world, and is generally racially bound and highly charged. As a primary example, both of us felt strongly that it was appropriate to maintain silence during the investigation and trial of O. J. Simpson. While we did not necessarily disagree with our black colleagues regarding Mr. Simpson's treatment, the behavior of other parties involved, or the behavior of the media, we nonetheless felt that the content and nature of the case was so highly sensitive as to effectively bar open dialogue. With the boomerang effect, the choice to remain silent or to channel comments is limited to the triggering condition. For example, though we each silenced our voice in regards to the O. J. Simpson trial, we did not feel restricted to exercise our voice freely on other topics.

Shifts in relationships, particularly those leading to an increase in the power held by white faculty, can lead to both internally and externally triggered reversions in voice. In any work situation, regardless of race, a change in the amount of authority held by one individual leads to a reassessment of interpersonal relationships on the job. The race factor, in our experience, seemed to heighten mistrust of white faculty, thereby extending the period of adjustment. However, we found that not only was the return to a heard/transformed voice possible, but it came more quickly than it had during the initial process of development.

Conclusion

For each of us, building a sense of voice was a common thread to our successful integration into a predominantly black college. This developmental process relied heavily on our ability to form and nurture strong friendships through which we were then able to examine both internal and external barriers to effective interracial relationships. In time, our sense of audience widened, thus enabling us to communicate freely in public forums with the assurance of being heard. Mutual trust between colleagues functioned as the foundation upon which we engaged in conversations of respect and intellectual reciprocity.

We recognize that our experiences are peculiar to one institution among many HBCUs, thus preventing broad generalizations. However, Willie's (1994) assessment of historically black institutions gives a strong argument for the theory that the black college, with its history of racial integration and its dedication to access, is peculiarly suited to nurture its minority constituents. Certainly, our experiences support this theory.

Further, we acknowledge that our understanding of the importance of voice and its relation to developing a sense of belonging may be, in part, gender specific. As Gilligan (1982) notes, many women form their self-identity within the context of relationship and make judgments from a standard of responsibility and care. However, scholars have also noted that, despite gender, the meaningful relationships formed by diverse individuals is directly related to their ability to work together effectively and find satisfaction in their jobs (Smith, 1985). We concur with Hill's (1991) understanding that it is relationships grounded upon mutual respect that allows diverse others to "sustain conversations of respect" for the sake of "forging over and over again a sense of a shared future" (p.42).

Last, our sense of inclusion at a black college and the positive, rewarding journey toward this status was no doubt influenced by the degree to which we were allowed to participate in decision making. "The well-being of a society is directly related to the degree and extent to which all of its citizens participate in its institutions," states Madrid (1990, p.19). We maintain that the same principle applies to any individual within an institutional context, whether he or she holds minority or majority status. Having a voice in the direction, mission, and future of an institution empowers its members, fosters a sense of ownership, and encourages the perception of equality. Smith (1985) found that the absence of voice in these matters contributed greatly to white minority faculty's dissatisfaction on black campuses. Further exploration into the perceptions of white minority faculty not actively participating in college governance would yield more insight into how shared decision making contributes to one's sense of belonging.

Our tenure at an HBCU has been an especially rewarding experience because it is intricately linked with our personal growth. We both attest to the fact that we have gained a deep perspective as a minority member of the institution, and a heightened sensitivity to the feelings and perceptions associated with being the "other. " But equally important, we have come to value a paradigm that recognizes, affirms, appreciates, and empowers the "other" by encouraging conversations of respect. It is in within this context that true integration becomes a real and meaningful possibility.

References

Brown, O. G. (1994). *Debunking the myth: Stories of African-American university students.* Bloomington, IN: Phi Delta Kappa Educational Foundation.

D'Souza, D. (1991). *Illiberal education: The politics of race and sex on campus.* New York: The Free Press.

Fields, C. D. (1996). A morale dilemma. *Black Issues in Higher Education,* 13(17), 22-29.

Fleming, J. (1984). *Blacks in college: A comparative study of students' success in black and in white institutions.* San Francisco, CA: Jossey-Bass Publishers, Inc.

Gilligan, C. (1982). *In a different voice: Psychological theory and women's development.* Cambridge, MA: Harvard University Press.

Hill, P. (1991). Multiculturalism: The crucial philosophical and organizational issues. *Change,* 3(7), 38-47.

hooks, b. (1989). *Talking back: Thinking feminist, thinking black.* Boston, MA: South End Press.

Madrid, A. (November/December, 1990). Diversity and its discontents. *Academe: Bulletin of the American Association of University Professors,* 23, 15-19.

Pascarella, E.T., & Terenzini, P.T. (1991). *How college affects students.* San Francisco, CA: Jossey-Bass Publishers, Inc.

Smith, S.L. (1985). Factors influencing adjustment of white faculty in predominantly black colleges. *Journal of Negro Education,* 54(2), 148-163.

Willie, C.V. (1994). Black colleges are not just for blacks anymore. *Journal of Negro Education,* 63(2), 153-163.

Willie, C.V., M.K. Grady, & R.O. Hope (1991). *African Americans and the doctoral experience.* New York: Teachers College Press.

Chapter 13 _____

Educating As Moral Responsibility

Karen Sides-Gonzales

The day I first stepped onto the grounds of St. Philip's College I knew I was home. Though I had yet to be interviewed for a job, there was no doubt that this was the place I wanted to be. St. Philip's is an inner city community college located on the east side of San Antonio, Texas, in an old and neglected neighborhood. It is one the oldest community colleges in the nation, with its beginnings in 1898 when the Episcopalian church founded it as a sewing school for black girls. It carries the unique distinction of being both a historically hlack and Hispanic-serving institution.

I will never forget the day I first came to St. Philip's to interview for a job. It was a bright, breezy, crisp fall day as I drove to the city's east side. As I neared the college, the beauty of the day was tainted by the sight of decaying buildings and small groups of people standing around sipping what I assumed to be beer out of cans held in small brown paper bags. I was reminded of a comment by a family member who had asked me why I wanted to work at that "black" school. He thought that surely I could do better. But, as I pulled into the parking lot of the St. Philip's campus, I saw a whole new world.

The campus was clean and inviting. Almost everyone I came across smiled at me and many said hello. Two individuals approached me offering directions. People were moving and talking to one another. The campus was alive with activity. I got the feeling that the students and faculty all had a sense of purpose, a goal, or at least a dream. As I continued on my way to be interviewed, I was greatly moved by the intensity of activity and the wonderful welcome I had received from people who had no idea who I was or why I was there. In anticipation of being hired, I made a mental note to explore what made this institution so different.

A Historical Perspective

To comprehend the personality of St. Philip's and its strength as an academic institution, an understanding of its history is critical. Facing incredible challenges that would have destroyed any other institution, St. Philip's has not only survived for one hundred years in an often racially hostile political and social climate, it has thrived. I share the common belief that its success can be traced to its original founding as a religious school and to one very critical decision by the leaders of the Episcopal church, the hiring of Miss Artemisia Bowden.

In 1902, St. Philip's hired Miss Bowden, the daughter of an ex-slave, to take the helm of the institution and lead it though what would prove to be very treacherous waters. Nearing bankruptcy and extinction on many occasions, Miss Bowden's unquestionable faith and determination were firmly rooted in her belief that the school had a *moral* obligation to serve the community and it simply could not fail. And indeed, it has not. A favorite story about Miss Bowden describes her standing on street corners with a cup in her hand asking for donations so that she might pay her faculty.

The tenet of "educating as moral obligation" was implemented by Miss Bowden and continues to be at the root of the academic, social, and spiritual center of St. Philip's College. Miss Bowden was quoted as saying, "It takes work, faith, patience, and persistence to make a 'goal' a reality." This view, along with her strong sense of moral obligation to the community brought the school from a small, poor, one-discipline institution with a handful of students, to a flourishing college with three campuses and over 9,000 students.

In the early part of this century, when the notion of "separate but equal" prevailed, Miss Bowden took the courageous stance that St. Philip's College would be an inclusive institution that served and showed respect for all people. This belief carried on in spite of the fact that the wealthy, predominantly white community provided little financial support. They were also successful in moving the school out of the center of the downtown business district, which is now the heart of San Antonio's high profile River Walk tourist market, to an area just east of downtown. The story has it that the white business community did not want the "black" school, its faculty, and students to be so visible, so they forced it out to an area where it (along with faculty, staff, and students) wouldn't be as readily seen. Many at this institution have expressed the belief that the move was intended to force the school to simply whither away and die. If this is true, and I have no reason to doubt it, then those responsible for driving the move could not have been more wrong. Through decades of persistent hard work, Miss Bowden was able to not only keep St. Philip's alive, she managed to form an affiliation with San Antonio Junior College. This was an amazing accomplishment and laid the groundwork for St. Philip's to become a member of the Alamo Community College District today.

It is within a historical context that the true spirit and energy of St. Philip's College can be understood. The college has an incredible legacy and is being led by individuals who understand how the ground gained by Miss Bowden could quickly and easily slip away if the institution strayed from its moral obligation of service to the community and to the individuals within that community. It is, perhaps, the very fabric of St. Philip's black and religious heritage and the legacy of Miss Artemisia Bowden that St. Philip's is the inclusive, open, caring, and supportive, as well as academically challenging, institution it is today.

Informal Attitudinal Survey

When first asked to write about my experiences working in a historically black college, I was a bit taken aback. I had never really stopped to think of my employment in terms of being white in a black college. I informally polled many of my white colleagues at St. Philip's College to get their reaction. Without exception, every person that I talked to had the same reaction that I did. We were all uncomfortable with talking about our work in terms of race and one individual refused to talk to me about it at all and simply said, "That is a non-issue." After some discussion, one person confided that on occasion it seemed that unless you were black, you would not be included in some decision-making processes. This individual felt some of the black leadership in the college did not believe that a white person was capable of understanding the depths of what it meant to be black in America and, therefore, not capable of making certain decisions. This person did not express these feelings with any anger or resentment, but rather with acceptance.

Interestingly, even though St. Philip's staff and faculty that I talked to didn't think of their employment in terms of race, most of my black friends and colleagues who are working in predominantly white institutions frequently mention themselves in the context of being black and of being outside the system. None of them have ever told me they thought of themselves as being a member of their institution's family.

There are probably many reasons for these differing reactions. In an informal dialogue with various faculty and staff colleagues, we talked about the possibility that white Americans have never really thought of themselves as being outside of the predominant culture. We also discussed the possibility that the grace and maturity earned by many historically black colleges, in spite of the gross injustices they have suffered, created an atmosphere of acceptance and inclusiveness that prevents anyone from feeling that they are outside of the predominant school culture. Whatever the reason, I believe that Miss Bowden's ghost still walks the halls of St. Philip's and is urging all of us to keep her work alive and to follow through on our moral obligation to serve our community inclusively and to serve it well.

Teaching and Learning

In talking to my colleagues, most frequently mention their students by name and talk about their students in very personal terms. I am amazed to find so many faculty who are aware of specific challenges facing individual students whether it is single parenthood, drug or alcohol abuse, physical or emotional abuse, or illness. Most faculty that I talked to could not only readily identify specific learning disabilities or problems, but they also talk about how they are trying to deliver their curriculum in such a way that every student has a chance to learn from his or her strength. In no instance did a faculty member mention a student in terms of his or her ethnicity.

Every day I see faculty members trying to improve their own technology skills that they might in turn help their students. I see faculty working to enhance instruction by integrating multimedia technologies and applications into their curriculum. Every semester, more faculty are developing on-line courses in order that they may broaden their reach into the community. Many faculty understand the importance of computing technology to the lives of their students and they have brought technology into their classrooms and place demands on their students to not only understand course content, but to be able to function technologically. Without question, faculty as a whole take their role as teacher, mentor, and guide very seriously. The result is an institution with a strong academic component and a very supportive student body.

St. Philip's, like any other higher education institution, has faculty and staff who are resistant to change, who don't put their students first, and who don't feel a moral obligation to support the school and community. But, unlike many other institutions, the number of staff and faculty who fall into this category is very, very small and the strength and power of those who embrace the higher ideals of the institution dominate the school culture. It is my belief that without a school culture and climate that supports this kind of dedicated service, it would at best only occur in small pockets, and at worst not happen at all. St. Philip's has been blessed with leadership that works hard to maintain and cultivate the kind of environment that Miss Bowden began building so many decades ago. This is heartening for anyone who entered the teaching profession simply for the opportunity to serve.

We Are Family

"We are family" is a phrase that St. Philip's employees and students hear every day from the administrative leadership, the faculty, and staff. I believe this is extremely important in helping all of us stay focused on our responsibilities, to always be supportive of our colleagues and our students, and to give everyone a sense of belonging. The simple feeling of belonging is powerful, powerful enough to hold an institution together. I often wonder how a theme of "We are family" would play in the corporate sector, or in most other institutions of higher education. My guess is that trying to get the theme to really take off and truly function as a unifying power would be met with laughter or disbelief. But, and I believe this can be directly tied to the college's historically black roots, dedication to and respect for the family is an exceptionally powerful emotion.

An example of the "We are family" theme at St. Philip's is the incredible ability of the school to pull together scores of volunteers among faculty, staff, students, and community members to orchestrate on- and off-campus events that serve the community. From supporting the Martin Luther King, Jr. Freedom March (one of the largest in the country), to the St. Philip's College Culture Fest to the Senior Citizen (Celebration of Life) Fest, the numbers of volunteers wanting to help make every service opportunity a resounding success is overwhelmingly evident. And, during the 1998-1999 academic year, as the college celebrates its one hundred year birthday, over seventy planned events are being orchestrated by St. Philip's volunteers.

Another example of the "We are family" theme at work is my observation that so many graduates never really leave St. Philip's. Hardly a week goes by that I do not see or hear about a student coming back to campus to either help the college in one activity or another, or just to visit with faculty and staff. I have heard students come back to campus with a desire in their hearts to let staff and faculty know how much St. Philip's means to them.

On more than one occasion, upon giving a new student directions on how to get to a specific building, or who to talk to about a certain course or program, students tell me this is why they come to St. Philip's; they feel as though everyone cares about them. One day, a very lost young man wandered into my office wanting to know where to go to find out about an on-line course. It only took a few clicks of my computer mouse to find the answers to his questions on the college's Web page. This student literally jumped for joy and thanked me profusely. He said at any other college he would have been shuffled around from one office or building to another, and may or may not have gotten the information he needed. And, because he knew the faculty and staff cared about his success, he was going to finish his degree at St. Philip's.

I remember thinking that helping this young man took so little, and he was so appreciative, that why wouldn't anyone at any institution do the same? I also wondered, if I had been working at any of my previous institutions, none of which embodied the notion of "family," would I have offered to do more than just send him scurrying over to another department? This simple little incident made me realize how strongly St. Philip's had drawn me in and how proud I was to be a part of an institution that had immediately adopted me as a family member. And, how without conscious effort, I was behaving in a manner consistent with the ideals first set forth by Miss Bowden and modeled by staff and faculty every day. In reflection, it was what seemed to be my inconsequentially small act of kindness that was at the heart of why I wanted to be an educator in the first place. It was a reminder that my youthful ideals were alive and well and were being actualized at St. Philip's College.

Of all the life altering experiences offered by St. Philip's College, "We are family" has had the most impact on me and I believe it is what allows the institution to thrive as a college filled with integrity and spirit. It has also clearly illustrated to me how seriously St. Philip's takes its moral responsibility to educate well and to educate inclusively. Having spent most of my career as an educator working at the university level and in the corporate sector, this working environment was a real about-face from what I was accustomed. My previous work experience emphasized beating the competition (even if your competition was your colleague down the hall), keeping the administration at bay, maintaining the territory at all cost, and meeting the "bottom line." For these reasons, it was with new life and vigor that I embraced the St. Philip's College ideals of service, responsibility, and personal empowerment. St. Philip's is not your typical institution. It is a personification of family.

Conclusion

At the known risk of being accused of being "Pollyanna-ish," or overly sentimental, I have written this essay from my heart and in a way that I hope members of other institutions might be able to learn and emulate best practice. Best practice in education, from the perspective I've gained from St. Philip's College, holds dear the following characteristics: service, responsibility, and personal empower-ment. This means actively practicing your moral responsibility to serve your community, nurturing and supporting the individual in an open and inclusive environment, keeping an eye on the future, and promoting the concept of community, community service, and volunteerism.

I believe that this institution, because it has embraced its heritage and has worked hard to live by its convictions, exemplifies "educating as moral responsibility." This concept is a far cry from most places of work where competition and "staying ahead of the other guy" abounds. This does not mean that St. Philip's coddles its students or fails to challenge them to achieve—far from it. St. Philip's works to challenge the individual to develop real world skills, and to learn and grow in a healthy family environment. The college is dedicated to providing the structure and support necessary for the individual to develop as a full and moral human being prepared to contribute to the community.

Armed with the knowledge of the history of the institution, I am very conscious of how precious St. Philip's is to so many people. Without question, I have become painfully aware that the struggle for equality and respect is far from over. Racial and socioeconomic inequality and hostility, though not always as overt as in times past, still abound. No doubt other HBCUs deal with these struggles on a continual basis as well.

Even though St. Philip's has experienced phenomenal growth, it is still not given the honor and respect it deserves from the community at large. Though the college student body is now about 20 percent black, 30 percent white, and 47 percent Hispanic, I often hear it referred to as the "black" school or even on occasion the "nigger" school. I've had people ask me if I was scared to go on "that" side of town, or if I was afraid to work there at night. I've even been asked what it is like to work with all those black people. I am continually amazed at the questions I'm asked and the comments I've heard from people in the community who are totally ignorant of the extraordinary achievements of St. Philip's College. It is as though many have no idea what a precious jewel St. Philip's is as an educational institution. Because of the public perception, it is not a surprise to hear faculty and staff refer to their own St. Philip's as the lost step-child of the district.

This tells me that Miss Bowden's struggle is not over and that there is much to be done to show the world that "we are *all* family." We should all ask ourselves why an institution that embodies the grace, maturity, and integrity of St. Philip's, and has such a strong academic track record, is not held up as a model of exemplary achievement. Why must it instead continually fight for community respect and recognition when it has already earned it one hundred times over? These questions are perplexing to me and I struggle to find answers.

Because of my opportunity to work in this institution, I am continually being transformed into a broader, kinder, and more purposeful thinker. It has become a practice of mine, and I know I am not alone, to think of Miss Bowden each morning as I come on campus and tell myself to do something that will make her proud of me. That is the power of a strong and healthy family, and without question Miss Bowden is the spiritual head of the St. Philip's family.

There is no doubt in my mind that there are many, many faculty, staff, and students who are also growing as moral human beings thanks to the legacy of Miss Artemisia Bowden and the current leadership's efforts to keep her dreams, her aspirations, and her accomplishments alive. St. Philip's will survive and thrive as it looks to its next 100 years because it embraces what Miss Bowden so powerfully taught. Educating is a moral responsibility.

Chapter 14 _____

Faculty Diversity at Historically Black Colleges and Universities: Context, Scope, and Meaning

Lenoar Foster, Andrea L. Miller, & Janet A. Guyden

In 1995, 59 percent of all faculty members in historically black colleges and universities (HBCUs) were African American. More than 25 percent of all faculty members in these institutions were white Americans. Faculty of Asian descent made up nearly 8 percent of the total faculty numbers, a statistic doubling their general faculty numbers in predominantly white institutions nationwide (New and Views, 1998). This level of diversity in faculty representation has led many in academe to conclude that the "only significant diversity in academic ranks in this country exists in black colleges and universities" (Slater, 1993, p.67). To fully understand the faculty diversity that has undergirded the foundations of higher education for African Americans in the United States and that continues to play a role in the contemporary education of black students at historically black institutions, Browning and Williams (1978) offer that "the development of black colleges in a sense turns on the issue of racial equality and the role of education in achieving or preventing attainment of it. Historically, the direction taken by the colleges was determined in large part by agreements in these two policy areas" (p.90). In a study of the self-concept of black colleges based on what they say about themselves in their catalogues, Gregory Kannerstein found that these agreements have, in large part, allowed HBCU institutions to integrate "academic values with ethical and moral values, of serving educational goals while serving the community, of being open to all while remaining committed to a specific constituency, of combating social injustice while never swerving in allegiance to American democracy" (Kannerstein, 1978, as cited in Willie, 1994, p.153) This duality of purpose continues to make faculty diversity an important ingredient in the achievement of the educational mission and goals of historically black colleges and universities.

History and Necessity as Context

The racial patterns of faculty composition in historically black colleges are, in part, a holdover from earlier days when white dominated religious and philanthropic societies took on the task of staffing segregated schools established for the freedmen shortly after the Civil War. Historically, the greatest growth in colleges and universities for African Americans occurred in the South during the thirty years following the Civil War, although earlier denominational efforts in the North had resulted in the establishment of Ashmun Institute (later Lincoln University) by the Presbyterian Church in Pennsylvania in 1854 and in the founding of Wilberforce University by the African Methodist Episcopal Church in Ohio in 1856. In the South the establishment of higher education institutions was led by "northern white benevolent societies and denominational bodies (missionary philanthropy) and black religious organizations (Negro philanthropy)" (Anderson, 1988, p.239). Such organizations included the American Missionary Association, the American Baptist Home Mission Society, the Presbyterian Board of Missions for Freedmen, the African Methodist Episcopal Church, the African Methodist Episcopal Zion Church, and the Freedmen's Aid Society of the Methodist Episcopal Church. Of these white missionary groups, Browning and Williams (1978) observe:

> the missionaries tended to mix social, economic, and religious ideas in their
> dedication to the task of uplifting the freed men and women. They were moved
> not only by their religious convictions but by the social and economic values
> that had produced the Yankee Protestant society of the North—particularly in
> New England. They were in agreement that someone needed to demonstrate
> that former slaves could be remade into the ideal of a Yankee, Calvinist,
> American citizen. Their common goals were to save souls, educate the minds,
> care for the bodies, and prepare the freed men and women for their
> responsibilities as new citizens of the South. (p.69)

With the exception of those institutions founded by black religious organizations, northern white mission societies were primarily responsible for administering and maintaining the majority of the early collegiate institutions established for African Americans in the South. For almost a quarter century after the establishment of these institutions, the majority of administrators and faculty were white idealistic missionaries who were assisted in their educational endeavors by a nominal group of blacks who had been educated in the North (Browning and Williams, 1978; Brubacher and Rudy, 1997; Harris, 1971). Slater (1993) notes, "Even well into the twentieth century, most black colleges were still controlled by and dependent on whites for operating funds. For the most part, these institutions were ruled by white administrations and staffed by white faculty" (p.67). So predominant was the presence of white faculty in these institutions that "it was not until 1926 that Mordecai Johnson became the first black president of Howard University—60 years after the institution was founded" (Slater, 1993, p.67).

Johnson (1971) observed that "faculty recruitment at all but a few black colleges is based on two elemental desiderata: (1) the need for faculty to teach the courses offered, and (2) the need for a sufficient number of persons with advanced degrees to meet the accreditation requirements of the regional accrediting agencies" (p.804). By 1895, black colleges had produced 1,150 college graduates (Brazzell, 1996), and many of that number took positions as faculty in black colleges supported by religious organizations and in the twelve public black institutions established in the South under the second Morrill Act of 1890.

From 1916 to 1942, a series of reports by the federal government and individual surveys by W.E.B. Dubois and the Phelps-Stokes Fund provided public information on the curricula and quality of education in black colleges. These reports were credited, in large part, with providing the stimulus for black colleges to seek approval by regional accrediting agencies, a process that would mark black colleges as legitimate enterprises of higher education. Anderson (1988) noted that "no formal accrediting agency took black colleges seriously until 1928, when the Southern Association of Colleges and Secondary Schools decided to rate black institutions separately" (p.250). As the stamp of accreditation increasingly marked the status and quality of higher education institutions in America from 1900 onwards, an important goal of black colleges was to be accredited by their respective regional accrediting associations. As accrediting requirements called for certain percentages of faculty to hold terminal and advanced degrees, black colleges experienced difficulties in varying degrees to comply with this provision. Johnson (1971) observed that institutions like the Atlanta University Center (now Clark Atlanta University), Fisk, Howard, and Tuskegee had little difficulty in attracting blacks with Ph.D. degrees, "Because these schools graduated most of the students who subsequently took doctor's degrees, they were in a somewhat privileged competitive position in securing the young graduate's services . . . . and because they provided the best employment opportunities" (p.805). Private and religiously affiliated black colleges continued to depend upon the services of white faculty, who had aligned themselves with these institutions for various religious, social, and political reasons, to meet the accrediting standards.

During the 1940s and 1950s, an increasingly valuable and available faculty pool for many black colleges comprised European immigrants, many of them Jewish scholars fleeing Europe to escape the tyranny of oppressive regimes and restrictions. As the civil rights movement of the late 1950s, 1960s, and 1970s pervaded the national landscape, eliminating de jure segregation laws, faculty diversity at both private and public black colleges was enhanced by the presence of young, liberal, and idealistic white faculty seeking to carry forth the hard won promises of the new American society grounded in equal rights and opportunities for all. Johnson (1971) noted that, "These young people brought with them some strange and exciting new ideas from such places as Berkeley, MIT, and the Peace Corps. They also brought a not inconsiderable capacity for work, which leavened the impact of their ideas" (p.806). In more contemporary times white faculty have been increasingly attracted to HBCU institutions because these institutions remain among the few higher education institutions where opportunities for academic employment remain open and viable, amid shrinking full-time and tenure track professorial ranks in academe at predominantly white institutions.

Because of the historical foundations of black colleges and universities and the varied roles (from egalitarian to paternalistic, from controlling to pacifying, from political and social alignments to career opportunism) that whites have played in the life and development of these institutions, public and internal dialogue about faculty diversity on black campuses has been pointed and excoriating. Johnson (1971) has called into question whether the multiracial composition of the faculty at many black colleges and universities is necessarily synonymous with "cosmopolitanism," and observed that, "The quality of non-black teachers varies among the different black schools. On many campuses, these teachers are all too often political refugees who neither understand the culture nor speak the language intelligibly; retired professors whose energy level does not always measure up to their awesome responsibilities; and wives of professors who are comfortably employed at neighboring white schools" (p.806). Critically, Johnson (1971), similiar to black campus voices where Afrocentric scholarly perspectives are increasingly playing an important role in educational direction and pedagogy, has questioned whether "the non-black presence on these campuses has always been in the best interests of black educational development" (p.805).

The historical causality underlying faculty diversity at black colleges and universities and the continuing internal debate occasioned by it are graphically illustrated by the taxonomy of roles of white faculty proposed by Warnat (1976). These roles include those of *Moron, Martyr, Messiah,* and *Marginal Man.* According to Warnat (1976), limited academic ability and limited or no access to white higher education institutions impel white faculty characterized as *Moron* to remain in the black college. For white faculty members working in black institutions under this archetype, "all personal incompetencies can then be blamed on the institutional setting, thereby absolving personal feelings of frustration and inadequacy" (p.335). The work of white faculty typed as *Martyr* is compared to that of "the zealous missionary who will do virtually anything in his power to relieve his guilt, including being punished for the errors committed by society" (Warnat, 1976, pp.335-336). Such faculty take on the "drudge work" of the institution and elicit the sympathy and condolence of black faculty for their willingness to tackle such responsibilities with a high measure of dedication. The major role of faculty typed as *Messiah* is "to attempt to provide the direction which they feel has been lacking" in the black institution in which they serve. Lastly, white faculty typed as *Marginal Man* live in two worlds and struggle to find their place and meaning in each. According to Warnat (1976), this white faculty member "joins the black college faculty, but continues to remain an alien because of his affiliation with the white social structure" (p.337). While this faculty member is motivated by the academic contribution that can be made to the advancement of the institution and its students, the task of "effectively combining conflicting cultures is unending" (p.338).

In the continuing public and internal discourse about white faculty at black colleges and universities, the nature of their relationships, their work with black students and with other black faculty, the perceptions they engender, the socialization and acculturation they undergo, the difficulties they may encounter in both academic and interpersonal encounters, and the acceptance and successes they experience vary widely (Foster and Guyden, 1998; Levy, 1967; Smith, 1982; Smith and Borgstedt, 1985; Slater, 1993).

Meaning and Scope of Diversity

Willie (1994) suggests that if one wishes to understand the heart and soul of American higher education, and the benefits that accrue to higher education from diverse perspectives, that the focus and outcomes of the educational experience provided by black colleges should be carefully examined. He notes:

> By teaching their students that they must not only know what is right but must do what is right, Black colleges have fashioned an analysis-action strategy of higher education that focuses on moral and ethical concerns. By teaching students to become politically active, Black colleges are repositories of creative dissent that help to keep this nation free. By insisting that education should enhance the individual as well as advance the community, Black colleges

discourage narcissism and help perpetuate democracy and community. By insisting that every person who wants to learn ought to have the opportunity to learn, Black colleges stand solidly against the excluding peril of elitism. (Willie, 1994, p.155)

Historically black colleges and universities have effectively operationalized the concept of "democratic pluralism" espoused by Hill (1991) in which frames of respect, appreciation, and tolerance for individuals and groups that are culturally different become lenses to appraise, assess, and "resist an oppressive social system rather than conform to it" (Willie, 1994, p.154). According to Hill (1991), academic institutions resting on this framework are strong because each group respects the differences of the other without giving up the right to be critical of each other. In such an environment, intellectual reciprocity characterizes "conversations of respect" and those involved in the conversations "expect to change at least intellectually as a result of the encounter" (Hill, 1991, p.43). Thus, the presence of white faculty on predominantly black campuses presents an unusual educational experience for both faculty and students alike. Smith and Borgstedt (1985) note the unique dynamics that occur in such an educational environment.

> The black college campus is an interesting laboratory for the study of interracial interaction. White faculty who have been socialized in the majority role are abruptly assuming a minority role within the black institution. Inherent within this new role is ambiguity related to role patterns and their current situation. Both white and black faculty and black students and administrators bring with them to their interaction their racial orientation and experiences from the dominant society. Their interaction is also influenced by the social context of the black college, which is the reverse of the dominant society. In this environment, the social climate is one of black-in-charge, white as subordinate. Because racial issues are very salient in the black colleges, white faculty who have dealt with race at a distance or only on an intellectual level are required to confront the whole issue of race and to explore their own reactions, personal prejudices, and other internal and external barriers to effective interracial relationships. (p.149)

Challenging to this educational context too is the behavior, both overt and covert, of black faculty, administrators, and students to white faculty as "other," "minority," and "representative of the dominant external culture" within the majority environment of the black institution.

A study of historically black colleges and universities from 1976 to 1994, conducted by the U.S. Department of Education (1996), revealed that there was little growth in white enrollment at private 4-year and 2-year HBCUs. As a result of these differing enrollment changes, the proportion of private 4-year students who were black remained high (94 percent) compared to the proportion at public 4-year HBCUs (80 percent). Interestingly, the same report noted that "the large enrollment increases at the graduate and first-professional levels were also stimulated by an influx of non-black students, which amounted to 35 percent of the graduate and 29 percent of the first-professional total in 1994" (U.S. Department of Education, 1996, p.6). Thus, large enrollments of white students at the undergraduate level at HBCU institutions remain small while professional and graduate school enrollments show some slight increase (this kind of growth represents efforts by college and university systems in the nineteen states where public HBCU institutions are located to desegregate these institutions by making them more attractive through professional and graduate education to numbers of white students who would otherwise attend predominantly white schools). Conclusions from *Miles to Go: Black Students and Postsecondary Education in the South*, a report commissioned by the Southern Education Foundation, revealed that, "In practice public higher education continues to be segregated. Historically black colleges and universities are overwhelmingly black, and traditionally white institutions remain the province of white students" (as cited in News & Trends, 1998, p.13). In light of these continuing statistics, the question of faculty diversity takes on greater urgency as HBCU institutions continue to provide education that is at once self-affirming and empowering to large numbers of African-American students, that is relevant and meaningful to incremental numbers of other diverse students, and that is inclusive of the external environment of the American society that is becoming more diverse in its representation.

Musil (1996) has observed that "to invite diversity on campus is not simply an act of charity. It is an act of raw self-interest. Simply put, it will make higher education better than it is. It expands our notion of learning. It widens what we study and how we study. It improves our pedagogy. It adds to our resources in human capital both in terms of the students and in terms of the people employed by colleges and universities" (p.225). For HBCU institutions, faculty diversity represents the raw interest of these institutions in their steadfast mission to educate students for the "goal of individual enhancement and community advancement, not one or the other but both" (Willie, 1994, p.154), and for empowerment, knowledge, and skill grounded in, according to what the late U.S. Supreme Court Justice Thurgood Marshall called "sufficient faith in the Constitution to confront the anomalies in society and insist that they conform with the basic principles upon which this nation was founded" (Marshall as cited in Willie, 1994, p.154). To this end white faculty become a resource for dialogue with diverse others in developing and creating a supportive "learning community" for the sake of a shared future, one, albeit, "where White and Black Americans are more racially segregated today in the nineties in our residential patterns than we have ever been in the history of the United States" (Massey & Denton, 1993, as cited in Musil, 1996, p.223).

Concluding Perspectives

Historically black colleges and universities have traditionally been welcoming of diverse faculty, particularly white faculty, out of historical and educational need. The confluence of this reality has produced outcomes (conscious and unconscious, covert and overt) that have contributed, in large measure, to the educational mission and value system that undergirds the educational experience provided by HBCU institutions. Succinctly, this mission has embraced the virtue and necessity of educating students to appreciate the richness and diversity of the human condition of which they are a unique and important component; to acknowledge differing ways of knowing and of contributing to the flow of societal and human history through connections of authentic learning and living; to challenge the realization of democratic ideals and principles through active and constructive participation in the democratic process; and to make substantive contributions to their communities and to the nation through the practice and observance of democratic ideals and principles. In providing the venue for this educational mission, HBCU institutions have continually challenged what constitutes the "correct knowledge and information about the Black experience as well as the White experience in this nation" (Willie, 1994, p.161).

For white faculty members in black colleges, the dynamics at work in the environment of a black majority provide a context of challenge and response. Chief among these challenges is the need for those participating in the process, white faculty member and the black majority constituency, to constantly re-examine the realities—or more accurately, their personal and institutional perspectives on the realities—of race, class, and gender. The opportunity the black college presents to white faculty and to its majority black constituency (both students and faculty) is the chance to broaden and challenge perceptions and perspectives within an atmosphere of mutual respect, civility, intellectual reciprocity, and equality. The response to this opportunity involves a validation of superficial differences, a recognition of deeper similarities, an acknowledgment of historical and contemporary inequities, and a commitment to eradicating structures and practices in a democratic society that hinder and negate the full potentialities of all citizens. As such, the eventual conflicts and transformations that can occur between students and faculty in black colleges do not make the institutions "microcosms" for experimenting with plausible solutions to race relations in the nation, but make them models of the kinds of frank and honest discourse, based in mutual respect and upon multiple perspectives and solutions, that should be taking place within the wider society. To this end faculty diversity facilitates and champions liberation from all sorts of myths and presumed superiorities and inferiorities. The effect becomes empowering through mutual interactions of authentic exchange and becomes efficacious for the living out of authentic truth in the wider society.

References

Anderson, J.D. (1988). *The education of blacks in the south, 1860-1935*. Chapel Hill, NC: The University of North Carolina Press.

Brazzell, J.C. (1996). Diversification of postsecondary institutions. In S.R. Komives, D.B. Woodard, Jr. (Eds.), *Student services: A handbook for the profession*, third edition (pp.43-63). San Francisco: Jossey-Bass Publishers, Inc.

Browning, J.E., & J.B. Williams (1978). History and goals of black institutions of higher learning. In C.V. Willie & R.R. Edmonds, *Black colleges in America* (pp.68-93). New York: Teachers College Press.

Brubacher, J.S., & W. Rudy (1997*). Higher education in transition: A history of American colleges and universities*. New Brunswick, NJ: Transaction Publishers.

Foster, L., & J.A. Guyden (1998). *Content analysis of the viewpoints of selected white faculty members at HBCUs*. Symposium presented at the Fifth National HBCU Faculty Development Network Conference, Miami, FL, October 15-18, 1998.

Harris, P.R. (1971). The Negro college and its community. *Daedalus,* 100(3), 720-731.

Hill, P.J. (1991). Multi-culturalism: The crucial philosophical and organizational issues. *Change*, 3(7), 38-47.

Johnson, T. (1971). The black college as system. *Daedalus*, 100(3), 798-812.

Levy, C. (1967). *The process of integrating white faculty into a predominantly Negro college*. Washington, DC: Department of Health, Education, and Welfare (ERIC Document Reproduction Service No. ED 052 744).

Musil, C.M. (1996). The maturing of diversity initiatives on American campuses: Multiculturalism and diversity in higher education. *American Behavioral Scientist*, 40(2), 222-233.

News and Trends (1998). Nation's black college students still face segregated systems. *AFT On Campus*, 18(2), 13.

News and Views (1998, Summer). White professors teaching at historically black colleges. *Journal of Blacks in Higher Education*, 20, 62.

Slater, R.B. (1993). White professors at black colleges. *Journal of Blacks in Higher Education*, 1(1), 67-70.

Smith, S.L (1982). *Dynamics of interracial relationships involving white faculty in black colleges: Review, systematization, and directives*. Paper presented at the annual meeting of the Council for Social Work Education, New York, NY, March, 1982.

Smith, S.L., & K.W. Borgstedt (1985). Factors influencing adjustment of white faculty in predominantly black colleges. *Journal of Negro Education*, 54(2), 148-163.

United States Department of Education (1996). *Historically black colleges and universities: 1976-1994* (NCES 96-902, by C.M. Hoffman, T.D. Synder, & B. Sonnenberg). Washington, DC: National Center for Education Statistics.

Warnat, W.I. (1976). The role of white faculty on the black college campus. *Journal of Negro Education*, 45(3), 334-338.

Willie, C.V. (1994). Black colleges are not just for blacks anymore. *Journal of Negro Education*, 63(2), 153-163.

Appendix _____

Historically Black Colleges and Universities in the United States

Listing of the 105 Four- and Two-Year Public and Private Institutions

4-YEAR PUBLIC INSTITUTIONS (40)	STATE	ORGANIZATION
Alabama A&M University	Alabama	4-yr. Public
Alabama State University	Alabama	4-yr. Public
University of Arkansas at Pine Bluff	Arkansas	4-yr. Public
University of the District of Columbia	District of Columbia	4-yr. Public
Delaware State University	Delaware	4-yr. Public
Florida A&M University	Florida	4-yr. Public
Albany State University	Georgia	4-yr. Public
Fort Valley State University	Georgia	4-yr. Public
Savannah State University	Georgia	4-yr. Public
Kentucky State University	Kentucky	4-yr. Public
Grambling State University	Louisiana	4-yr. Public
Southern University A&M College	Louisiana	4-yr. Public
Southern University at New Orleans	Louisiana	4-yr. Public
Bowie State University	Maryland	4-yr. Public
Coppin State College	Maryland	4-yr. Public
Morgan State University	Maryland	4-yr. Public
University of Maryland Eastern Shore	Maryland	4-yr. Public
Alcorn State University	Mississippi	4-yr. Public
Jackson State University	Mississippi	4-yr. Public
Mississippi Valley State University	Mississippi	4-yr. Public
Harris-Stowe State College	Missouri	4-yr. Public
Lincoln University	Missouri	4-yr. Public
Elizabeth City State University	North Carolina	4-yr. Public
Fayetteville State University	North Carolina	4-yr. Public
North Carolina A&T State University	North Carolina	4-yr. Public

4-YEAR PUBLIC INSTITUTIONS	STATE	ORGANIZATION
North Carolina Central University	North Carolina	4-yr. Public
Winston-Salem State University	North Carolina	4-yr. Public
Central State University	Ohio	4-yr. Public
Langston University	Oklahoma	4-yr. Public
Cheyney State University	Pennsylvania	4-yr. Public
Lincoln University	Pennsylvania	4-yr. Public
South Carolina State University	South Carolina	4-yr. Public
Tennessee State University	Tennessee	4-yr. Public
Prairie View A&M University	Texas	4-yr. Public
Texas Southern University	Texas	4-yr. Public
Norfolk State University	Virginia	4-yr. Public
Virginia State University	Virginia	4-yr. Public
Bluefield State College	West Virginia	4-yr. Public
West Virginia State University	West Virginia	4-yr. Public
University of the Virgin Islands	U.S. Virgin Islands	4-yr. Public

4-YEAR PRIVATE INSTITUTIONS (49)	STATE	ORGANIZATION
Miles College	Alabama	4-yr. Private
Oakwood College	Alabama	4-yr. Private
Selma University	Alabama	4-yr. Private
Stillman College	Alabama	4-yr. Private
Talladega College	Alabama	4-yr. Private
Tuskegee University	Alabama	4-yr. Private
Arkansas Baptist College	Arkansas	4-yr. Private
Philander Smith College	Arkansas	4-yr. Private
Howard University	District of Columbia	4-yr. Private
Bethune-Cookman College	Florida	4-yr. Private
Edward Waters College	Florida	4-yr. Private
Florida Memorial College	Florida	4-yr. Private
Clark Atlanta University	Georgia	4-yr. Private
Interdenominational Theological Center	Georgia	4-yr. Private
Morehouse College	Georgia	4-yr. Private
Morehouse School of Medicine	Georgia	4-yr. Private
Morris Brown College	Georgia	4-yr. Private
Paine College	Georgia	4-yr. Private
Spelman College	Georgia	4-yr. Private
Dillard University	Louisiana	4-yr. Private
Xavier University	Louisiana	4-yr. Private
Rust College	Mississippi	4-yr. Private
Tougaloo College	Mississippi	4-yr. Private
Barber-Scotia College	North Carolina	4-yr. Private
Bennett College	North Carolina	4-yr. Private
Johnson C. Smith University	North Carolina	4-yr. Private
Livingstone College	North Carolina	4-yr. Private
Shaw University	North Carolina	4-yr. Private
St. Augustine's College	North Carolina	4-yr. Private
Wilberforce University	Ohio	4-yr. Private
Allen University	South Carolina	4-yr. Private

4-YEAR PRIVATE INSTITUTIONS	**STATE**	**ORGANIZATION**
Benedict College	South Carolina	4-yr. Private
Claflin College	South Carolina	4-yr. Private
Morris College	South Carolina	4-yr. Private
Voorhees College	South Carolina	4-yr. Private
Fisk University	Tennessee	4-yr. Private
Knoxville College	Tennessee	4-yr. Private
Lane College	Tennessee	4-yr. Private
Lemoyne-Owen College	Tennessee	4-yr. Private
Meharry Medical College	Tennessee	4-yr. Private
Huston-Tillotson College	Texas	4-yr. Private
Jarvis Christian College	Texas	4-yr. Private
Paul Quinn College	Texas	4-yr. Private
Southwestern Christian College	Texas	4-yr. Private
Texas College	Texas	4-yr. Private
Wiley College	Texas	4-yr. Private
Hampton University	Virginia	4-yr. Private
Saint Paul's College	Virginia	4-yr. Private
Virginia Union University	Virginia	4-yr. Private
2-YEAR PUBLIC INSTITUTIONS (11)	**STATE**	**ORGANIZATION**
Bishop State Community College	Alabama	2-yr. Public
Fredd State Technical College	Alabama	2-yr. Public
Gadsden State Comm. College, Valley Street	Alabama	2-yr. Public
J.F. Drake Technical College	Alabama	2-yr. Public
Lawson State Community College	Alabama	2-yr. Public
Trenholm State Technical College	Alabama	2-yr. Public
Southern University at Shreveport	Louisiana	2-yr. Public
Coahoma Community College	Mississippi	2-yr. Public
Hinds Community College	Mississippi	2-yr. Public
Denmark Technical College	South Carolina	2-yr. Public
St. Philip's College	Texas	2-yr. Public
2-YEAR PRIVATE INSTITUTIONS (5)	**STATE**	**ORGANIZATION**
Concordia College	Alabama	2-yr. Private
Shorter College	Arkansas	2-yr. Private
Lewis College of Business	Michigan	2-yr. Private
Mary Holmes College	Mississippi	2-yr. Private
Clinton Junior College	South Carolina	2-yr. Private

Source: United States Department of Education, White House Initiative on Historically Black Colleges and Universities, 600 Independence Avenue, S.W., The Portals Building, Suite 605, Washington, DC 20202-5120.

About the Editors _____

LENOAR FOSTER is an associate professor of educational leadership at the University of Montana where he teaches courses in secondary school administration and higher education. He received his B.S. degree (1974) in secondary education, his M.Ed. degree (1977) in secondary education and curriculum, and his Ed.D. degree (1987) in educational administration and higher education from the University of Nevada, Reno. Foster is the recipient of the Phi Delta Kappa Expectation of Excellence Award from the College of Education at the University of Nevada, Reno, and has been a Stanford University William Coe Fellow in American history. He has been a high school teacher, department chair, curriculum coordinator, dean of students, principal, and university department chair, and he has taught at the University of Nevada, Reno, and the University of San Francisco. His research interests and publications are in the areas of the secondary principalship, school reform, distributed learning in higher education, and higher education administrative and faculty issues. Foster currently serves as editor of *Connections: NASSP Journal of Secondary and Higher Education*, a national research journal published by the National Association of Secondary Principals, and is a member of the governing board for the Association for the Study of Higher Education Reader Series.

JANET A. GUYDEN is an associate professor of educational leadership in the Department of Educational Leadership and Human Services at Florida A&M University, Tallahassee, Florida, where she teaches courses in educational administration. She received her B.A. degree (1968) in English from Howard University, her M.Ed. degree (1977) in counselor education from Worchester State College, and her Ph.D. (1992) in educational administration from Georgia State University. Guyden has been a secondary school teacher, coordinator of an adult education program, and a counselor in clinical and educational settings. At Paine College, Augusta, Georgia, she served as director of the college counseling center and as dean for admissions, recruitment, and financial aid. Guyden joined the faculty in the Department of Educational Policy Studies at Georgia State University in 1992 where she coordinated the Ph.D. program in higher education. She joined the faculty in the Department of Educational Leadership and Human Services at Florida A&M University in July 1997 and currently serves as interim department chair. Her research interests focus on the impacts of organizational culture in historically black colleges and universities.

ANDREA L. MILLER is interim vice president for academic and student affairs at Shelby State Community College in Memphis, Tennessee. She received her B.S. degree (1976) from Lemoyne-Owen College in biology, and her M.S. degree (1978) and Ph.D. (1980) in cell and molecular biology from Atlanta University. She received additional training at Los Alamos National Laboratory in Los Alamos, New Mexico, and at the Marine Biological Laboratory in Woods Hole, Massachusetts. Miller has over twenty years of experience at the postsecondary level in both teaching and administrative positions. She has taught at Clark College (Atlanta, Georgia), the University of Cincinnati College of Medicine, LeMoyne-Owen College (Memphis, Tennessee), and the University of Nevada, Reno. Miller was previously assistant dean and chair of the Department of Biology at LeMoyne-Owen College, assistant dean in the College of Human and Community Services at the University of Nevada, Reno, and vice president for academic affairs/dean of faculty at LeMoyne-Owen College. She has also served as the program director of a five-million dollar National Science Foundation collaborative grant for eleven colleges and universities in the Mid-South region. Miller's current research interests are in the areas of student retention, student outcomes assessment, and institutional effectiveness.

About the Contributors _____

TONI P. ANDERSON is assistant professor of music at Morris Brown College, Atlanta, Georgia. She has been a member of the music faculty at Morris Brown College since 1985 and served as chair of the Music Department from 1993 to 1996. Anderson received her B.M. degree (1979) in music education from Lamar University, her M.M. degree (1982) in vocal performance from the New England Conservatory of Music, and her Ph.D. (1997) in higher education from Georgia State University. A music scholar and performer, Anderson has conducted extensive research on the historic choral ensemble, the Fisk Jubilee Singers. As a mezzo-soprano, she has performed in concerts, oratorios, operas, and recitals throughout the eastern United States.

FRED BALES is associate professor of communications and adviser to the *Xavier Herald* at Xavier University of Louisiana in New Orleans, Louisiana. Among his teaching assignments are news writing, feature writing, and law and ethics. He received his B.A. degree (1962) from DePauw University in economics, his M.A. degree (1965) from Indiana University in journalism, and his Ph.D. (1980) from the University of Texas at Austin in communications. He was a reporter and editor at the *Courier-Journal* (Louisville) from 1968 to 1975 and a Fulbright lecturer in the Philippines in 1989-90. From 1979 to 1997, he was a faculty member at the University of New Mexico where he was a chair of the Department of Journalism and recipient of the university's Student Service Award. His academic specialties are media criticism and media ethics.

ROY C. DELAMOTTE was professor of Bible and ethics at Paine College, Augusta, Georgia, from 1961 to 1991. He received his B.A. degree (1939) from Millsaps College in English, his B.D. degree (1943) from the Candler School of Theology, Emory University, and his Ph.D. (1953) from Yale University in world religions. As a United Methodist minister, he was left without a church in the Mississippi Annual Conference in 1955 for demanding racial integration in the Methodist ministry. During a six-year pastorate in Tennessee, he taught ethics part time at Morristown College, Morristown, Tennessee, from 1956 to 1957. He came to Paine College in 1961 and taught Bible and ethics until his retirement in 1991. He has had two novels published: *The Stained Glass Jungle*

(1962), on power politics in the Methodist Church, and *The Valley of Time* (1967) on TVA in east Tennessee. His scholarly publications are *Rumi: Songbird of Sufism* (1980), and *The Alien Christ* (1980) on the Gospel of Thomas. His current research work is on the Second Seminole War in Florida and the origins of abolitionism.

FREDERICK P. FRANK is professor of educational leadership at Florida A&M University, Tallahassee, Florida. He has been a member of the faculty at Florida A&M University since January 1997. He has held faculty positions at Georgia State University, Northern Illinois University, the Ohio State University, and the State University of New York at Buffalo. Frank received the Bachelor of Music Education degree (1961) and the Master of Music Education degree (1966) from Syracuse University and a Ph.D. (1973) in educational administration from the State University of New York at Buffalo. His current research and writing interests are in the application of information systems to school settings and structural approaches to school reform.

BARBARA STEIN FRANKLE is associate dean for academic affairs and professor of history at LeMoyne-Owen College, Memphis, Tennessee, where she has been a faculty member since 1971. She received her B.A. degree (1961) from Mount Holyoke College in Victorian studies, her M.A. degree (1963) from the University of Wisconsin, Madison, in British history, and her Ph.D. (1969) from the University of Wisconsin, Madison, in the comparative history of modern Britain and the United States. Frankle has directed several diversity projects through the Ford Foundation Campus Diversity Institute, and was a delegate to the foundation's 1998 International Seminar on Diversity and Democracy in Higher Education in the Union of South Africa. She directs the Service Learning program at LeMoyne-Owen College. She has also given extensive national presentations on campus community relations, diversity programs, general education, and service learning.

KARL HENZY is assistant professor of English at Morgan State University, Baltimore, Maryland, where he teaches courses in modern literature, the humanities, and composition. He received his B.A. degree (1984) and M.A. degree (1987) from the University of Connecticut, and his Ph.D. (1993) from the University of Delaware. Henzy has been a member of the faculty at Morgan State University since 1993. He has aided in the development of Morgan State's humanities program into a fully multicultural curriculum with a worldwide focus. He has lectured on the pedagogical issues involved in teaching world literature, on the traditional African epic-drama, and on Chinua Achebe's *Things Fall Apart*. He has published scholarly articles on modern British literature, including an essay on D.H. Lawrence's foreign women characters, which will appear in a book published by Greenwood Press in 1999. Dr. Henzy is on the editorial board of the *D.H. Lawrence Review*.

BARBARA JUR was an adjunct professor at Florida A&M University, Tallahassee, Florida, from 1973 to 1975 and curriculum coordinator for the Upward Bound/Special Services Program from 1975-1977. She received her B.A. degree (1966) from the University of Chicago in sociology, her M.S. degree (1971) from Ohio State University in mathematics, and her Ed.D. (1985) from U.S. International University in curriculum design. At Florida A&M University, she taught a variety of mathematics courses, ranging from fundamental mathematics through trigonometry. While at Florida A&M University, she began her research on success indicators and factors for developmental students. At present, Jur is associate dean of mathematics at Macomb Community College in Warren, Michigan. She maintains her research interest in developmental education and also chairs the Subcommittee on Quantitative Literacy for the Mathematical Association of America.

JULIANA S. LANCASTER is assistant professor of psychology at Morris Brown College, Atlanta, Georgia, where she has been employed since 1993. She received her B.A. degree (1974) in psychology from the University of South Florida, and her M.A. degree (1982) in developmental psychology, and her Ph.D. (1985) in cognitive psychology from Emory University. Lancaster was initially hired at Morris Brown in the position of research specialist in institutional research. She assumed a full-time faculty position in the Department of Psychology in 1995. Her research interest is in the area of human memory and decision making. She has recently initiated a series of studies on recognition and recall errors in memory.

MATTHEW A. REDINGER was a visiting assistant professor of history at Bennett College from 1993 to 1995 and at North Carolina Agricultural and Technical State University during the 1995-1996 academic year. He received his B.A. degree (1986) and his M.A. degree (1988), both in history, at the University of Montana. He received his Ph.D. (1993) in history at the University of Washington. At both Bennett College and North Carolina A&T State University, Redinger taught courses in the history of the United States and world civilizations. While at Bennett, he was also advisor to the college Model United Nations team. Redinger is now an assistant professor of history at Montana State University-Billings, where he teaches history courses in western civilization, modern United States, Latin America, and historical methodology. He also advises the university's highly successful Phi Alpha Theta honor society and spends his time researching and writing on topics including United States foreign policy, private interest groups, and United States-Mexican relations in the twentieth century.

STEPHEN L. ROZMAN is professor of political science and dean of the Social Science Division at Tougaloo College, Tougaloo, Mississippi, where he teaches courses in international relations, comparative politics, and political theory. He received his B.A. degree (1962) from the University of Minnesota in political science, his M.A. degree (1965) from the University of Florida in Inter-American Studies, and his Ph.D. (1968) from the University of Florida in political science. Rozman has been a member of the faculty at Tougaloo College since 1972. His recent activities include serving as co-director of the HBCU Faculty Development Network, director of faculty development grants at Tougaloo College funded by the Bush Foundation, and coordinator of a new international studies emphasis program at Tougaloo College. He is also president of Mississippi Partners, a partnership with Guyana in the Partners of the Americas people-to-people developmental program.

AMY SIBULKIN is an assistant professor of psychology at Tennessee State University, Nashville, Tennessee. She received her B.A. degree (1976) in psychology from Clark University, and her M.S. (1979) and Ph.D. (1981) degrees from Cornell University in developmental psychology. Her current research uses national-level survey data to explain the difference in college graduation rates between young African American and white college students. Sibulkin currently co-directs a federally-funded project designed to increase successful applications to graduate and professional programs among Tennessee State University undergraduates in the fields of psychology and education through a research mentoring program, a computer lab, and an information resource center.

KAREN SIDES-GONZALES is an instructional designer at St. Philip's College in San Antonio, Texas, where she produces and evaluates faculty development programs. She received her B.A. degree in art (1984) and M.A. degree (1986) in multidisciplinary studies from the University of the Incarnate Word, and her Ed.D. (1993) in institutional management from Pepperdine University. Sides-Gonzales has been employed by St. Philip's College since January 1997. She has been particularly involved in the development of programs to promote the integration of contemporary learning theory and instructional technologies into the college curriculum. She also serves on an array of campus committees including the diversity, the centennial, and the institutional technology planning committees. Her current research interest is the application of holistic teaching and learning models in technologically enhanced classes.

JESSE SILVERGLATE is professor of history and director of academic computing at Florida Memorial College, Miami, Florida, where he teaches courses in world civilization, introduction to social sciences, group dynamics, and community psychology. He has been a member of the faculty at Florida Memorial College since 1970. Silverglate received his B.A. degree (1963) from Rutgers University in history, his M.A. degree (1963) from the University of Wisconsin in European intellectual history, his M.S. Ed. degree (1980) in educational counseling and administration from the University of Miami, and his Ph.D. (1969) in modern European history from the University of Wisconsin. For the past seven years at Florida Memorial College he has been extensively involved in assisting faculty and students to incorporate technology into the teaching and learning process. His current research interests are in the effective coordination of traditional and technological teaching methodologies. Silverglate has published several articles on the Nuremberg war crimes, and he has conducted numerous workshops on incorporating the computer and the Internet into the classroom learning environment. He is a founding member and serves on the steering committee of the HBCU Faculty Development Network and was recognized as the social science division Professor of the Year in 1998 at Florida Memorial College.

MARK THOMSON is an assistant professor of chemistry at Xavier University of Louisiana, New Orleans, Louisiana, where he teaches courses in general, inorganic, and environmental chemistry. He received his B.S. degree (1987) from the University of Utah in chemistry and his Ph.D. (1995) from Colorado State University in inorganic chemistry. He has been a member of the faculty at Xavier University of Louisiana since 1995. For the past several years, he has been the coordinator of the general chemistry lab program. His current research interests include the development of new experiments for use in introductory chemistry courses for both science and nonscience students.